MEDIEVAL EUROPE
A SHORT SOURCEBOOK

MEDIEVAL EUROPE
A SHORT SOURCEBOOK

EDITED BY

C. WARREN HOLLISTER
University of California, Santa Barbara

JOE W. LEEDOM
Hollins College

MARC A. MEYER
University of Rochester

DAVID S. SPEAR
University of California, Santa Barbara

Alfred A. Knopf New York

Cover photo of "The Falcon Hunt" is located in the Metropolitan Museum of Art, Robert Lehman Collection, 1975.

First Edition
9876

Library of Congress Cataloging in Publication Data:

Main Entry under title:

Medieval Europe.

  Includes index.
  1. Europe—History—476-1492—Sources.
2. Middle Ages—History—Sources. I. Hollister,
C. Warren (Charles Warren), 1930–
D113.M4   940.1   81-14747
ISBN 0-394-34189-9   AACR2

Manufactured in the United States of America

PREFACE

This book of readings is new but not untested. In its previous incarnation it was a longer, two-volume work, xeroxed and bound, and used by students in medieval history at the University of California, Santa Barbara. We thank the UCSB Office of Instructional Development for supporting this earlier project. On the basis of student response and our own experience, the collection has been shortened and thoroughly revised into its present form.

The xeroxed prototype was assigned in conjunction with C. Warren Hollister's textbook, *Medieval Europe: A Short History*. Because literary passages and sources on social history abound in the Hollister text, they have been minimized in the present sourcebook. Again, because St. Thomas Aquinas proves the existence of God in the textbook, he does not repeat himself in the sourcebook. We believe that the textbook and sourcebook together provide an appropriate balance, and we have been at pains to avoid redundancy between the two. Owing to limitations of length, and to our decision to stress certain major themes, many well-known medieval sources are absent. But we are confident that the sources we have chosen constitute an effective instructional tool, proven in the classroom and polished through revision.

We are grateful to Professors Ralph V. Turner of Florida State University and Marcia L. Colish of Oberlin College for their valuable comments, and to several hundred undergraduate students at UCSB for their encouraging and candid evaluations. For the flaws that remain we assume full responsibility.

JOE W. LEEDOM
MARC A. MEYER
DAVID S. SPEAR
C. WARREN HOLLISTER

ABOUT THE AUTHORS

Warren Hollister is Professor of History at the University of California, Santa Barbara, and his three coeditors are past or present doctoral students at UCSB. Joe W. Leedom taught medieval history for two years at the University of Maryland as a Visiting Assistant Professor and is now on the regular history faculty at Hollins College, Roanoke, Virginia. Marc A. Meyer is an Assistant Professor at the University of Rochester. David S. Spear is completing his Ph.D. dissertation. All have published in a variety of areas of medieval history.

CONTENTS

PART 3   THE LATE MIDDLE AGES

Introduction

Many students dislike reading historical sources, yet many professors assign them nonetheless. In our own view, a history course that does not require the reading of original documents is a contradiction in terms. Contemporary sources are the foundations on which historical scholarship is built—the raw materials with which all historians work. Source materials are often difficult to absorb because they lack the tidiness and clarity that one finds in a good work of historical interpretation, or in a good textbook. But one cannot hope to understand the historical edifice without examining its foundations.

This collection of translated documents has been designed for use in connection with Warren Hollister's *Medieval Europe: A Short History* (Fifth Edition, 1982), but it can be used with other textbooks as well. Some of the translations are our own; some are the work of others. When translations were already available that were accurate, readable, and not prohibitively expensive, we used them—and we thank the translators and publishers who gave us permission to do so. The editorial headnote preceding each document provides essential information on its historical context but does not summarize its contents. We prefer to let the sources speak for themselves.

They will not always speak clearly; the human past was more complex and ambiguous than most textbooks make it out to be. But it is our hope that many readers will appreciate the challenge of being led beyond the generalizations of textbooks and lectures into the underlying human reality. In this book, as in others like it, the reader is led very gently. The documents that follow are a minute sampling of the historical records of the Middle Ages, carefully chosen and edited to illustrate historical trends and events that we regard as significant. In place of the documentary jungle through which the historical scholar must grope, we have provided a small, well-tended garden. In this respect, our book of readings offers only a foretaste of the historian's craft.

Reading an historical source is rather like reading a newspaper: both should be approached with a healthy touch of skepticism. When an event is reported, the careful reader will ask a series of questions about the accuracy and objectivity of the report: did the reporter witness the event? If not, how reliable were the sources used? Is the reporter caught up in some personal hostility or enthusiasm that might affect the tone of the report, or the selection of certain facts to the exclusion of others? Is the reporter reputable or reckless, shrewd or gullible?

Reports of past events are known to historians as *narrative sources*, and they must always be evaluated by the criteria suggested above. Whenever possible, relevant information about the narrators quoted in this sourcebook will be provided in an editorial headnote, just as a good newspaper provides the names and affiliations of the writers of its major articles and columns. If your own newspaper does not provide such information, beware of it. Likewise, in reading a work of nonfiction or in viewing a documentary film, you should always ask who produced it and for what purpose.

Many of our documents are not narrative accounts but official edicts, laws, charters, creeds, and letters. Known generally as *record sources*, these documents bring us face to face with the past, without the distorting lens of the biased, careless, or misinformed reporter. They are like the verbatim accounts that newspapers sometimes provide of speeches, diplomatic agreements, and court decisions. But here again, they must be read with discrimination and with certain questions in mind. First and most obviously, is the document absolutely authentic, or has it been forged or tampered with? (The speeches of members of Congress often appear in the *Congressional Record* in much improved form, and some were never delivered at all.) If authentic, does the source tell us what was occurring or what its framer(s) hoped might occur? Does a religious creed reflect general belief or is it a response to a growing number of people who believed otherwise? Does a law providing severe penalties for arson suggest that arson was being reduced or that it was increasing to dangerous proportions? Was a particular law, edict, or creed strictly enforced or largely ignored? Is a particular charter typical or atypical? Does a particular law code create new legal conditions or simply perpetuate old ones? What portions of the document are merely conventional formulas (like "Sincerely yours," or "I believe in a new beginning for this great country of ours, where Americans, regardless of creed or race, can live together in peace and prosperity,'' etc.), and what parts contain the meat of the message? Above all, what were the cultural attitudes and historical circumstances underlying the creation of the record source, and how does the source reflect them? Again, our editorial headnotes will provide some guidance in answering these questions.

In short, we hope that students who use this book will not simply read the sources but think critically about them as well. The development of a discriminating, sophisticated approach to historical documents can sharpen one's ability to evaluate evidence of all sorts—from campaign oratory, sales pitches, college catalogues, and books about biorhythms and UFOs to the evening television news and the morning paper.

Part One

THE EARLY MIDDLE AGES

During the turbulent centuries between about A.D. 300 and 1050, Western Europe underwent wave after wave of invasions. As a result of the first wave, Roman imperial government disintegrated in the West, giving way by A.D. 500 to a group of loosely organized Germanic kingdoms. Most of these kingdoms were themselves destroyed or transformed by subsequent invasions. East Roman armies reconquered Italy in the mid-sixth century but quickly lost much of it to the assaults of the Germanic Lombards. In the early eighth century, Muslim armies overwhelmed the Visigothic kingdom of Spain and struck deep into France. Between these major invasions Europe was afflicted by warfare between and within its kingdoms. The population declined, cities shriveled into villages, and commerce ebbed. Europe became a land of isolated agricultural settlements surrounded by forests and wastelands.

In the course of this troubled era, the cultural traditions of the Classical, Christian, and Germanic past gradually fused into a new, Western European civilization. Its great unifying force was the Christian Church, which had spread through the Roman Empire and eventually converted it. When Rome collapsed in the West, the Church remained to preserve its memory and perpetuate its culture. Christian missionaries labored to convert and civilize pagan tribes. Benedictine monasteries, planted in Germanic forests, became centers of devotion, learning, and agrarian enterprise, while in Rome, where emperors had once ruled the West, popes now claimed the allegiance of all Christians and directed the efforts of far-flung missionaries.

In the decades around A.D. 800, the emerging culture of Western Christendom experienced a period of political unification and expansion under a Frankish dynasty known as the Carolingians. The most celebrated of the Carolingian kings, Charlemagne, worked closely with the Roman popes and Benedictine monks to conquer and convert pagan tribes, to reform the Church, and to encourage learning.

In the years following Charlemagne's death in 814, his empire broke into pieces as a result of internal instability and attacks from without. Europe was struck by new waves of non-Christian invaders—Hungarian horsemen from the East, Muslim pirate bands from the South, and Viking seafarers from the North. These were to be the last invasions that Europe would suffer. Out of the chaos that they brought, strong Christian monarchies emerged in England and Germany. The kingdom of France—the western part of Charlemagne's former empire—remained decentralized, with a weak monarchy and increasingly strong regional principalities: Anjou, Poitou, Champagne, Normandy, and others. Italy survived the invasions to become a land of increasingly vigorous commercial cities.

By A.D. 1050 Europe was once again expanding. Hungary, Scandinavia, and Poland had been Christianized and brought under the loose jurisdiction of the Roman popes. Commerce was reviving, towns were growing along Europe's river valleys, and the population was increasing once again. The old civilization of Rome had evolved, through centuries of turmoil and struggle, into the civilization of Western Europe.

CHAPTER 1

The Transformation of the Roman World

The documents in this chapter illustrate two major themes: (1) the Christianization of the Roman Empire, and (2) the administrative and military problems leading to the Empire's collapse in the West.

The process of Christianization progressed during the fourth century A.D. from the abolition of imperial persecutions of Christians to the establishment of imperial persecutions of non-Christians. The conversion of Constantine (document 1) and the edict granting Christians the same toleration that other religions enjoyed (document 2) were followed by imperial efforts to resolve theological disputes within the Christian community (document 3). Such involvement forced the emperors to take sides in the debate between two contending Christian groups: the Trinitarians (who believed that God was a Trinity of three equal Persons: Father, Son, and Holy Spirit) and the Arians (who believed that the Son was subordinate to the Father). By the end of the fourth century it had become imperial policy to tolerate only the Trinitarian Christians and to ban the religious activities of Arians and all non-Christian sects (document 4). Meanwhile the Christian Church was attracting many of the keenest minds of the age. The writings of St. Augustine, who interpreted Christianity in the intellectual context of Classical Antiquity, shaped Christian thought across the Middle Ages and beyond (document 5).

During the fourth and fifth centuries, the Roman Empire suffered from internal stresses and barbarian invasions. Imperial taxes were becoming increasingly severe and inequitable. Civic officials, who had abandoned their cities to avoid financial ruin, were ordered to resume their municipal duties (document 6). Others responded to the tax burden by fleeing the Empire to live among the barbarians (documents 7 and 8). The victory of the Visigoths over the Romans at Adrianople in 378 (document 9) was followed by a period of growing Germanic military pressure. The emperors were driven to increasingly desperate measures—urging slaves to enroll in the Roman army, pleading that civilians join in the defense of their localities (again, document 6). But these edicts failed to halt the disintegration of the Western Empire. In 476 imperial rule came to an end in the West when the barbarian general Odoacer deposed the last of the Western emperors, Romulus Augustulus (document 10). The Roman Empire endured in the East for another thousand years, centered on its great capital of Constantinople, but the Western provinces passed into the hands of Germanic kings.

Reading 1

Eusebius on Constantine's Conversion

The conversion of Constantine, the first Christian emperor, was of decisive importance to Roman and Christian history. Eusebius, bishop of Caesarea, a contemporary and admirer of Constantine's, ascribes the conversion to a miracle. Eusebius also makes it clear that Constantine regarded the Christian God primarily as a bringer of victory. Constantine was not disappointed. Shortly after the events described here, he won control of Italy and the Western Empire by defeating his rival, the Emperor Maxentius, at the Battle of the Milvian Bridge (312). A subsequent victory over the the Eastern Emperor Licinius (324) brought the entire Roman Empire under Constantine's authority.

Constantine now sought divine assistance, having become convinced that he needed more powerful aid than his military forces could afford him, on account of the wicked and magical enchantments that the tyrant [Maxentius] so diligently practiced. For Constantine regarded the possession of arms and a large army of secondary importance, believing that the helping power of Deity was invincible and unshakable. He considered, therefore, on what God he might rely for protection and assistance. While engaged in this inquiry, it occurred to him that, of the many emperors who had preceded him, those who had rested their hopes in a multitude of gods, and served them with sacrifices and offerings, had in the first place been deceived by flattering predictions, and oracles which promised them all prosperity, and at last had met with an unhappy end, while not one of their gods had stood by to warn them of the impending wrath of heaven. One emperor alone had pursued an entirely opposite course: having condemned their error and honored the Supreme God during his whole life, that emperor had found him to be the Saviour and Protector of his empire and the Giver of every good thing. Reflecting on this . . . Constantine judged it to be folly indeed to join in the idle worship of those who were no gods and, after such convincing evidence, to err from the truth; and he therefore felt it incumbent on him to honor his father's God alone.[1]

Accordingly he called on Him with earnest prayer and supplications that He would reveal to him who He was, and stretch forth His right hand to help him in his present difficulties. And while he was thus praying with fervent entreaty, a most marvelous sign appeared to him from heaven, the account of

From Eusebius of Caesarea, *Life of Constantine*, tr. E. C. Richardson; *Library of Nicene and Post-Nicene Fathers*, I, 2nd Series; New York, Christian Literature Company, 1890, pp. 489–491.

[1]Constantine's father, Constantius I (294-306), was a monotheist but not a Christian. His deity was the Sun God.

which it might have been hard to believe had it been related by any other person. But since the victorious emperor himself long afterwards declared it to the writer of this history, when he was honored with his acquaintance and society, and confirmed his statement by an oath, who could hesitate to accredit the relation, especially since the testimony of after-time has established its truth? He said that about noon, when the day was already beginning to decline, he saw with his own eyes the trophy of a cross of light in the heavens, above the sun, and bearing the inscription, CONQUER BY THIS. At this sight he himself was struck with amazement, and his whole army also, which followed him on the expedition, and witnessed the miracle.

He said, moreover, that he doubted within himself what the import of this apparition could be. And while he continued to ponder and· reason on its meaning, night suddenly came on; then in his sleep the Christ of God appeared to him with the same sign which he had seen in the heavens, and commanded him to make a likeness of that sign which he had seen in the heavens, and to use it as a safeguard in all engagements with his enemies.

At the dawn of day he arose, and communicated the marvel to his friends; and then, calling together the workers in gold and precious stones, he sat in the midst of them, and described to them the figure of the sign he had seen, bidding them represent it in gold and precious stones. And this representation I myself have had an opportunity of seeing.

Now it was made in the following manner. A long spear, overlaid with gold, formed the figure of the cross by means of a transverse bar laid over it. On the top of the whole was fixed a wreath of gold and precious stones; and within this, the symbol of the Saviour's name, two letters indicating the name of Christ by means of its initial characters, the letter P being intersected by X in its center[2] and these letters the emperor was in the habit of wearing on his helmet at a later period. From the cross-bar of the spear was suspended a cloth, a royal piece, covered with a profuse embroidery of most brilliant precious stones; and which, being also richly interlaced with gold, presented an indescribable degree of beauty to the beholder. This banner was of a square form, and the upright staff, whose lower section was of great length, bore a golden half-length portrait of the pious emperor and his children on its upper part, beneath the trophy of the cross, and immediately above the embroidered banner.

The emperor constantly made use of this sign of salvation as a safeguard against every adverse and hostile power, and commanded that others similar to it should be carried at the head of all his armies.

These things were done shortly afterwards. But at the time above specified, being struck with amazement at the extraordinary vision, and resolving to

---

[2]The Chi-Rho, ☧ ,the first two letters in the Greek spelling of Christ.

worship no other God save Him who had appeared to him, he sent for those who were acquainted with the mysteries of His doctrines, and inquired who that God was, and what was intended by the sign of the vision he had seen.

They affirmed that He was God, the only begotten Son of the one and only God: that the sign which had appeared was the symbol of immortality, and the trophy of that victory over death which He had gained in time past when sojourning on earth. They taught him also the causes of His advent, and explained to him the true account of His incarnation. Thus he was instructed in these matters and was impressed with wonder at the divine manifestation which had been presented to his sight. Comparing, therefore, the heavenly vision with the interpretation given, he found his judgment confirmed; and, in the persuasion that the knowledge of these things had been imparted to him by Divine teaching, he determined thenceforth to devote himself to the reading of the Inspired writings.

Moreover, he made the priests of God his counselors, and deemed it incumbent on him to honor the God who had appeared to him with all devotion. And after this, being fortified by well-grounded hopes in Him, he hastened to quench the threatening fire of tyranny.

Reading 2

The Edict of Milan, 313

The first imperial edict to prohibit the persecution of Christians was issued in 311 by the pagan emperor Galerius, as a deathbed response to the clear failure of the last imperial persecution. Galerius permitted Christians to practice their religion so long as they did so without offending public order. In 313 a much more sweeping edict of toleration was issued by Constantine and his co-emperor, Licinius. Although not actually issued from Milan, the edict promulgates an agreement that the two emperors had previously concluded there.

When we, Constantine Augustus and Licinius Augustus, had happily met at Milan, and were conferring about all things which concern the advantage and security of the state, we thought that amongst other things which seemed likely to profit men generally, the reverence paid to the Divinity merited our first and chief attention. Our purpose is to grant both to the Christians and to all others full authority to follow whatever worship each man has desired;

From *A New Eusebius: Documents Illustrative of the History of the Church to A.D. 337,* ed. J. Stevenson; London, 1957, pp. 300-302. By permission of the Society for Promoting Christian Knowledge.

whereby whatsoever Divinity dwells in heaven may be benevolent and propitious to us, and to all who are placed under our authority. Therefore we thought it salutary and most proper to establish our purpose that no man whatever should be refused complete toleration, who has given up his mind either to the cult of the Christians, or to the religion which he personally feels best suited to himself; to the end that the supreme Divinity, to whose worship we devote ourselves under no compulsion, may continue in all things to grant us his wonted favour and beneficence. Wherefore your Dignity should know that it is our pleasure to abolish all conditions whatever which were embodied in former orders directed to your office about the Christians, that what appeared utterly inauspicious and foreign to our Clemency should be done away and that every one of those who have a common wish to follow the religion of the Christians may from this moment freely and unconditionally proceed to observe the same without any annoyance or disquiet. These things we thought good to signify in the fullest manner to your Carefulness, that you might know that we have given freely and unreservedly to the said Christians toleration to practise their cult. And when you perceive that we have granted this favour to the said Christians, your Devotion understands that to others also freedom for their own worship and cult is likewise left open and freely granted, as befits the quiet of our times, that every man may have complete toleration in the practice of whatever worship he has chosen. This has been done by us that no diminution be made from the honour of any religion. Moreover in regard to the legal position of the Christians we have thought fit to ordain this also, that if any appear to have bought, whether from our exchequer or from any others, the places at which they were used formerly to assemble, concerning which definite orders have been given before now, and that by a letter issued to your office—that the same be restored to the Christians, setting aside all delay and doubtfulness, without any payment or demand of price.

All these things must be delivered over at once and without delay by your intervention to the corporation of the Christians. And since the said Christians are known to have possessed, not those places only whereto they were used to assemble, but others also belonging to their corporation, namely to their churches, and not to individuals, we comprise them all under the above law, so that you will order them to be restored without any doubtfulness or dispute to the said Christians, that is to their corporation and assemblies; provided always as aforesaid, that those who restore them without price, as we said, shall expect a compensation from our benevolence. In all these things you must give the aforesaid Christians your most effective intervention, that our command may be fulfilled as soon as may be, and that in this matter, as well as others, order may be taken by our Clemency for the public quiet. So far we will ensure that, as has been already stated, the Divine favour toward us which we have already experienced in so many affairs shall continue for all time to give us prosperity and successes, together with happiness for the State. But that the tenor of our gracious ordinance may be brought to the knowledge of all men, it will be your duty by a proclamation of your own to publish everywhere and bring to the notice of all men this present document, that the command of this our benevolence may not be hidden.

Reading 3

The Nicene Creed, 325

The Nicene Creed is a product of the Trinitarians' victory over the Arians at the Council of Nicaea, summoned by Constantine in 325. The outcome of this first universal council of the Church was strongly influenced by Constantine, who had himself been persuaded by important churchmen to support the Trinitarian position. The Nicene Creed expresses what would become the orthodox Christian position on the Trinity and the incarnation of Christ. It rejects explicitly the doctrine of the Alexandrian churchman Arius, who taught that only God the Father was eternal and that God the Son was His creation.

We believe in one God, the Father Almighty, maker of all things visible and invisible; and in one Lord Jesus Christ, the Son of God, the only-begotten of his Father, of the substance of the Father, God of God, Light of Light, true God of true God, begotten not made, being of one substance with the Father; by whom all things were made, both in heaven and in earth. Who for us men and for our salvation came down from heaven and was incarnate and was made man. He suffered and the third day he rose again, and ascended into heaven. And he shall come again to judge both the living and the dead. And we believe in the Holy Spirit. And whosoever shall say that there was a time when the Son of God was not, or that before he was begotten he was not, or that he was made of things that were not, or that he is of a different substance or essence from the Father, or that he is a creature, or subject to change or conversion—all that say so, the Catholic and Apostolic Church anathematizes[1] them.

From *The Seven Ecumenical Councils*, tr. A.C. McGiffert and E.C. Richardson; *Library of Nicene and Post-Nicene Fathers*, V, XIV, 2nd Series; New York, Charles Scribner's, 1900, p. 3.

[1]"Anathema" is a curse, carrying the full authority of the Church, that banishes the recipient from the Christian community.

Reading 4
Selections from the Code of Theodosius II

Around the year 438 the Emperor Theodosius II (408–450) published a law code intended as a convenient reference to all imperial edicts since the time of Constantine that still remained valid. The excerpts reproduced below are edicts of Emperor Theodosius I (378–395), issued in his name and in those of his several co-emperors. Notice the marked shift in imperial religious policy since the Edict of Milan.

Emperors Gratian, Valentinian, and Theodosius Augustuses: An Edict to Eutropius, Praetorian Prefect [A.D. 380]:

Crowds shall be kept away from the unlawful congregations of all the heretics. The name of the One and Supreme God shall be celebrated everywhere; the observance, destined to remain forever, of the Nicene faith, as transmitted long ago by Our ancestors and confirmed by the declaration and testimony of divine religion, shall be maintained. The contamination of the Photinian pestilence, the poison of the Arian sacrilege, the crime of the Eunomian perfidy,[1] and the sectarian monstrosities, abominable because of the ill-omened names of their authors, shall be abolished even from the hearing of men.

On the other hand, that man shall be accepted as a defender of the Nicene faith and as a true adherent of the Catholic religion who confesses that Almighty God and Christ the Son of God are One in name, God of God, Light of Light, who does not violate by denial the Holy Spirit which we hope for and receive from the Supreme Author of things; that man who esteems, with the perception of inviolate faith, the undivided substance of the incorrupt Trinity. The latter beliefs are surely more acceptable to Us and must be venerated.

Those persons, however, who are not devoted to the aforesaid doctrines shall cease to assume, with studied deceit, the alien name of true religion, and they shall be branded upon the disclosure of their crimes. They shall be removed and completely barred from the threshold of all churches, since We forbid all heretics to hold unlawful assemblies within the towns. If factions should attempt to do anything, We order that their madness shall be banished and that they shall be driven away from the very walls of the cities, in order

---

From *The Theodosian Code and Novels and the Sirmondian Constitutions*, tr. Clyde Pharr (copyright 1952 by Clyde Pharr, renewed 1980 in the name of Roy Pharr), pp. 440, 451, 473. Reprinted by permission of Princeton University Press.

[1]The Photinians and Eunomians, like the Arians, were Christian groups whose doctrines differed from the orthodox Catholic position and who were thus denounced as heretics by orthodox believers.

that Catholic churches throughout the whole world may be restored to all orthodox bishops who hold the Nicene faith.

Emperors Theodosius, Arcadius, and Honorius Augustuses to Rufinus, Praetorian Prefect [A.D. 391]:

If any man should dare to immolate a victim for the purpose of sacrifice, or to consult the quivering entrails,[2] according to the example of a person guilty of high treason he shall be reported by an accusation which is permitted to all persons, and he shall receive the appropriate sentence, even though he has inquired nothing contrary to, or with reference to, the welfare of the Emperors. For it is sufficient to constitute an enormous crime that any person should wish to break down the very laws of nature, to investigate forbidden matters, to disclose hidden secrets, to attempt interdicted practices, to seek to know the end of another's life, to promise the hope of another person's death.

If any person should venerate, by placing incense before them, images made by the work of mortals and destined to suffer the ravages of time, and if, in a ridiculous manner, he should suddenly fear the effigies which he himself has formed, or should bind a tree with fillets, or should erect an altar of turf that he has dug up, or should attempt to honor vain images with the offering of a gift, which even though it is humble, still is a complete outrage against religion, such a person, as one guilty of the violation of religion, shall be punished by the forfeiture of that house or landholding in which it is proved that he served a pagan superstition. For We decree that all places shall be annexed to Our fisc,[3] if it is proved that they have reeked with the vapor of incense, provided, however, that such places are proved to have belonged to such incense burners.

If any person should attempt to perform any such kind of sacrifice in public temples or shrines, or in the buildings or fields of others, and if it is proved that such places were usurped without the knowledge of the owner, the offender shall be compelled to pay twenty-five pounds of gold as a fine. If any person should connive at such a crime, he shall be held subject to the same penalty as that of the person who performed the sacrifice.

It is Our will that this regulation shall be so enforced by the judges, as well as by the defenders and decurions[4] of the several cities, that the information

---

[2]The examination of animal entrails was a pagan procedure to foretell the success or failure of a venture.

[3]Fisc: property of the emperor.

[4]Decurions were municipal officials responsible for the civil administration of Roman towns. They functioned as judges, sheriffs, and tax collectors. If the city proved unable to meet its tax quota, the decurions were expected to pay the shortfall from their private fortunes. This liability made the office, which became hereditary, an unendurable burden in the late Empire. See below, pp. 18.

learned by the defenders and decurions shall be immediately reported to the courts, and the crimes so reported shall be punished by the judges. Moreover, if the defenders and decurions should suppose that any such crime should be concealed through favoritism or overlooked through carelessness, they shall be subjected to judicial indignation. If the judges should be advised of such crimes and should defer punishment through connivance, they shall be fined.

Reading 5

St. Augustine on Christian Doctrine

St. Augustine of Hippo (354–430), the greatest philosopher of late Antiquity, devoted his intelligence and his mastery of Greco-Roman thought to the development of Christian theology. Following the tradition of the Greek philosopher Plato, he preferred introspection and deductive reasoning to observation and inductive reasoning. In the passage below, Augustine sets forth his deeply influential theory of the nature of evil. St. Thomas Aquinas, writing in the thirteenth century, used a portion of Augustine's argument to explain how evil could exist in a world created by a God of infinite power and goodness (see Hollister, *Medieval Europe*, p. 307).

When it is asked what we should believe about religion, the answer is not to be found in the nature of things, where those the Greeks call "physicists" look; nor should we fear if Christians are ignorant of the power and number of the elements; or the motion, order, and defects of heavenly bodies or constellations; or the species and nature of animals, plants, stones, springs, rivers, or mountains; or the periods of space and time; or signs of imminent storms; or the vast number of these sorts of things that they either have ascertained or feel they have ascertained. Because even these men, with such eminent intellect, earnest study, abundant leisure, some exploring these things through human conjectures, others through pursuing history, even they have not learned everything; indeed many of the things in whose understanding they have gloried are more frequently matters of opinion than science. For the Christian it is enough to believe that the cause of creation, in heaven or on earth, visible or invisible, is nothing but the bounty of the creator, who is the one true God; and that nothing exists but He Himself and what is from Him; and that He is a trinity, the Father, and the Son begotten of the Father, and the Holy Spirit

St. Augustine, *The Enchiridion on Faith, Hope, and Love*; in J. P. Migne, Patrologia Latina, vol. 40, pp. 235–239; tr. Joe W. Leedom.

proceeding from the Father, one and the same Spirit of the Father and the Son.

All things were created by this supreme, equal, great, and immutably good Trinity; yet they were not created supremely, equally, and immutably good. But still, each one is good, and as a group they are very good, because all together they constitute a universe of admirable beauty. Even that which is called evil, if ordered and placed in its position, effectively commends the good, inasmuch as good, when compared to evil, is more pleasing and more praised. And omnipotent God, whom even the pagans recognize as the most powerful, as the greatest good, would not allow a single particle of evil in His work unless He brings forth good from evil through His goodness and omnipotence. What, then, is that which is called evil, except the privation of good? For just as wounds and illnesses, in the bodies of animals, are nothing but the privation of health, so when a cure is produced, the evils that were there—illnesses and wounds—do not retreat and go to some other place, but cease to exist, because they are not a thing, only a defect in the substance of a body that is essentially good but accidentally made evil by the privation of that good called health. So it is that whatever are the flaws of souls, they are the privation of good; and, when they are cured, do not transfer elsewhere, but no longer exist in the state of health, and thus they are no more.

Therefore all natural things are good, for the creator of all nature is supremely good. Yet because natural things are not, like their creator, supremely and immutably good, it is possible that goodness be added to and subtracted from them. And goodness diminished is evil. Yet necessarily a particle of the thing's nature remains, providing it exists, because whatever type or however small its nature, the goodness that is its nature cannot be consumed without the thing itself being destroyed.

Rightly is an incorruptible nature lauded, and furthermore, if it were incorruptible and its ruin impossible, it would be unquestionably worthy of praise. When, therefore, it is corrupted, its corruption is evil because it is a privation of so much good. If there is no privation of good, there is no decay; where there is decay, there is diminution of the good. So while a thing is being corrupted, there is in it goodness being diminished; and it follows that if anything of its nature cannot be corrupted, what is left will actually be an incorruptible nature; and it will arrive at such great goodness through corruption. And if the corruption continues, at least the thing also continues to have goodness, which cannot be denied it by corruption; while if it be completely and totally consumed, then neither is any good left, because it will cease to exist. And for that reason it is impossible for corruption to consume the good totally unless the being is consumed. Therefore all nature is good, great if it cannot be corrupted, less if it can be; and it is absolutely impossible to deny, unless one is stupid and ignorant, that it is still good. On account of which, if it is consumed by corruption, the corruption does not itself remain, because there is no subsisting nature where it can dwell.

In sum, there is nothing to be called evil if nothing is good. A good entirely missing evil is entirely good, and in one in which there is some evil, the good is either flawed or capable of being flawed. There can be no evil where there is no good. From this comes an odd idea: because any nature, as a natural thing, is good, it appears that to say a bad thing is bad is to say that what is good is evil, and that unless there is good there is no evil. Because all things are good, because evil does not exist as a thing, then nothing can be evil if something is not good.

This being so, when Vergil's verse pleases us,

> "Happy is he who understands the causes of things,"

it does not seem that our consequent felicity requires that we know the origins of great motions in the physical world which are concealed in the hidden purposes of nature

> "Whence the tremors of the earth come, whose power swells the seas
> Bursting their shores, and returning to their proper place"

and others like this. But we should know the causes of good and evil, as far as humanly possible in this error-ridden and tumultuous life, so that these same errors and tumults can be overcome. We must hold on to that happiness which turmoils cannot shake nor errors mislead.

Reading 6

More Selections from the Theodosian Code

The following imperial edicts, two of which were added to the Theodosian collection after it was originally compiled, illustrate the burden of taxation and the Empire's declining military fortunes. In earlier times, membership on municipal councils had been sought as an honor, but in the late Empire it carried such heavy financial responsibilities that the imperial government was forced to freeze council members in their office and make their status hereditary (above, p. 15, footnote 4).

Again from the Clyde Pharr translation (above, document 4), pp. 344, 361, 170, 172, 544. Reprinted by permission of Princeton University Press.

The Emperor Constantine Augustus to Evagrius, Praetorian Prefect [A.D. 326]:

Since We have learned that the municipal councils are being left desolate by those persons who are obligated to them through birth status and who are requesting imperial service for themselves through supplications to the Emperor and are running away to the legions and various governmental offices, We order all municipal councils to be admonished that if they should apprehend any persons with less than twenty terms of service in governmental offices, either in evading the duties that devolve upon their birth status or in insinuating themselves into the imperial service and holding in contempt the nomination to a municipal office, they shall drag such persons back to the municipal councils. They shall know that henceforth the regulation shall be observed that if any person should desert his municipal council and enter the imperial service, he shall be recalled to the municipal council, not only if he has been born to that status, but also if he should possess an adequate amount of property to perform his compulsory municipal public services and should take refuge in the imperial service, or if he has been freed by our special grant of imperial favor from such duties.

The same Augustus to Count Annius Tiberianus [A.D. 329]:

You shall inform all governors of the provinces that Our Clemency has decreed that sons of veterans shall be bound to the compulsory services of decurions. Thus even those who flatter themselves with the rank of Most Perfect shall be forced into the municipal council and shall perform the necessary public services.

The same Augustus [A.D. 329]:

If persons who are nominated to a magistracy should flee, they shall be sought out; and if with an obstinate spirit they should be able to hide, their goods shall be granted to those persons who at the present time are called in their places to the compulsory public services of the duumvirate, with the provision that if the fugitives should afterwards be found, they shall be forced to assume for two entire years the burdens of the duumvirate. All persons who attempt to avoid the duties of compulsory public services shall be held subject to the same conditon.

Emperors Arcadius, Honorius, and Theodosius II Augustuses to the Provincials [A.D. 406]:

In the matter of defense against hostile attacks, We order that consideration be given not only to the legal status of soldiers, but also to their physical strength. Although We believe that freeborn persons are aroused by love of country, We exhort slaves also, by the authority of this edict, that as soon as possible they shall offer themselves for the labors of war, and if they receive their arms as men fit for military service, they shall obtain the reward of freedom, and they shall also receive two solidi each for travel money. Especially, of course, do We urge this service upon the slaves of those persons who are retained in the armed imperial service, and likewise upon the slaves of federated allies and of conquered peoples, since it is evident that they are making war also along with their masters.

Emperors Theodosius II and Valentinian III Augustuses to the Roman People [A.D. 440]:

As often as the public welfare demands, We consider that the solicitude of all of you must be summoned as an aid, in order that the provisions which will profit all may be fulfilled by all, and We do not believe that it is burdensome to Our provincials that the regulation is made for the safety of all that they shall undertake the responsiblility of resisting the brigands.[1]

Genseric,[1] the enemy of Our Empire, is reported to have led forth from the port of Carthage a large fleet, whose sudden excursion and fortuitous depredation must be feared by all shores. Although the solicitude of Our Clemency is stationing garrisons throughout various places and the army of the most invincible Emperor Theodosius, Our Father, will soon approach, and although We trust that the Most Excellent Patrician, Our Aetius,[2] will soon be here with a large band and the Most Illustrious Master of Soldiers, Sigisvuldus, does not cease to organize guards of soldiers and federated allies for the cities and shores, nevertheless, because it is not sufficiently certain, under summertime opportunities for navigation, to what shore the ships of the enemy can come, We admonish each and all by this edict that, with confidence in the Roman strength and the courage with which they ought to defend their own, with their own men against the enemy, if the occasion should so demand, they shall use those arms which they can, but they shall preserve the public discipline and the moderation of free birth unimpaired. Thus they shall guard Our provinces and their own fortunes with faithful harmony and with joined shields. Of course, this hope for each man's exertions is published, namely, that whatever a victor takes away from an enemy shall undoubtedly be his own.

Emperors Theodosius II and Valentinian III Augustuses to Maximus, Praetorian Prefect for the second time [A.D. 440]:

Justice must be preserved both publicly and privately in all matters and transactions, and We must adhere to it especially in those measures that sus-

---

[1]King of the Vandals, then occupying North Africa and raiding Roman Mediterranean ports. (In 455 they pillaged Rome.)

[2]Aetius was commander of the Roman legions in Gaul.

tain the sinews of the public revenues, since such measures come to the aid of the diminished resources of Our loyal taxpayers with useful equity. Very many persons reject this idea, since they serve only their domestic profits and deprive the common good wherein is contained their true and substantial welfare, although such welfare clearly comes better to each person when it profits all persons, especially since this necessity for tribute so demands, and without such tribute nothing can be provided in peace or in war. Nor can the continuity of such tax payments remain any further if there should be imposed upon a few exhausted persons the burden which the more powerful man declines, which the richer man refuses, and which, since the stronger reject it, only the weaker man assumes.

Reading 7
Salvian Compares the Romans and Barbarians

Salvian, a well-traveled priest of the fifth-century Western Empire, paints a somber picture of the imperial tax system of his time. He writes not as an objective reporter but as a moralist condemning the corruption and wickedness of late-Roman society, and the laggard faith and morals of his Christian contemporaries. Although Salvian's account is marked by rhetorical exaggeration, the evils that he describes were quite real.

In what respects can our customs be preferred to those of the Goths and Vandals, or even compared with them? And first, to speak of affection and mutual charity (which, our Lord teaches, is the chief virtue, saying, "By this shall all men know that ye are my disciples, if ye have love one to another"), almost all barbarians, at least those who are of one race and kin, love each other, while the Romans persecute each other. For what citizen does not envy his fellow citizen? What citizen shows to his neighbor full charity?

The Romans oppress each other with exactions, nay, not each other: it would be quite tolerable if each suffered what he inflicted. It is worse than that; for the many are oppressed by the few, who regard public exactions as their own peculiar right, who carry on private traffic under the guise of collecting the taxes. And this is done not only by nobles, but by men of lowest rank; not by judges only, but by judges' subordinates. For where is the city—even the town or village—which has not as many tyrants as it has officials? . . .

From Salvian Presbyter, *On God's Governance*, in *Readings in European History*, ed. and tr. James H. Robinson; Boston, Ginn & Company, 1904, vol. I, pp. 28–29.

What place is there, therefore, as I have said, where the substance of widows and orphans, nay even of the saints, is not devoured by the chief citizens? . . . None but the great is secure from the devastations of these plundering brigands, except those who are themselves robbers.

Nay, the state has fallen upon such evil days that a man cannot be safe unless he is wicked. Even those in a position to protest against the inquity which they see about them dare not speak lest they make matters worse than before. So the poor are despoiled, the widows sigh, the orphans are oppressed, until many of them, born of families not obscure, and liberally educated, flee to our enemies that they may no longer suffer the oppression of public persecution. They doubtless seek Roman humanity among the barbarians, because they cannot bear barbarian inhumanity among the Romans. And although they differ from the people to whom they flee in manner and in language; although they are unlike as regards the fetid odor of the barbarians' bodies a..d garments, yet they would rather endure a foreign civilization among the barbarians than cruel injustice among the Romans.

So they migrate to the Goths, or to some other tribe of the barbarians who are ruling everywhere, and do not regret their exile. For they would rather live *free* under an appearance of slavery than live as captives under an appearance of liberty. The name of Roman citizen, once so highly esteemed and so dearly bought, is now a thing that men repudiate and flee from. . . .

Reading 8

Priscus Describes a Roman Citizen who Lives among the Barbarians

Priscus, A Greek inhabitant of the fifth-century Roman Empire, served on an imperial ambassadorial mission to the court of Attila the Hun in 448. He tells here of his encounter with a Greek-speaking man who was living among the "Scythians"— a name applied very loosely at the time to barbarian tribes coming from southern Russia. Priscus's "Scythians" were a tributary tribe to the Huns and were settled in present-day Hungary. The Greek whom Priscus meets had once been a prosperous merchant of the Eastern Empire but had been taken prisoner in a barbarian raid. Having been granted his freedom, he chose not to return.

He considered his new life among the Scythians better than his old life among the Romans, and the reasons he urged were as follows: "After war the

From Priscus of Panium, *An Embassy to the Huns*, in *Readings in European History*, ed. and tr. James H. Robinson; Boston, Ginn & Company, 1904, vol. I, pp. 30–33.

Scythians live at leisure, enjoying what they have got, and not at all, or very little, disturbed. The Romans, on the other hand, are in the first place very liable to be killed, if there are any hostilities, since they have to rest their hopes of protection on others, and are not allowed, by their tyrants, to use arms. And those who do use them are injured by the cowardice of their generals, who cannot properly conduct war.

"But the condition of Roman subjects in time of peace is far more grievous than the evils of war, for the exaction of the taxes is very severe, and unprincipled men inflict injuries on others because the laws are practically not valid against all classes. A trangressor who belongs to the wealthy classes is not punished for his injustice, while a poor man, who does not understand business, undergoes the legal penalty—that is, if he does not depart this life before the trial, so long is the course of lawsuits protracted, and so much money is expended on them. The climax of misery is to have to pay in order to obtain justice. For no one will give a hearing to the injured man except he pay a sum of money to the judge and the judge's clerks."

In reply to this attack on the Empire, I asked him to be good enough to listen with patience to the other side of the question. "The creators of the Roman Republic," I said, "who were wise and good men, in order to prevent things from being done at haphazard, made one class of men guardians of the laws, and appointed another class to the profession of arms, who were to have no other object than to be always ready for battle, and to go forth to war without dread, as though to their ordinary exercise, having by practice exhausted all their fear beforehand. Others again were assigned to attend to the cultivation of the ground, to support themselves and those who fight in their defense by contributing the military corn supply. . . . To those who protect the interests of the litigants a sum of money is paid by the latter, just as a payment is made by the farmers to the soldiers. Is it not fair to support him who assists and requite him for his kindness? . . .

"Those who spend money on a suit and lose it in the end cannot fairly put it down to anything but the injustice of their case. And as to the long time spent on lawsuits, that is due to anxiety for justice, that judges may not fail in passing accurate judgments by having to give sentence offhand; it is better that they should reflect, and conclude the case more tardily, than that by judging in a hurry they should both injure man and transgress against the Deity, the institutor of justice. . . .

"The Romans treat their slaves better than the king of the Scythians treats his subjects. They deal with them as fathers or teachers, admonishing them to abstain from evil and follow the lines of conduct which they have esteemed honorable; they reprove them for their errors like their own children. They are not allowed, like the Scythians, to inflict death on their slaves. They have numerous ways of conferring freedom; they can manumit not only during life, but also by their wills, and the testamentary wishes of a Roman in regard to his property are law."

My interlocutor shed tears, and confessed that the laws and constitution of the Romans were fair, but deplored that the officials, not possessing the spirit of former generations, were ruining the state.

Reading 9
Jordanes on the Coming of the Visigoths

Jordanes, a Christian writer of partly Germanic ancestry, wrote his *Gothic History* in the middle of the sixth century. Since the events decribed below occurred more than 170 years earlier, in 376–378, Jordanes cannot be regarded as an eyewitness any more than could somebody writing today about the wars of Napoleon. But Jordanes plagarized freely Cassiodorus's somewhat earlier history of the Goths (now lost), which was itself heavily indebted to a still earlier history by a certain Ablabius (whose works have perished). Ablabius, in turn, is said to have drawn his information from Greek literary sources and Gothic sagas.

Jordanes' account of the entry of the Visigoths into the Roman Empire (376) and their victory at Adrianople (378) is more or less consistent with other accounts and can be generally trusted. The events occurred immediately before the accession of the strongly Trinitarian emperor Theodosius I (see document 4), in a period when imperial religious policy was shifting back and forth between Arianism and Trinitarianism. As the account opens, the Ostrogoths (East Goths) had just been conquered by the Huns.

The Visigoths, who were inhabitants of the western country, were terrified as their [Ostrogothic] kinsmen had been, and knew not how to plan for safety against the race of the Huns. After long deliberation by common consent they finally sent ambassadors into Romania to the Emperor Valens, brother of Valentinian, the elder Emperor, to say that if he would give them part of Thrace or Moesia to keep, they would submit themselves to his laws and commands. That he might have greater confidence in them, they promised to become Christians, if he would give them teachers who spoke their language. When Valens learned this, he gladly and promptly granted what he had himself intended to ask. He received them into the region of Moesia and placed them there as a wall of defense for his kingdom against other tribes. And since at that time the Emperor Valens, who was infected with the Arian

From *The Gothic History of Jordanes*, tr. Charles C. Mierow; Princeton, Princeton University Press, 1915, pp. 88–90.

perfidy, had closed all the churches of our party, he sent as preachers to them those who favored his sect. They came and straightway filled a rude and ignorant people with the poison of their heresy. Thus the Emperor Valens made the Visigoths Arians rather than Christians. Moreover, from the love they bore them, they preached the gospel both to the Ostrogoths and to their kinsmen the Gepidae, teaching them to reverence this heresy, and they invited all people of their speech everywhere to attach themselves to this sect. They themselves, as we have said, crossed the Danube and settled Dacia Ripensis, Moesia and Thrace by permission of the Emperor.[1]

Soon famine and want came upon them, as often happens to a people not yet well settled in a country. Their princes and the leaders who ruled them in place of kings, that is Fritigern, Alatheus and Safrac, began to lament the plight of their army and begged Lupicinus and Maximus, the Roman commanders, to open a market. But to what will not the "cursed lust for gold" compel men to assent? The generals, swayed by avarice, sold them at a high price not only the flesh of sheep and oxen, but even the carcasses of dogs and unclean animals, so that a slave would be bartered for a loaf of bread or ten pounds of meat. When their goods and chattels failed, the greedy trader demanded their sons in return for the necessities of life.

Now it came to pass in that troublous time that Lupicinus, the Roman general, invited Fritigern, a chieftain of the Goths, to a feast and, as the event revealed, devised a plot against him. But Fritigern, thinking no evil, came to the feast with a few followers. While he was dining in the praetorium he heard the dying cries of his ill-fated men, for, by order of the general, the soldiers were slaying his companions who were shut up in another part of the house. The loud cries of the dying fell upon ears already suspicious, and Fritigern at once perceived the treacherous trick. He drew his sword and with great courage dashed quickly from the banqueting-hall, rescued his men from their threatening doom and incited them to slay the Romans. Thus these valiant men gained the chance they had longed for—to be free to die in battle rather than to perish of hunger—and immediately took arms to kill the generals Lupicinus and Maximus. Thus that day put an end to the famine of the Goths and the safety of the Romans, for the Goths no longer as strangers and pilgrims, but as citizens and lords, began to rule the inhabitants and to hold in their own right all the northern country as far as the Danube.

When the Emperor Valens heard of this at Antioch, he made ready an army at once and set out for the country of Thrace. Here a grievous battle took place and the Goths prevailed. The Emperor himself was wounded and fled to a farm near Adrianople. The Goths, not knowing that an emperor lay hidden in so poor a hut, set fire to it (as is customary in dealing with a cruel foe), and

---

[1] Along the southern border of the middle Danube.

thus he was cremated in royal splendor. Plainly it was a direct judgment of God that he should be burned with fire by the very men whom he had perfidiously led astray when they sought the true faith, turning them aside from the flame of love into the fire of hell. From this time the Visigoths, in consequence of their glorious victory, possessed Thrace and Dacia Ripensis as if it were their native land.

Reading 10

Jordanes on the Fall of the Western Empire

Jordanes, again using earlier sources, is here describing events that occurred between 60 and 75 years before he wrote. As in the previous selection, Jordanes exhibits a distinct pro-Gothic bias, and his sympathies have prompted him to exclude certain details from his account. We know from other sources, for example, that Emperor Zeno invited Theodoric to Constantinople and honored him there in order to halt a five-year plundering expedition that Theodoric had been conducting against the Eastern Empire. The Ostrogothic invasion of Italy resulted from a pact between Theodoric and Zeno to get rid of Odoacer. And Theodoric persuaded Odoacer to stop fighting by promising to spare his life and share power with him. A few days later Theodoric had Odoacer murdered along with all his soldiers and their families. In short, this passage teaches us not only about the later fifth century but also about the problem of dealing with sources that are at once informative and biased. A biographer of an American president would doubtless study the releases of his press secretary but would be advised to seek other sources as well.

The passage begins with the appointment of the young Romulus Augustulus, the last of the Western emperors.

Now when Augustulus had been appointed Emperor by his father Orestes in Ravenna, it was not long before Odoacer, king of the Torcilingi, invaded Italy, as leader of the Sciri, the Heruli and allies of various races. He put Orestes to death, drove his son [Romulus] Augustulus from the throne and condemned him to the punishment of exile in the Castle of Lucullus in Campania [A.D. 476]. Thus the Western Empire of the Roman race, which Octavianus Augustus, the first of the Augusti, began to govern in the seven hundred

From *The Gothic History of Jordanes*, tr. Charles C. Mierow; Princeton, Princeton University Press, 1915, pp. 119–120, 134–139.

and ninth year from the founding of the city, perished with this Augustulus in the five hundred and twenty-second year from the beginning of the rule of his predecessors and those before them, and from this time onward kings of the Goths held Rome and Italy. Meanwhile Odoacer, king of nations, subdued all Italy and then at the very outset of his reign slew Count Bracila at Ravenna that he might inspire a fear of himself among the Romans. He strengthened his kingdom and held it for almost thirteen years, until the appearance of Theodoric, of whom we shall speak hereafter.

When the [Eastern] Emperor Zeno heard that Theodoric had been appointed king over his own people [the Ostrogoths], he received the news with pleasure and invited him to come and visit him in Constantinople, sending an escort of honor. Receiving Theodoric with all due respect, he placed him among the princes of his palace. After some time Zeno increased his dignity by adopting him as his son-at-arms and gave him a triumph[1] in the city at his expense. Theodoric was made Consul Ordinary also, which is well known to be the supreme good and highest honor in the world. Nor was this all, for Zeno set up before the royal palace an equestrian statue to the glory of this great man.

Now while Theodoric was in alliance by treaty with the Empire of Zeno and was himself enjoying every comfort in the city, he heard that his tribe, dwelling as we have said in Illyricum, was not altogether satisfied or content. So he chose rather to seek a living by his own exertions, after the manner customary to his race, rather than to enjoy the advantages of the Roman Empire in luxurious ease while his tribe lived apart.

Therefore Theodoric departed from the royal city and returned to his own people. In company with the whole tribe of the Goths, who gave him their unanimous consent, he set out for Hesperia. He went in straight march through Sirmium to the places bordering on Pannonia and, advancing into the territory of Venice as far as the bridge of the Sontius, encamped there. When he had halted there for some time to rest the bodies of his men and pack-animals, Odoacer sent an armed force against him, which he met on the plains of Verona and destroyed with great slaughter. Then he broke camp and advanced through Italy with greater boldness. Crossing the river Po, he pitched camp near the royal city of Ravenna, about the third milestone from the city in the place called Pineta. When Odoacer saw this, he fortified himself within the city. He frequently harassed the army of the Goths at night, sallying forth stealthily with his men, and this not once or twice, but often; and thus he struggled for almost three whole years. But he labored in vain, for all Italy at last called Theodoric its lord and the Empire obeyed his nod. But Odoacer, with his few adherents and the Romans who were present, suffered daily from

[1] A ceremonial procession traditionally accorded victorious Roman military commanders.

war and famine in Ravenna. Since he accomplished nothing, he sent an embassy and begged for mercy. Theodoric first granted it and afterwards deprived him of his life.

It was in the third year after his entrance into Italy, as we have said, that Theodoric, by advice of the Emperor Zeno, laid aside the garb of a private citizen and the dress of his race and assumed a costume with a royal mantle, as he had now become the ruler over both Goths and Romans.

CHAPTER 2

The Heirs of
Classical Civilization

With the collapse of Western imperial government in 476 and the establishment of Christian Germanic kingdoms in its place, the cultures of the Eastern Empire and Western Europe began to drift apart. The vast lands that Rome had once ruled came to be divided into two distinct civilizations: Byzantium (East Rome) and Western Christendom. A third civilization emerged when the Arab conquests of the seventh and eighth centuries spread the religion and culture of Islam through much of the Middle East, and westward across the formerly Roman territories of North Africa and Spain.

The three civilizations of medieval Western Eurasia—Byzantine, Western Christian, and Islamic—were all influenced by the earlier Greco-Roman culture. All were, to some degree, heirs of Classical civilization. And all were committed to monotheistic religions that drew inspiration from ancient Judaism. Mohammed taught that Jesus, Moses, and the Old Testament prophets were, like himself, servants and spokesmen of the one God.

The sources in this chapter deal first with Byzantine Civilization (documents 1–3), then with early Western Christendom through the seventh century (documents 4–7), and finally with Islam (documents 8–10). The Byzantine sources begin with an account of one of the holy men who functioned as spiritual heroes and centers of community devotion in early Byzantine society (document 1). There follows a selection from the *Corpus Juris Civilis* (the "Body of Civil Law"), assembled under the sixth-century emperor Justinian, which was to exert a commanding influence on medieval jurisprudence (document 2). We conclude with an account of the overwhelming defeat at Manzikert in 1071, which crippled the Byzantine Empire permanently (document 3). The sources from the early-medieval West all emphasize, in one way or another, the creative role of the popes and Benedictine monks in preserving and expanding Classical-Christian culture in the Germanic kingdoms (documents 4–7). Our Islamic documents begin with an excerpt from the Koran, the holy book in which the Islamic faith is rooted (document 8). They continue with Mohammed's Constitution of Medina, the political-religious community that served as a model for the future governance of the Islamic Empire (document 9). The two final sources illustrate Islamic medical science (document 10) and, a much-neglected topic, Islamic humor (document 11).

Reading 1

The Life of St. Daniel the Stylite

A disciple of the pillar-saint Simeon Stylites, St. Daniel was born in Syria in 409 and died near Constantinople in 493. He was a shrewd, uncomplicated man who gave practical advice to people of the neighborhood and travelers from afar. And he served as a living example of heroic Christian sanctity. The author of the *Life* was a younger contemporary of Daniel's, perhaps a disciple and certainly an eyewitness to many of Daniel's activities. Like the authors of other saints' lives throughout the Middle Ages, Daniel's biographer writes with the purpose of inspiring others to admire and emulate his spiritual hero. If Daniel had faults, we will not discover them here.

Daniel's career was paralleled by those of numerous Byzantine saints who, to a far greater extent than in the West, played intimate, unifying roles in their urban communities.

Before all things it is right that we should give glory to Jesus Christ our God, Who for us was made man and for our salvation endured all things according to the Dispensation; for His sake, too, prophets were killed, and just men crucified themselves because of this faith in Him and by His grace, after having kept patience under their sufferings unswervingly unto the end, they received a crown of glory. These men our Master and Saviour Christ gave us as an example that we might know that it is possible for a man by the patient endurance of his sufferings to please God and be called His faithful servant. . . .

The servant of God [St. Daniel] fell into an ecstasy, as it were, and saw a huge pillar of cloud standing opposite him and the holy and blessed Simeon [another famous pillar saint] standing above the head of the column and two men of goodly appearance, clad in white, standing near him in the heights. And he heard the voice of the holy and blessed Simeon saying to him, "Come here to me, Daniel." And he said, "Father, father, and how can I get up to that height?" Then the saint said to the young men standing near him, "Go down and bring him up to me." So the men came down and brought Daniel up to him and he stood there. Then Simeon took him in his arms and kissed him with a holy kiss, and then others called him away, and escorted by them he was borne up to heaven leaving Daniel on the column with the two men. When holy Daniel saw him being carried up to heaven he heard the voice of St. Simeon, "Stand firm and play the man." But he was confused by fear and by that fearful voice, for it was like thunder in his ears. When he came to himself again he

From *Three Byzantine Saints*, ed. and tr. E. Dawes and N.H. Baynes; Crestwood, N.J., St. Vladimir's Seminary Press, 1948, pp. 7, 18–19, 29, 36, 43–44, 70–71.

declared the vision to those around him. Then they said to the holy man, "You must mount on to a pillar and take up St. Simeon's mode of life and be supported by the angels." . . .

Now the blessed Emperor Leo [457–474] of pious memory had heard from many of these things and desired for a long time to see the man. Therefore he sent for the pious Sergius, who carried the saint's messages, and through him he asked that the saint would pray and beseech God to grant him a son. And Daniel prayed, and through God's good pleasure the emperor's wife, the Empress Verina, thereafter conceived and begot a son, whereupon the emperor immediately sent and had the foundations laid of a third column. . . .

It happened about the same time that Gubazius, the king of the Lazi, arrived at the court of the Emperor Leo, who took him up to visit the holy man. When he saw this strange sight Gubazius threw himself on his face and said, "I thank You, heavenly King, that by means of an earthly king You have deemed me worthy to behold great mysteries; for never before in this world have I seen anything of this kind." And these kings had a point in dispute touching the Roman policy; and they laid the whole matter open to the servant of God and through the mediation of the holy man they agreed upon a treaty which satisfied the claims of each. After this the emperor returned to the city and dismissed Gubazius to his native land, and when the latter reached his own country he related to all his folk what he had seen. Consequently the men who later on came up from Lazica to the city [of Constantinople] invariably went up to Daniel. Gubazius himself, too, wrote to the holy man and besought his prayers and never ceased doing so to the end of his life. . . .

At about that time the blessed Emperor Leo heard from many about a certain Titus, a man of vigor who dwelt in Gaul and had in his service a number of men well trained for battle; so he sent for him and honored him with the rank of count that he might have him to fight on his behalf if he were forced to go to war. This Titus he sent to the holy man for his blessing; on his arrival the saint watered him with many and divers counsels from the holy writings and proved him to be an ever-blooming fruit-bearing tree; and Titus, beholding the holy man, marveled at the strangeness of his appearance and his endurance and just as good earth when it has received the rain brings forth much fruit, so this admirable man Titus was illuminated in mind by the teaching of the holy and just man and no longer wished to leave the enclosure, for he said, "The whole labor of man is spent on growing rich and acquiring possessions in this world and pleasing men; yet the single hour of his death robs him of all his belongings; therefore it is better for us to serve God rather than men." With these words he threw himself down before the holy man begging him to receive him and let him be enrolled in the brotherhood. And Daniel, the servant of the Lord, willingly accepted his good resolve. Thereupon that noble man Titus sent for all his men and said to his soldiers, "From now on I am the soldier of the heavenly King; aforetime my rank among men made me your captain and yet I was unable to benefit either you or myself, for I only urged you on to slaughter and bloodshed. From today, however, and henceforth I bid farewell to all such things; therefore those of you who wish it, remain here with me, but I do not compel any one of you, for what is done under compulsion is not acceptable. See, here is the money, take some, each of you, and go to your homes." Then he brought much gold and he took and placed it in front of the column and gave to each according to his rank. Two of them, however, did not choose to take any, but remained with him. All the rest embraced Titus and went their ways.

When the emperor heard this he was very angry and sent a messenger up to the holy man to say to Titus, "I brought you up from your country because I wanted to have you quite near me and I sent you to the holy man to pray and receive a blessing, but not that you should separate yourself from me." Titus replied to the messenger, "From now on, since I have listened to the teaching of this holy man, I am dead to the world and to all the things of the world. Whatever the just man says about me to you, tell to the emperor, for Titus your servant is dead." Then the messengers went outside into the enclosure to the holy man and told him everything. And the holy man sent a letter of counsel by them to the emperor, beseeching him and saying, "You yourself need no human aid; for owing to your perfect faith in God you have God as your everlasting defender; do not therefore covet a man who today is and tomorrow is not; for the Lord does all things in accordance with His will. Therefore dedicate your servant to God Who is able to send your Piety in his stead another still braver and more useful; without your approval I never wished to do anything."

And the emperor was satisfied and sent and thanked the holy man and said, "To crown all your good deeds there yet remained this good thing for you to do. Let the man, then, remain under your authority, and may God accept his good purpose." Not long afterwards they were deemed worthy of the holy robe, and both made progress in the good way of life; but more especially was this of Titus, the former count. . . .

Let us now in a short summary review his whole life down to the end of his time on earth.

Our all-praiseworthy father Daniel said good-bye to his parents when he was twelve years old, then for twenty-five years he lived in a monastery; after that during five years he visited the fathers and from each learned what might serve his purpose, making his anthology from their teachings. At the time when the crown of his endurance began to be woven the saint had completed his forty-second year, and at that age he came by divine guidance, as we have explained above, to this our imperial city. He dwelt in the church for nine years, standing on the capital of a column, thus training himself beforehand in the practice of that discipline which he was destined to bring to perfection. For he had learned from many divine revelations that his duty was to enter upon the way of life practiced by the blessed and sainted Simeon.

For three and thirty years and three months he stood for varying periods on the three columns, as he changed from one to another, so that the whole span of his life was a little more than eighty-four years.

During these he was deemed worthy to receive "the prize of his high calling"; he blessed all men, he prayed on behalf of all, he counseled all not to be covetous, he instructed all in the things necessary to salvation, he showed hospitality to all, yet he possessed nothing on earth beyond the confines of the spot on which the enclosure and religious houses had been built. And though many, amongst whom were sovereigns and very distinguished officials occupying the highest posts, wished to present him with splendid possessions he never consented, but he listened to each one's offer and then prayed that he might be recompensed by God for his pious intention.

Reading 2

The Institutes of Justinian

During the early years of the reign of the Byzantine emperor Justinian (reigned 527–565), a commission of imperial lawyers headed by Tribonian carried out the emperor's order to systematize and produce official texts of the whole of Roman law still in effect. The result of this immense effort, the *Corpus Juris Civilis*, included all valid imperial statutes since the time of Hadrian (the *Codex*) along with a synthesis of the authoritive writings of Roman legal officials (the *Digest*) and an introductory textbook on the fundamental principles of Roman law (the *Institutes*). It is from the *Institutes*, completed in 533, that the following passages are drawn.

PROLOGUE

In the name of our Lord Jesus Christ. The emperor Caesar Flavius Justinian, conqueror of the Alamanni, Goths, Franks, Germans, Antes, Alani, Vandals and Africans, rightly fortunate and renowned, victorious and triumphant, ever Augustus, to the young [scholars] desirous of legal knowledge.

The imperial majesty should not only be embellished with arms but also strengthened by laws, so that the times of both war and peace can be ordered

From *Corpus Juris Civilis*, ed. Paul Krueger. 1882 vol. I, pp. 2–4; tr. Marc Anthony Meyer, Berlin.

correctly and that the Roman emperor [*princeps*] may emerge not only victorious in battle with enemies but also, eliminating the iniquities of villains through legal means, may be as solicitous of the law as he is triumphant over conquered foes.

1. We have reached each of these objectives through the greatest vigilance and foresight, and by the will of God. And the barbarian nations brought under our subjection know of our military achievements, and Africa as well and many other provinces have been restored after a very long time to Roman domination through our victories, and with divine guidance we have achieved and proclaimed our empire. Truly, all of the people are now also governed by laws that have been promulgated or compiled by us.

2. And after bringing the revered constitutions, previously in a confused state, into lucid harmony, we turned our attention to the great mass of venerable jurisprudence and, as if crossing the open sea, we completed—by the favor of heaven—a nearly hopeless task.

3. And when, with God's help, this had been done, we called together Tribonian, a great man and teacher and ex-quaestor of our sacred palace, and Theophilus and Dorotheus, both illustrious men—all of whose ingenuity and legal expertise and tried obedience to our orders we have had ample proof. We issued a special mandate that by our authority and with our encouragement they should compose the *Institutes* so that you might acquire your first knowledge of the law not from old stories but through the splendor of the emperor [and] that your ears and minds might receive nothing useless or false but that which is deemed proper in these matters. And whereas in the past at least four years would go by before the imperial constitutions were read, you can now do this from the beginning, meriting such honor and discovering with such happiness that the beginning and the end of your legal studies proceed from the mouth of the emperor.

7. Therefore, with all endeavor and eager study, receive these our laws and show yourselves so learned that you may cherish the marvelous hope that, at the end of your legal studies, you may even be able to order our state [*res publica*] in that part given over to you. . . .

ON JUSTICE AND LAW

Justice is the constant and perpetual desire to give to each person his own due right [*ius*].

1. Jurisprudence [*iurisprudentia*] is the acquaintance with both human and divine things, the knowledge of what is just and what unjust.

3. These are the precepts of law [*ius*]: to live honestly, not to injure another, and to render to each his own.

4. The two aspects of this study are public and private: public law is that

which pertains to the Roman state, private is that which concerns the benefit of the individual. This is to say, therefore, that private law has three parts—indeed, it consists of natural precepts or either those of nations or of states.

ON NATURAL LAW, THE LAW OF NATIONS AND CIVIL LAW

Natural law [*ius naturale*] is that which nature has instilled in all animals, because this law is not characteristic of humankind but of all animals which are born on land and in the air and in the sea. From this derives the association of man and woman which we call marriage, as well as procreation and the rearing of off-spring because we see that animals are imbued with the experience of this law.

1. Civil law [*ius civile*] and the law of nations [*ius gentium*], however, are divided in this way: all peoples who are governed by laws [*leges*] and customs [*mores*] use law which is in part particular to themselves and in part common to all men. The law that each people has established for itself is particular to that state and is called civil law as being specifically of that state. Yet, what natural reason has established among all men is kept equally by all peoples and is called the law of nations, as it were, the law common to all peoples. And hence, the Roman people observe partly their own particular law [and] partly that which is common to all peoples. . . .

3. Our law is derived from written or unwritten [sources], just as among the Greeks: some laws are written, others unwritten. . . .

4. A 'law' [*lex*] is that which the Roman people commanded on a question submitted by a senatorial magistrate, like a consul. A 'plebiscite' [*plebiscitum*] is that which the plebs ordered put by a plebian magistrate, like a tribune. The plebs, however, differ from the people as a 'species' is distinguished from a 'genus' because the term 'people' means all the citizens, including as well patricians and senators, while the name 'plebians' signifies the other citizens, excluding the patricians and the senators. Yet, with the passing of the *lex Hortensia*[1] the plebiscites came to be no less valid than the laws.

5. A 'senatusconsultum' is that which the senate orders and directs, for when the Roman people had increased in its number, it became difficult to call it together in one place for the enactment of a law, [and thus,] it seemed best instead to invoke the senate in place of the people.

6. The emperor's voice has the force of law as well since, by the 'law of kings' [*lex regia*] which regulated his authority [*imperium*], the people conceded to him and placed in him all their power and authority. Thus, whatever

---

[1]In 287 B.C. the "struggle of the orders" culminated in the promulgation of the *lex Hortensia*, which decreed that plebiscites were to be as fully valid as laws [*leges*] proper.

the emperor directed by letter or decreed in a hearing or ordered by edict is to be conceived as law: these are what are called "constitutions." Some of these, of course, are special cases which are not to be used as precedents, for the emperor did not intend this to go beyond the individual because he views one person favorably because of merits or inflicts a penalty on another or offers relief to another. Others, however, when general in intent, undoubtedly apply to everyone.

7. Furthermore, praetorian[2] edicts have no ordinary authority as law. We normally call this the law of honor because those who bear honor, that is a magistrate, have given their authority to this law. And curule aediles[3] as well issued edicts concerning certain cases and that kind of edict is part of honorary law.

8. The responses of the learned [jurists] are sentences and opinions of those to whom it was permitted to lay down the law; for in ancient times it was instituted that there were those who publicly interpreted the law—who are called jurisconsults—to whom the right of responding [in legal matters] was given by the caesar. All of their sentences and opinions [when unanimous] held such authority that judges were not permitted to differ from their responses, so that it is a constitution.

9. Unwritten law is that which usage has approved, for long-observed customs take on the effect of law by consent of those who observe them. . . .

11. And, natural laws, which are followed by all nations alike, deriving from divine providence, remain always firm and unchangeable: truly, those which each state constitutes for itself often subject to alteration whether by the tacit approval of the people or else by subsequent legislation.

[2]The *praetor* was responsible for the administration of justice in both the Republic and Empire periods, but the authority of this high office was restricted by the superior authority of the consul. When Roman authority was established outside the boundaries of Italy, the praetors acted as provincial governors of the Senate; but with the dictatorship of Sulla in the first century B.C., these officers were required to remain in the capital to preside over criminal courts.

[3]In their capacity as market officers the curule aediles were responsible for important features of the Roman law of sale.

Reading 3

Michael Psellus, Describes the Battle of Manzikert 1071

In August 1071 a Byzantine army led by Emperor Romanus Diogenes was routed by the invading Seljuk Turks under their sultan, Alp Arslan. As a result of the Turkish victory the Byzantines lost Asia Minor, which had for many centuries been the Empire's best source of revenues and soldiers. Having captured Emperor Romanus, the Turks released him in return for a tremendous ransom and an annual tribute.

The author of this account, Michael Psellus, was a contemporary though not an eyewitness. He was a master of philosophy at the academy at Constantinople and one of the most celebrated and influential scholars of the age, whose keen intellect was matched only by his vanity and ambition. Psellus died a few years after the battle.

With his usual contempt of all advice, whether on matters civil or military, [Romanus] at once set out with his army and hurried to Caesarea. Having reached that objective, he was loath to advance any further and tried to find excuses for returning to Byzantium, not only for his own sake but for the army's. When he found the disgrace involved in such a retreat intolerable, he should have come to terms with the enemy and put a stop to their annual incursions. Instead, whether in desperation, or because he was more confident than he should have been, he marched to the attack without taking adequate measures to protect his rear. The enemy, seeing him advance, decided to lure him on still farther and ensnare him by cunning. They therefore rode on ahead of him and then retired again, as though the retreat was planned. By carrying out this maneuver several times, they succeeded in cutting off some of our generals, who were taken captive.

Now I was aware—though he was not—that the Sultan himself, the king of the Persians and Kurds [Alp Arslan, the Seljuk leader], was present in person with his army, and most of their victories were due to his leadership. Romanus refused to believe anyone who detected the Sultan's influence in these successes. The truth is, he did not want peace. He thought he would capture the barbarian camp without a battle. Unfortunately for him, through his ignorance of military science, he had scattered his forces; some were concentrated round himself, others had been sent off to take up some other position. So, instead of opposing his adversaries with the full force of his army, less than half were actually involved.

From Michael Psellus, *Chronographica*, in *Fourteen Byzantine Rulers*, tr. E.R.A. Sewter, New York, Penguin Books, 1966, pp. 353–356.

Although I cannot applaud his subsequent behavior, it is impossible for me to censure him. The fact is, he bore the whole brunt of the danger himself. His action can be interpreted in two ways. My own view represents the mean between these two extremes. On the one hand, if you regard him as a hero, courting danger and fighting courageously, it is reasonable to praise him; on the other, when one reflects that a general, if he conforms to the accepted rules of strategy, must remain aloof from the battle-line, supervising the movements of his army and issuing the necessary orders to the men under his command, then Romanus's conduct on this occasion would appear foolish in the extreme, for he exposed himself to danger without a thought of the consequences. I myself am more inclined to praise than to blame him for what he did.

However that may be, he put on the full armor of an ordinary soldier and drew sword against his enemies. According to several of my informants he actually killed many of them and put others to flight. Later, when his attackers recognized who he was, they surrounded him on all sides. He was wounded and fell from his horse. They seized him, of course, and the Emperor of the Romans was led away, a prisoner, to the enemy camp, and his army was scattered. Those who escaped were but a tiny fraction of the whole. Of the majority some were taken captive, the rest massacred.

I do not intend at this moment to write of the time spent by the emperor in captivity, or of the attitude adopted towards him by his conqueror. That must wait till later. A few days after the battle, one of those who escaped, arriving before his comrades, brought the terrible news to the city. He was followed by a second messenger, and by others. The picture they painted was by no means distinct, for each explained the disaster in his own fashion, some saying that Romanus was dead, others that he was only a prisoner; some again declared that they had seen him wounded and hurled to the ground, while others had seen him being led away in chains to the barbarian camp. In view of this information, a conference was held in the capital, and the empress considered our future policy. The unanimous decision of the meeting was that, for the time being, they should ignore the emperor, whether he was a prisoner, or dead, and that Eudocia and her sons should carry on the government of the Empire.

Reading 4

Pope Gelasius I on Priestly and Royal Power

In 494 Pope Gelasius I set forth, in this letter to the East Roman emperor, the classic papal argument on the superiority of priestly to royal power—the so-called "doctrine of the two swords." Gelasius' words would be repeated by popes and other churchmen throughout the Middle Ages.

. . . Two there are, august emperor, by which this world is chiefly ruled, the sacred authority [*auctoritas*] of the priesthood and the royal power [*potestas*]. Of these the responsibility of the priests is more weighty in so far as they will answer for the kings of men themselves at the divine judgment. You know, most clement son, that, although you take precedence over all mankind in dignity, nevertheless you piously bow the neck to those who have charge of divine affairs and seek from them the means of your salvation, and hence you realize that, in the order of religion, in matters concerning the reception and right administration of the heavenly sacraments, you ought to submit yourself rather than rule, and that in these matters you should depend on their judgment rather than seek to bend them to your will. For if the bishops themselves, recognizing that the imperial office was conferred on you by divine disposition, obey your laws so far as the sphere of public order is concerned lest they seem to obstruct your decrees in mundane matters, with what zeal, I ask you, ought you obey those who have been charged with administering the sacred mysteries? Moreover, just as no light risk attends pontiffs who keep silent in matters concerning the service of God, so too no little danger threatens those who show scorn—which God forbid—when they ought to obey. And if the hearts of the faithful should be submitted to all priests in general who rightly administer divine things, how much more should assent be given to the bishop of that see which the Most High wished to be pre-eminent over all priests, and which the devotion of the whole church has honored ever since. As your piety is certainly well aware, no one can ever raise himself by purely human means to the privilege and place of him whom the voice of Christ has set before all, whom the church has always venerated and held in devotion as its primate. The things which are established by divine judgment can be assailed by human presumption; they cannot be overthrown by anyone's power.

From Pope Gelasius' letter to Emperor Anastasius, in *The Crisis of Church and State, 1050-1300*, ed. Brian Tierney; Englewood, N.J., Prentice-Hall, Inc., 1964, pp. 13–14. Reprinted by permission.

Reading 5

The Rule of St. Benedict

The Rule of St. Benedict (*c.* 480–544), based in part on earlier models, spread throughout Western Christendom to govern the lives of countless monks and nuns of the Middle Ages and beyond. The excerpts that follow stress two fundamental elements in Benedictine monasticism: humility and poverty.

PROLOGUE

Hear, my son, the precept of your master, and incline the ear of your heart, willingly receive and faithfully fulfill the admonition of your loving Father, that you may return by the labor of obedience to Him from Whom you had departed through the sloth of disobedience. Therefore, my little speech is now addressed to you—whoever you are—that, renouncing your own will, you take up the strong and bright weapons of obedience to fight for the Lord Christ, our true King. In the first place, whatever good work you begin to do, beg Him with most earnest prayer to perfect it; that He Who has now vouchsafed to count us in the number of His sons may not be grieved at any time by our evil deeds. For we must always serve Him with the good things He has given us, that not only may He never, as an angry father, disinherit His children, but may never, as an irate lord, incensed by our sins, deliver us to everlasting punishment, as most wicked servants who would not follow Him to glory. . . .

If we wish to dwell in the tabernacle of His kingdom, we will not reach it unless we approach by our good deeds. But let us ask the Lord with the prophet, saying to Him: "Lord, who will dwell in Your tabernacle, or who will rest upon Your holy mountain?" After this question, brothers, let us hear the Lord answering, and showing us the way to His tabernacle, and saying: "He who walks without stain and works justice; he who speaks the truth in his heart [and] has not spoken wickedly with his tongue; he who has done no evil to his neighbor and has not taken up a reproach against his neighbor." He who has brought the malignant one to nothing, casting him out of his heart with all his suggestions, and has taken his evil thoughts, while still new, and dashed them down on Christ. These are the ones who, fearing the Lord, are not puffed up with their own good works, but knowing that the good which is in them comes not from themselves but from the Lord, they magnify the Lord Who works in them, saying with the prophet: "Not to us, Lord, not to us but to Your name give the glory. . . ."

From *Patrologiae Cursis Completus, sive Latinorum*, ed. J.P. Migne, vol. 66, columns 215–218, 371–376, 551–552, 839–840, tr. Marc Anthony Meyer.

Therefore, a school of the Lord's service has been instituted by us, in which institution we hope will be ordered nothing harsh or nothing rigorous. But if anything is somewhat strictly laid down, according to the dicates of equity, for the amendment of vices or the preservation of charity, do not on account of this flee in dismay from the road of salvation, whose beginning cannot but be straight. But as we go forward in our life and faith, we will, with hearts enlarged and with unspeakable sweetness of love, run in the way of God's commandments; so that never departing from His guidance, but persevering in His teaching in the monastery until death, we may by patience share in the sufferings of Christ, that we may deserve to be consorts of His kingdom.

CHAPTER SEVEN: ON HUMILITY

The Holy Scripture cries out to us, brothers, saying: "Everyone who exalts himself will be humbled, and he who humbles himself shall be exalted." In saying this, it teaches us all exaltation is a kind of pride, against which the prophet shows himself to be on his guard when he says: "Lord, my heart is not exalted nor my eyes lifted up; nor have I walked in great things, nor in wonders above me." And why? "If I did not think humbly, but exalted my soul, like a child who is weaned from his mother, so will you requite my soul." Hence, brothers, if we wish to arrive at the highest point of humility and quickly reach that heavenly exaltation to which we can only ascend by the humility of this present life, we must by our ever-ascending actions erect such a ladder as that which Jacob beheld in his dream, by which the angels appeared to him descending and ascending [*Genesis* 28]. This descent and ascent signify nothing else but that we descend by exaltation and ascend by humility. And the ladder thus erected is our life in the world which, if the heart is humble, is lifted up by the Lord to heaven. The sides of the same ladder we understand to be our body and soul, in which the call of God has placed various degrees of humility or discipline, which we must ascend.

The first degree of humility, then, is that a man must always keep the fear of God before his eyes [and] avoid all forgetfulness; and that he must remember all that God has commanded and that those who despise God will be consumed in hell for their sins; and that he must consider that life everlasting is prepared for those who fear Him. And keeping himself at all times from sin and vice, whether of the thoughts, the tongue, the eyes, the hands, the feet, or his own will, let him quickly hasten to cut off the desires of the flesh. Let him consider that he is always seen from heaven by God, and that his actions are everywhere seen by the eye of the Divine Majesty and are every hour reported to Him by His angels. . . . Since, therefore, the eyes of the Lord see good and evil, and the Lord is always looking down from the heavens upon the children of men to see who has understanding or is seeking God, and since the works of our hands are reported to Him, our Maker and Creator, day and night by the angels appointed to watch over us, we must always be on guard, brothers, lest, as the prophet says in the psalm, God should see us at any time descending into evil and become unprofitable, and lest, though He would spare us now, because He is merciful and expects our conversion, He should say to us in the future: "These things you did and I held my peace."

The second degree of humility is that a man should not love his own will, nor delight in gratifying his own desires; but should carry out in his own deeds that saying of the Lord: "I came not to do my own will, but the will of Him who sent me." And again, Scripture says "Self-will has punishment, but necessity wins a crown."

The third degree of humility is that for the love of God a man should surrender himself in all obedience to his superior, imitating the Lord of whom the apostle says: "He was made obedient even to death."

The fourth degree of humility is that if in this very obedience hard and contrary things, or even injuries, are done to him, he should embrace them patiently with silent consciousness, and not grow weary or submit, as the Scripture says: "He who will persevere to the end will be saved." And again: "Let your heart take courage and wait for the Lord. . . ."

The fifth degree of humility is to hide from one's abbot none of the evil thoughts that beset one's heart, nor the sins committed in secret, but humbly confess them. Concerning which the Scripture exhorts us, saying: "Make known the way to the Lord, and hope in Him." And again: "Confess to the Lord, for He is good, for His mercy endures forever." The prophet also says: "I have made known to You my offence, and my iniquities I have not hidden. I said I will confess against myself my iniquities to the Lord, and You have forgiven the wickedness of my heart."

The sixth degree of humility is for a monk to be contented with the vilest and worst of everything and in all that is enjoined him to esteem himself a bad and worthless laborer, saying with the prophet: "I have been brought to nothing, and I knew it not; I have become like a beast before You, yet I am always with You."

The seventh degree of humility is that he should not only call himself with his tongue lower and viler than all else, but also believe himself with intimate affection of the heart to be so, humbling himself, and saying with the prophet: "I am a worm and no man, the shame of men and the outcast of the people; I have been exalted, and cast down and confounded." And again: "It is good for me that You have humbled me so that I may learn Your commandments."

The eighth degree of humility is for a monk to do nothing except what is authorized by the common rule of the monastery or by the example of his seniors.

The ninth degree of humility is that a monk should refrain his tongue from speaking, keeping silence until a question is asked him, as the Scripture shows: "In much talking you will not avoid sin" and "The talkative man will not be directed upon the earth."

The tenth degree of humility is that he should not be easily or quickly moved to laughter, because it is written: "The fool lifts up his voice in laughter."

The eleventh degree of humility is that when a monk speaks he should do so gently and without laughter, humbly and with gravity, or with few words and reasonable speech, as it is written: "A wise man is known in a few words."

The twelfth degree of humility is that a monk, not only in his heart but also in his very body, should always show his humility to all who see him; that is, in work, in the oratory, in the monastery, in the garden, on the road, in the field, or wherever he may be, whether sitting, walking or standing, with head always bent down, and eyes fixed on the earth; that he always thinks of the guilt of his sins and imagines himself already present before the terrible judgment of God, always saying in his heart what the publican said with his eyes fixed on earth: "Lord, I am a sinner and am not worthy to raise my eyes to heaven." And again with the prophet: "I am bowed down and humbled on every side."

Therefore, having ascended all these degrees of humility, the monk will presently arrive at the love of God which, being perfect, casts out fear; whereby he will begin to keep, without labor, and as it were naturally and by custom, all those precepts which he had once observed only out of fear; no longer through dread of hell, but for the love of Christ, and of a good habit and a delight in virtue, which God will deem to make manifest by the Holy Spirit in His laborer, now cleansed from sin and vice.

CHAPTER THIRTY THREE: IF MONKS SHOULD HAVE ANYTHING OF THEIR OWN

Above all let the vice of private ownership be cut off from the monastery by the roots. Let no one presume to give or receive anything without leave of the abbot, or to keep anything as their own—either book or writing tablet or pen or anything whatsoever—since they are permitted to have neither body nor will in their own power. But let them hope to receive all necessities from the abbot of the monastery; nor let them keep anything which the abbot has not given or permitted. Let all things be common to all, as it is written; nor let anyone say or assume that anything is his own. But if anyone shall be found to indulge in this most horrible vice, and after one or two admonitions he does not make amends, let him be subjected to correction.

Reading 6

Select Letters of Pope Gregory the Great

St. Gregory the Great (pope 590–604) was one of the most learned popes of the early Middle Ages and perhaps the ablest. His letter to John bishop of Ravenna (letter A), better known as *The Book of Pastoral Care*, was written shortly after his accession to the papacy. A wise and authoritative guide to the responsibilities of bishops, it achieved tremendous popularity across Western Christendom. Gregory's letter to Emperor Maurice (letter B), echoing Pope Gelasius' two-swords doctrine, discloses the precarious semi-independent position of the papacy in central Italy. Rome and the lands around it were under Byzantine rule in Gregory's time as a result of Justinian's reconquest (535–555), but imperial authority was being undermined by the attacks of Lombard warriors. Despite the unsettled conditions in Rome, Gregory worked effectively toward the reform and expansion of Western Christendom. The monks whom he sent to pagan England in 596 (letters C and D) succeeded in converting the southern kingdom of Kent, thereby launching a missionary process that would eventually bring all of England into the Christian fold.

A. LETTER TO JOHN BISHOP OF RAVENNA, BETTER KNOWN AS THE BOOK OF PASTORAL CARE

With kind and humble intent you reprove me, dearest brother, for having wished by hiding myself to flee from the burdens of pastoral care; as to which, lest to some they should appear light, I express with my pen in the book before you all my own estimate of their heaviness, in order both that he who is free from them may not unwarily seek them, and that he who has sought them may tremble for having gotten them. . . .

What manner of man ought to come to rule? A man ought by all means be drawn to be an example of good living who already lives spiritually, dying to all passions of the flesh; who disregards wordly prosperity; who is afraid of no adversity; who desires only inward wealth; whose intention the body, in good accord with it, thwarts not at all by its frailness, nor the spirit greatly by its disdain—one who is not led to covet the things of others but gives freely of his own; who through the bowels of compassion is quickly moved to pardon, yet is never bent down from the fortress of rectitude by pardoning more than is necessary; who perpetrates no unlawful deeds, yet deplores those perpetrated

From Letters of Pope Gregory the Great, Tr. James Barmby, in *Library of Nicene and Post-Nicene Fathers*, vol. XII, pp. 1, 7, 24–25, 71, 175–177, 202–203, 205–206.

by others as though they were his own; who out of affection of the heart sym-
pathizes with another's infirmity and so rejoices in the good of his neighbor as
though it were his own advantage; who so insinuates himself as an example to
others in all he does that among them he has nothing, at any rate of his own
past deeds, to blush for; who studies so to live that he may be able to water
even dry hearts with the streams of sacred learning; who has already by the use
and trial of prayer that he can obtain what he has requested from the Lord,
having already been told, as it were, through the voice of experience, "While
you are still speaking, I will say, here am I." For if by chance anyone should
come to us asking us to intercede for him with some great man, who was incensed against him, but unknown to us, we should at once reply, we cannot go
to intercede for you since we have no familiar acquaintance with that man. If,
then, a man blushes to become an intercessor with another man on whom he
has no claim, with what idea can anyone grasp the duty of intercession with
God for the people, who does not know himself to be in favor with Him
through the merit of his own life? And how can he ask pardon of Him for
others while ignorant whether towards himself He is appeased? And in this
matter there is still another thing to be more anxiously feared; namely, lest one
who is supposed to be competent to appease wrath should himself provoke it
on account of guilt of his own. For we all know well that when one who is in
disfavor is sent to intercede with an incensed person the mind of the latter is
provoked to greater severity. Wherefore, let one who is still tied and bound
with earthly desires beware lest by more grievously incensing the strict Judge,
while he delights himself in his place of honor, he becomes the cause of ruin to
his subordinates. . . .

How the ruler, while living well, ought to teach and admonish those who
are placed under him: Since, then, we have shown what manner of man the
pastor ought to be, let us now set forth after what manner he should teach. For
as long before us Gregory Nazianzen[1] of reverend memory has taught, one and
the same exhortation does not suit all, since all people are not bound together
by similarity of character. For the things that profit some often hurt others;
seeing that also for the most part herbs which nourish some animals are fatal
to others; and the gentle hissing that quiets horses incites puppies; and the
medicine which abates one disease aggravates another; and the bread which in-
vigorates the life of the strong kills little children. Therefore, according to the
quality of the listeners the discourse ought to be fashioned by teachers to suit
all and each for their different needs, and yet never deviate from the art of

---

[1]Gregory of Nazianzus (d. 389) is one of the four great Greek doctors of the church and is associated with the final defeat of the Arian heresy in the East. Gregory was made bishop of Constantinople in 380, but the difficulties he encountered forced him to resign within a few weeks and
he ended his life in contemplation near Arianzus in Iona.

common edification. For what are the intent minds of listeners but, so to speak, a kind of tight tension of strings in a harp, which the skillful player strikes variously that he may produce a tune not at variance with itself? And for this reason the strings render back a consonant modulation, that they are struck indeed with one quill, but not with one kind of stroke. Whence every teacher also, that he may edify all in the one virtue of charity, ought to touch the hearts of his listeners out of one doctrine, but not with one and the same exhortation. . . . Differently, then, men and women are to be admonished because on the former heavier injunctions and on the latter lighter ones are to be laid so that [men] may be exercised by great things, but women overwhelmingly converted by light ones. Differently to be admonished are young and old men because for the most part severity of admonition directs the former to improvement, while kind remonstrance disposes the latter to better deeds. . . .

How the preacher, when he has accomplished his task, should return to himself lest either his life or his preaching puff him up. But since often, when preaching is abundantly poured forth in fitting ways, the mind of the preacher is elevated in itself by a hidden delight in self-display, great care is necessary that he may gnaw himself with the laceration of fear, lest he who recalls the diseases of others to health by remedies should himself swell through neglect of his own; lest in helping others he deserts himself, lest in lifting up others he falls. For some the greatness of their virtue has often been the occasion of their perdition, causing them, while inordinately secure in confidence of strength, to die unexpectedly through negligence. For virtue strives with vice—the mind flatters itself with a certain delight in it—and it comes to pass that the soul of a well intentioned man casts aside the fear of its circumspection and rests secure in self-confidence; and to it, now torpid, the cunning seducer enumerates all things that it has done well, and exalts it in swelling thoughts as though superexcellent beyond all beside it. Whence it is brought about that before the eyes of the just Judge the memory of virtue is a pitfall of the soul; because, in calling to mind what it has done well, while it lifts itself up in its own eyes, it falls before the Author of humility.

B. LETTER TO THE EMPEROR MAURICE, c. 591–592.

The piety of my lords in their most serene commands, while set on refuting me on certain matters, in sparing me have by no means spared me. For by the use therein of the word "simplicity" they politely call me silly. It is true indeed that in Holy Scripture, when simplicity is used in a good sense, it is often carefully associated with prudence and uprightness. . . .

Indeed if the captivity of my land were not increasing day by day, I would gladly pass over in silence contempt and ridicule of myself. But this does afflict me exceedingly, that from my bearing the charge of falsehood it ensues also that Italy is daily led captive under the yoke of the Lombards. And, while my representations are not believed, the strength of the enemy is increasing. This, however, I suggest to my most pious lord, that he would think anything that is bad of me, but with regards to the advantage of the Republic and the cause of the rescue of Italy, not easily lend his pious ears to anyone, but believe facts rather than words. Moreover, let our lord, in virtue of his earthly power, not too hastily disdain priests, but with excellent consideration, on account of Him Whose servants they are, so rule over them as also to pay the reverence that is due to them. For in Holy Scripture priests are sometimes called gods and sometimes angels. For even through Moses it is said of him who is to be put upon his oath, "Bring him unto the gods"—that is "unto the priests. . . ." Why, then, should it be strange if your piety were to condescend to honor those to whom even God Himself in His word gives honor, calling them angels or gods? Ecclesiastical history also testifies that when accusations in writing against bishops had been given to the emperor Constantine of pious memory, he received the written accusations; but calling together the bishops who had been accused, he burnt before their eyes the documents he had received, saying, "You are gods, constituted by the true God. Go and settle your causes among yourselves, for it is not fit that we should judge gods." Yet in this sentence, my pious lord, he conferred more on himself by his humility than on them by the reverence paid to them. For before him there were pagan princes in the Republic who knew not the true God but worshipped gods of wood and stone; and yet they paid the greatest honor to their priests. What wonder then if a Christian emperor should condescend to honor the priests of the true God, when pagan princes, as we have already said, knew how to bestow honor on priests who served gods of wood and stone?

These things, then, I suggest to the piety of my lords, not in my behalf but in behalf of all priests. For I am a man who is a sinner. And since I offend against Almighty God incessantly every day, I surmise that there will be some amends for this at the tremendous judgment, that I am stricken incessantly every day by blows. And I believe that you appease the same Almighty God all the more as you more severely afflict me who serve Him badly. For I had already received many blows, and when the commands of my lords came in addition, I found consolations that I want not hoping for. For if I can, I will briefly enumerate these blows.

First, the peace which without any cost to the Republic I had made with the Lombards who were in Tuscany was withdrawn from me. Then, the peace having been broken, the [imperial] soldiers were removed from the Roman city. And indeed some were slain by the enemy, but others were placed at Narni and Perugia, and Rome was left that Perugia might be held. After this a still heavier blow was the arrival of Agilulph,[2] so that I saw with my own eyes Romans tied by the neck with ropes like dogs to be taken to Gaul for sale. And, because we who were in the city under the protection of God escaped his hand, a reason was then sought for making us look culpable—particularly because corn ran short, which cannot by any means be kept for long in large quantities in this city, as I have written more fully in another letter. On my own account, I was in no way disturbed since I declare, my conscience bearing witness, that I was prepared to suffer any adversity whatever so long as I came out of all these things with the safety of my soul. But for the glorious men, Gregory the praefect and Castorius the military commander, I have been distressed to a great degree, seeing that they did not neglect to do all that could be done and endured most severe toil in watching and guarding the city during the siege; and after all this were smitten by the heavy indignation of my lord. As to them, I clearly understand that it is not their conduct but my person that goes against them. For having along with me labored in trouble, they are alike troubled after labor.

Now as to the piety of my lord holding over me the formidable and terrible judgment of Almighty God, I ask you by the same Almighty God to do this no more. . . . [And] this I say briefly, that, unworthy sinner as I am, I rely more on the mercy of Jesus when He comes than on the justice of your piety. And there are many things that men are ignorant of with regards to this judgment; for perhaps He will blame what you praise and praise what you blame. Therefore, among all these uncertainties I return to tears only, praying that the same Almighty God may both direct our most pious lord with His hand and in that terrible judgment find him free of all defaults. And may He make me so to please men, if need be, as not to offend His eternal grace.

C. LETTER TO THE MISSIONARIES GOING TO ENGLAND, DATED AUGUST 596

Gregory, servant of the servants of God, to the servants of our Lord Jesus Christ.

Since it had been better not to have begun what is good than to return from it when begun, you must, most beloved sons, fulfill the good work which you have started with the help of the Lord. Let, then, neither the toil of the journey nor the tongues of evil-speaking men deter you; but with all constancy

---

[2]Agilulph of Turin succeeded the great Lombard king Authari in c. 591 and also took the dead king's Catholic wife, Theodolinda of Bavaria, as his queen. Many of Gregory's letters are addressed to the powerful Theodolinda, who was herself partly responsible for the conversion of the Lombards to Catholicism.

and fervor go on with what under God's guidance you have begun, knowing that great toil is followed by the glory of an eternal reward. Humbly obey in all things your leader Augustine[3] who is returning to you [and] whom we have appointed your abbot, knowing that whatever may be fulfilled in you through his admonition will in all ways profit your souls. May Almighty God protect you with his grace, and grant to me to see the fruit of your work in the eternal country, that I may be found together with you in the joy of the reward, for in truth I desire to labor. God keep you safe, most beloved sons.

D. LETTER TO BRUNECHILD QUEEN OF THE FRANKS, DATED 596

Gregory to Brunechild, etc.

The Christianity of your excellence had long been so truly known to us that we do not in the least doubt your goodness but rather hold it to be in all ways certain that you will devoutly and zealously concur with us in the case of faith and supply most abundantly the succour of your religious sincerity. Being for this reason well assured and greeting you with paternal charity, we inform you that it has come to your knowledge how the nation of the English, by God's authority, is anxious to become Christian, but that the priests who are in their neighborhood have no pastoral solicitude with regards to them. And lest their souls should by chance perish in eternal damnation, it has been our care to send to them the bearer of these presents, Augustine, the servant of God, whose zeal and earnestness are well known to us, with other servants of God, that through them we might be able to learn their wishes, and as far as possible, you also striving with us, to take thought to their conversion. We have also charged them that for carrying out this design they should take with them preachers from the neighboring regions. Therefore, your excellency, habitually prone to good works [and] on account of our request as well as with regards to the fear of God, deign to hold him in all ways as commended to you and earnestly bestow on him the favor of your protection, and lend the aid of your patronage to his labor, and, that he may have the fullest fruit thereof, provide for his going secure under your protection to the above-mentioned nation of the English to the end that our God, who has adorned you in this world with good qualities well pleasing to Him, may cause you to give thanks here and in eternal rest with his saints. . . .

---

[3]Augustine became the first archbishop of Canterbury in 597 and died *c.* 604 and was succeeded by other members of the original mission to England.

Reading 7
A Description of the Synod of Whitby, 664

As Pope Gregory's monks and their successors spread Roman Christianity through England, they encountered rival missionaries from the Celtic monasteries of Ireland and southern Scotland. Celtic Christians, isolated from Rome and the Continent by the barbarian invasions, had developed distinctive customs and modes of organization: they used a different formula for calculating the date of Easter, they employed a different tonsure (below, note 2), and their church was organized around monasteries rather than bishoprics. Celtic and Roman-Benedictine missionaries had both been active in the conversion of the kingdom of Northumbria (northern England and southeastern Scotland). In 664, King Oswiu (or Oswy) of Northumbria summoned a council to meet at the Benedictine nunnery of Whitby to decide between the two forms of Christian practice. Although much of the argument at Whitby turned on the seemingly minor issue of the Easter date, far more was actually at stake. Northumbria had become the most powerful kingdom in England, and the decision at Whitby brought Northumbria out of the Celtic backwater into the papal-Benedictine mainstream. The champion of the papal cause at Whitby was the celebrated Benedictine missionary, Wilfrid of Hexham, better known as Wilfrid of Ripon. The account below was written by Eddius, one of his disciples and perhaps an eyewitness, shortly after Wilfrid's death.

On a certain occasion while Colman was bishop of York and metropolitan archbishop, during the reign of Oswiu and Alhfrith,[1] abbots, priests, and clerics of every rank gathered at Whitby Abbey in the presence of the most holy abbess Hilda, the two kings, and bishops Colman and Agilberht [of the West Saxons], to discuss the proper time for celebrating Easter: whether the practice of the British, Irish and the northern province of keeping it on the Sunday between the fourteenth and twenty-second day of the moon was correct or whether they ought to give way to the Roman plan for fixing it for the Sunday between the fifteenth and twenty-first days of the moon. Bishop Colman, as was proper, was given the first chance to state his case. He spoke with complete confidence, as follows: "Our fathers and theirs before them, clearly

From Eddius, "The Life of St. Wilfred of Hexham," in *Lives of the Saints*, tr. J.F. Webb; New York, Penguin Books, 1965, pp. 141–143.

[1]King Oswiu and his son, King Alhfrith, ruled jointly for a time. Oswiu controlled the entire kingdom of Northumbria, of which Deira, Alhfrith's area of jurisdiction, was a part. The young king died shortly after the synod of Whitby and his father survived another six years, dying in 670.

inspired by the Holy Spirit, as was Columba, stipulated that Easter Sunday should be celebrated on the fourteenth day of the moon if that day were a Sunday, following the example of St. John the Evangelist 'who leaned on the Lord's breast at supper,' the disciple whom Jesus loved. He celebrated Easter on the fourteenth day of the moon, as did his disciples, and Polycarp and his disciples, and as we do on their authority. Out of respect to our fathers we dare not change, nor do we have the least desire to do so. I have spoken for our party. Now let us hear your side of the question.''

Agilberht, the foreign prelate, and his priest Agatho bade St. Wilfrid, priest and abbot [of Hexham], use his winning eloquence to express in his own words the case of the Roman Church and Apostolic See. His speech was, as usual, humble. ''This question has already been admirably treated by a gathering of our most holy and learned fathers, three hundred and eighteen strong, at Nicaea, a city in Bithynia. Among other things they decided upon a lunar cycle recurring every nineteen years. This cycle gives no room for celebrating Easter on the fourteenth day of the moon. This is the rule followed by the Apostolic See and by nearly the whole world. At the end of the decrees of the fathers of Nicaea come these words: 'Let him who condemns any one of these decrees be anathema.' ''

At the end of Wilfrid's speech Oswiu asked them, with a smile on his face, ''Tell me, which is greater in the Kingdom of Heaven, Columba or the apostle Peter?''

Then the whole synod with one voice and one accord cried: ''The Lord Himself settled this question when He declared, 'Thou art Peter and upon this rock I will build my Church and the gates of hell shall not prevail against it. And I will give you the keys of the Kingdom of Heaven; and whatsoever thou shalt bind on earth shall be bound in Heaven and whatsoever thou shalt loose on earth shall be loosed in Heaven.' '' To this the king added, showing his wisdom: ''He is the keeper of the door and the keys. I will neither enter into strife and controversy with him, nor will I condone any who do. As long as I live I shall abide by his every decision.''

Bishop Colman was told that if, out of respect for his own country's customs, he should reject the Roman tonsure[2] and method of calculating Easter, he was to resign his see in favor of another and better candidate. This he did.

---

[2]The Roman method of tonsure, the shearing of the hair upon entry into the monastic or clerical order, provided for a bald spot on the top of the head, whereas the Irish method simply extended the length of the forehead.

Reading 8
Select Passages from "The Cow"
(Sura 2) from the Koran

Mohammed (d. 632) makes it clear that Allah, the God of Islam, is also the
God of the Old and New Testaments, and that the new religion is actually the
fulfillment of Judaism and Christianity. He respects Jews and Christians as
"People of the Book" (the Bible) but chides those among them who reject the
teachings of God's final prophet. The passage concludes with a summary of
Islamic ethics as revealed by Allah to Mohammed.

In the Name of Allah, the Compassionate, the Merciful. This Book is not
to be doubted. It is a guide to the righteous, who have faith in the unseen and
are steadfast in prayer; who bestow in charity a part of what We have given
them; who trust what has been revealed to you [Mohammed] and to others before you, and firmly believe in the life to come. These are rightly guided by
their Lord; these shall surely triumph. . . .

Believers, Jews, Christians, and Sabaeans—whoever believes in Allah and
the Last Day and does what is right—shall be rewarded by their Lord; they
have nothing to fear or to regret. . . .

When Moses said to his people: "Allah commands you to sacrifice a
cow," they relied: "Are you making game of us?" "Allah forbid that I should
be so foolish!" he rejoined. "Call on your Lord," they said, "to make known
to us what kind of cow she shall be." Moses replied: "Your Lord says: 'Let
her be neither an old cow nor a young heifer, but in between.' Do, therefore as
you are bidden." "Call on your Lord," they said, "to make known to us what
her color shall be." Moses replied: "Your Lord says: 'Let the cow be yellow, a
rich yellow pleasing to the eye.' " "Call on your Lord," they said, "to make
known to us the exact type of cow she shall be; for to us cows look all alike. If
Allah wills we shall be rightly guided." Moses replied: "Your Lord says: 'Let
her be a healthy cow, not worn out with ploughing the earth or watering the
field; a cow free from any blemish.' " "Now you have told us all," they
answered. And they slaughtered a cow, after they had almost succeeded in
evading the sacrifice. . . .

To Moses We gave the Scriptures and after him We sent other apostles.
We gave Jesus the son of Mary veritable signs and strengthened him with the
Holy Spirit. Will you then scorn each apostle whose message does not suit your
fancies, charging some with imposture and slaying others? They say: "Our

From *The Koran*, tr. N.J. Dawood; New York, 1968, pp. 326–356. Reprinted by permission of Penguin
Books, Ltd.

hearts are sealed.'' But Allah has cursed them for their unbelief. They have but little faith.

And now that a Book confirming their Scriptures has been revealed to them by Allah, they deny it, although they know it to be the truth and have long prayed for help against the unbelievers. May Allah's curse be upon the infidels! Evil is that for which they have bartered away their souls. To deny Allah's own revelation, grudging that He should reveal His bounty to whom He chooses from His servants! They have incurred Allah's most inexorable wrath. An ignominious punishment awaits the unbelievers. . . .

The unbelievers among the People of the Book, and the pagans, resent that any blessings should have been sent down to you from your Lord. But Allah chooses whom He will for His mercy. His grace is infinite.

If We abrogate any verse or cause it to be forgotten We will replace it by a better one or one similar. Do you not know that Allah has power over all things? Do you not know that it is to Allah that the kingdom of heaven and the earth belongs and that there is none besides Him to protect or help you? . . .

Who but a foolish man would renounce the faith of Abraham? We chose him in this world, and in the world to come he shall dwell among the righteous. When his Lord said to him: ''Submit,'' he answered: ''I have submitted to the Lord of the Creation.''

Abraham enjoined the faith on his children, and so did Jacob, saying: ''My children, Allah has chosen for you the true faith. Do not depart this life except as men who have submitted to Him.'' . . .

They say: ''Accept the Jewish or the Christian faith and you shall be rightly guided.'' Say: ''By no means! We believe in the faith of Abraham, the upright one. He was no idolater.'' Say: ''We believe in Allah and that which is revealed to us; we believe in what was revealed to Abraham, Ishmael, Isaac Jacob, and the tribes; to Moses and Jesus and the other prophets. We make no distinction between any of them, and to Allah we have surrendered ourselves.'' . . .

Your God is one God. There is no god but Him. He is the Compassionate, the Merciful. . . .

Righteousness does not consist in whether you face towards the east or the west. The righteous man is he who believes in Allah and the Last Day, in the angels and the Scriptures and the prophets; who for the love of Allah gives his wealth to his kinsfolk, to the orphans, to the needy, to the wayfarers, and to the beggars, and for the redemption of captives; who attends to his prayers and pays the alms-tax; who is true to his promises and steadfast in trial and adversity and in times of war. Such are the true believers; such are the God-fearing. . . .

Believers, fasting is decreed for you as it was decreed for those before you; perchance you will guard yourselves against evil. Fast a certain number of days, but if any one of you is ill or on a journey let him fast a similar number of days later on; and for those that can afford it there is a ransom: the feeding of a poor man. He that does good of his own accord shall be well rewarded; but to fast is better for you, if you but knew it. . . .

Fight for the sake of Allah those that fight against you, but do not attack them first. Allah does not love the aggressors.

Kill them wherever you find them. Drive them out of the places from which they drove you. Idolatry is worse than carnage. But do not fight them within the precincts of the Holy Mosque unless they attack you there; if they attack you put them to the sword. Thus shall the unbelievers be rewarded: but if they mend their ways, know that Allah is forgiving and merciful. . . .

Give generously for the cause of Allah and do not with your own hands cast yourselves into destruction. Be charitable; Allah loves the charitable.

Make the pilgrimage and visit the Sacred House [the Ka'ba at Mecca] for His sake. If you cannot, send such offerings as you can afford and do not shave your heads until the offerings have reached their destination. But if any of you is ill or suffers from an ailment of the head, he must pay a ransom either by fasting or by alms-giving or by offering a sacrifice. . . .

You shall not wed pagan women, unless they embrace the faith. A believing slave-girl is better than an idolatress, although she may please you. Nor shall you wed idolaters, unless they embrace the faith. A believing slave is better than an idolater, although he may please you. These call you to Hell-fire; but Allah calls you, by His will, to Paradise and to forgiveness. He makes plain His revelations to mankind, so that they may take heed. . . .

Women are your fields: go, then, into your fields as you please. Do good works and fear Allah. Bear in mind that you shall meet Him. Give good news to the believers. . . .

Women shall with all justice have rights similar to those exercised against them, although men have a status above women. Allah is mighty and wise. . . .

Attend regularly to your prayers, including the middle prayer, and stand up with all devotion before Allah. When you are exposed to danger pray while riding or on foot; and when you are restored to safety remember Allah, as He has taught you what you did not know. . . .

There shall be no compulsion in religion. True guidance is now distinct from error. He that renounces idol-worship and puts his faith in Allah shall grasp a firm handle that will never break. Allah hears all and knows all.

Allah is the Patron of the faithful. He leads them from darkness to the light. As for the unbelievers, their patrons are false gods who lead them from light to darkness. They are the heirs of Hell and shall abide in it for ever. . . .

Fear the day when you shall all return to Allah; when every soul shall be requited according to its deserts. None shall be wronged. . . .

The Apostle [Mohammed] believes in what has been revealed to him by his Lord, and so do the faithful. They all believe in Allah and His angels, His scriptures, and His apostles: We discriminate against none of His apostles. They say: "We hear and obey. Grant us your forgiveness, Lord; to You we shall all return. Allah does not charge a soul with more than it can bear. It shall be requited for whatever good and whatever evil it has done. Lord, do not be angry with us if forget or lapse into error. Lord, do not lay on us the burden You laid on those before us. Lord, do not charge us with more than we can bear. Pardon us, forgive us our sins, and have mercy upon us. You alone are our Protector. Give us victory over the unbelievers."

Reading 9

The "Constitution of Medina," 622

In 622, Mohammed left his home city of Mecca, where he had won only a small following, to become the civil and religious leader of the city of Yathrib—later renamed Medina, "the Prophet's City." From Medina, Mohammed's followers made war on Mecca—raiding its caravans, blockading its commerce, and eventually accepting its submission. The sacred community that Mohammed forged in Medina, at once a state and a church, foreshadowed the later organization of the Islamic Empire under the caliphs. The Constitution of Medina, the first official document of the Islamic political community, also foreshadowed the relatively tolerant policy of the Islamic Empire toward its Jewish inhabitants.

The Prophet wrote a document concerning the emigrants and the helpers in which he made a friendly agreement with the Jews and established them in their religion and their property, and stated the reciprocal obligations, as follows:

In the name of God the Compassionate, the Merciful. This is a document from Muhammud the prophet [governing the relations] between the believers and Muslims of Quraysh and Yathrib [Medina], and those who followed them and joined them and labored with them. They are one community [umma] to the exclusion of all other men. The Quraysh emigrants according to their present custom shall pay the blood-price within their company and shall redeem their prisoners with the kindness and justice common among believers. . . . Be-

From Ibn Ishaq's "Life of the Prophet," in *The Life of Mohammed, a Translation of Ishaq's Sirat Rasul Allah*, ed. and tr. A. Guillaume; New York, 1955, pp. 231–233. By permission of Oxford University Press.

lievers shall not leave anyone destitute among them by not paying his redemption money or blood-price in kindness.

A believer shall not take as an ally the freedman of another Muslim against him. The God-fearing believers shall be against the rebellious or him who seeks to spread injustice, or sin or enmity, or corruption between believers; the hand of every man shall be against him even if he be a son of one of them. A believer shall not slay a believer for the sake of a believer nor shall he aid an unbeliever against a believer. God's protection is one, the least of them may give protection to a stranger on their behalf. Believers are friends one to the other to the exclusion of outsiders. To the Jew who follows us belong help and equality. He shall not be wronged nor shall his enemies be aided. The peace of the believers is indivisible. No separate peace shall be made when believers are fighting in the way of God. Conditions must be fair and equitable to all. In every foray a rider must take another behind him. The believers must avenge the blood of one another shed in the way of God. The God-fearing believers enjoy the best and most upright guidance. No polytheist [the heathen Arabs of Medina] shall take the property or person of Quraysh under his protection nor shall he intervene against a believer. Whosoever is convicted of killing a believer without good reason shall be subject to retaliation unless the next of kin is satisfied [with blood-money], and the believers shall be against him as one man, and they are bound to take action against him.

It shall not be lawful to a believer who holds by what is in this document and believes in God and the last day to help an evil-doer [*muhdith*] or to shelter him. The curse of God and His anger on the day of resurrection will be upon him if he does, and neither repentance nor ransom will be upon him if he does, and neither repentance nor ransom will be received from him. Whenever you differ about a matter it must be referred to God and to Muhammud.

The Jews shall contribute to the cost of war so long as they are fighting alongside the believers. The Jews of the Bani Auf are one community with the believers [the Jews have their religion and the Muslims have theirs], their freedmen and their persons except those who behave unjustly and sinfully, for they hurt but themselves and their families. . . . Loyalty is a protection against treachery. The freedmen of Tha'laba are as themselves. The close friends of the Jews are as themselves. None of them shall go out to war save with the permission of Muhammud, but he shall not be prevented from taking revenge for a wound. He who slays a man without warning slays himself and his household, unless it be one who has wronged him, for God will accept that. The Jews must bear their expenses and the Muslims their expenses. Each must help the other against anyone who attacks the people of this document. They must seek mutual advice and consultation, and loyalty is a protection against treachery. A man is not liable for his ally's misdeeds. The wronged must be helped. The Jews must pay with the believers so long as war lasts. Yathrib shall be a sanctuary for the people of this document. A stranger under protection shall be as his host doing no harm and committing no crime. A woman shall only be given protection with the consent of her family. If any dispute or controversy likely to cause trouble should arise it must be referred to God and to Muhammud the prophet of God. God accepts what is nearest to piety and goodness in this document. Quraysh and their helpers shall not be given protection. The contracting parties are bound to help one another against any attack on Yathrib. If they are called to make peace and maintain it they must do so; and if they make a similar demand on the Muslims it must be carried out except in the case of a holy war. Every one shall have his portion from the side to which he belongs; the Jew of al-Aus, their freedmen and themselves have the same standing with the people of this document in pure loyalty from the people of this document.

Loyalty is a protection against treachery: He who acquires it ought to acquire it for himself. God approves of this document. This deed will not protect the unjust and the sinner. The man who goes forth to fight and the man who stays at home in the city is safe unless he has been unjust and sinned. God is the protector of the good and God-fearing man and Muhammud is the prophet of God.

Reading 10
A Tenth-Century Guide for Physicians

These excerpts illustrate not only the sophistication of Islamic medicine but also the contribution of Jewish scholars to Islamic culture. Drawing from both ancient Greek and Arabic sources, Isaac Israeli (d. 955) provides much sensible advice along with recurring warnings against quacks.

1. Since it is the nature of living creatures to seek their sustenance and to concern themselves with those things that maintain their being; so, too, is man, whose image is the image of God, necessarily bound to strive and to concern himself with those things whereby are maintained his being, his existence, and his survival before concerning himself with other knowledge and occupations in which others than he participate, for man is nearest to himself. Therefore, the usefulness of the practice of medicine is very great indeed, and man is always bound and obliged to put it in the forefront of his studies.

From Isaac Israeli's "Guide for Physicians," in *Islam:Religion and Society*, ed. and tr. Bernard Lewis; New York, 1974, vol. II, pp. 182–188. By permission of Harper & Row.

2. Since the science of medicine is very vast and the life of man too short to reach its end, therefore expert physicians must be distinguished and separated from the fools. The [former] busy themselves constantly with the study of books and pore over them by night and day, and devote themselves to this above other men who do not join them in this work.

14. Just as you must read all the books written on the practice of medicine, so too must you know the relevant principles of natural science, of which medicine is a branch. You must also be proficient in the methods of logic so that you may be able effectively to refute the fools who pass as physicians, to confound them, and to make them respect you.

20. The better you know and understand the temperament and characteristics of the patient when he is healthy, and the more you feel his pulse and examine his urine, the more easily will you cure him.

21. If you can carry out your treatment effectively with diet or with healing foods, then do not use drugs, for most of them are enemies and antagonists of nature, especially the purgatives.

30. Be most diligent in visiting and healing poor and needy patients, for there is no greater charity than this.

39. Fix your fee with the patient when his illness is at its worst, for when he gets better he will forget what you have done for him.

40. The more you charge for your work and the more costly is your treatment, the more will your work be respected by men. Only those for whom you work for nothing will think lightly of your skill.

48. There is a foolishness widespread among the common people. They regard themselves as physicians for certain ailments and believe that a man with an internal inflammation must not eat anything, not even very light food, because they think that food stops up the windpipe and prevents the cough. Thus they enfeeble his nature and sap his strength. They also believe that they should not give the patient anything to drink with this sickness. Some of them withhold bread from anyone with a fever. In his very country I have see a case where the physician ordered a clyster [enema] for a patient, in order to soften his nature, and then the patient stood up to walk with it and he fainted and died, and from that day onward all the people of the city avoided using a clyster for any patient because they thought that it was as deadly as a sword, and they made it a law, and no physician may use a clyster there. There are notions about medicine which they regard as true and right, though they are clearly false. Thus they think that young male chicks are colder than females, that vinegar, since it arises from wine, must not be included in the diet of a patient. They also believe that women are hotter than men and that the sneeze is the end of the disease. Because they see that when they go barefoot and get cold out of doors in the cold air, their stomachs are loosened because of the

cold and the recoil of the loose matter in the body and bowels, they think that all things cold are aperients according to the degree of their coldness and many other such absurdities.

Reading 11

Two Muslim Jokes of Ubayd-i Zakani's Kulliyyat

This final Islamic source requires no editorial comment.

A. In the time of the Caliph Wathiq a woman laid claim to prophethood. The Caliph asked her, "Was Muhammad a Prophet?" "Certainly," she replied. "Then," said the Caliph, "since Muhammad said, 'There will be no Prophet after me,' your claim is false." The woman replied, "He said, 'There will be no prophet after me.' He did not say, 'There will be no Prophetess after me!'"

B. A tumbler scolded his son and said, "You do no work and you waste your life in idleness. How often must I tell you to practice somersaults and to learn how to dance on a rope and to make a dog jump through a hoop so that you can achieve something with your life. If you don't listen to me, I swear by God I Shall abandon you to the *madrasa* [law school] to learn their dead and useless science and to become a scholar so as to live in contempt and misery and adversity and never be able to earn a penny wherever you go."

From *Islam: Religion and Society*, ed. and tr. Bernard Lewis; New York, 1974, vol. II, pp. 279-280. By permission of Harper & Row.

3

Carolingian Europe

The eighth century saw a revival of Classical-Christian culture in the kingdom of the Franks under a powerful new dynasty, the Carolingians. The cultural surge owed much to the work of English Benedictine missionary-scholars such as St. Boniface, who labored to reform the Carolingian Church and to convert pagan Germanic tribes to the northeast of Christian Frankland. Like the monks whom Gregory the Great had sent to England more than a century before, St. Boniface worked under the supervision of the papacy (document 1). It was Boniface, acting as a representative of Pope Zacharias, who crowned the first Carolingian king, Pepin the Short, bringing to an end the rule of the Merovingian dynasty (document 2). King Pepin reciprocated by leading an army into Italy, at the papacy's urging, to rescue Rome from the Lombard menace. Defeating the Lombards in battle, Pepin granted the papacy authority over extensive territories in central Italy known thereafter as the Papal States or the Patrimony of St. Peter. The papacy justified its claim to these lands by asserting that they had been given originally to Pope Sylvester I by the emperor Constantine back in the early fourth century. At just the right moment an imperial letter known as the "Donation of Constantine" conveniently came to light to provide documentary evidence for the papal position (document 3).

Charlemagne (768–814), Pepin's son and successor, extended the boundaries of the Carolingian realm by military conquests (document 4). He appointed loyal dukes and counts as regional governors throughout his dominions and supervised them through traveling royal agents known as *missi dominici*—"envoys of the lord" (document 5). Charlemagne's patronage and encouragement gave rise to an intellectual and cultural revival centering on major bishoprics and Benedictine abbeys (document 6) and on the royal court, where Charlemagne assembled a group of scholars from the length and breadth of Western Christendom. This "Carolingian Renaissance" continued through the reigns of Charlemagne's successors (document 7). It contributed much to the solidifying of Europe's Classical-Christian foundations.

Reading 1

Letters of St. Boniface

These three documents show Boniface first as a servant of the pope and of Catholic orthodoxy (document A), next as a missionary among Germanic pagans (document B), and finally as a pastoral adviser (document C). They reveal something of the communications network connecting churchmen in Rome, England, Frankland, and pagan Germany—and, in the letter to Abbess Bugga, the hazards of travel within Christendom. The letter of Bishop Daniel of Winchester, with its deep-set confidence in the intellectual plausibility of Christianity as against the "idol worship" of rival religions, will help to explain the eventual success of Christian missions to central and eastern Europe.

A. THE OATH OF BISHOP BONIFACE GIVEN TO POPE GREGORY II, DATED 30 NOVEMBER , 722.

In the name of the Lord God and of our Savior Jesus Christ. In the sixth year of Leo, by the grace of God emperor, in the sixth year of his consulship and in the fourth year of his son, the Emperor Constantine, in the sixth indiction:

I, Boniface, by the grace of God bishop, promise to you, blessed Peter, chief of the Apostles, and to your vicar, the blessed Pope Gregory [II] and to his successors, in the name of the Father, the Son, and the Holy Spirit, the indivisible Trinity, and of this, thy most sacred body, that I will show entire faith and sincerity toward the holy catholic doctrine and will persist in the unity of the same, so God help me—that faith in which, beyond a doubt, the whole salvation of Christians consists. I will in no wise agree to anything which is opposed to the unity of the Church Universal, no matter who shall try to persuade me; but I will, as I have said, show in all things a perfect loyalty to you and to the welfare of your Church, to which the power to bind and loose is given by God, and to your vicar and his successors.

But, if I shall discover any bishops who are opponents of the anci~nt institutions of the holy Fathers, I will have no part nor lot with them, but so far as I can will restrain them or, if that is impossible, will make a true report to my apostolic master. But if (which God forbid!) I should be tempted into any action contrary to this my promise, in any way or by any device or pretext whatsoever, may I be found guilty at the last judgment and suffer punishment of

From *The Letters of St. Boniface*, tr. E. Emerton; New York, Columbia University Press, 1940, nos. viii, xv, xix.

Ananias and Sapphira, who dared to defraud you by making a false declaration of their property.

This text of my oath, I, Boniface, a humble bishop, have written with my own hand and laid above thy most sacred body. I have taken this oath, as is prescribed, in the presence of God, my witness and my judge, and I pledge myself to observe it.

B. A LETTER WRITTEN BY BISHOP DANIEL OF WINCHESTER, ENGLAND, ADVISING BONIFACE ON THE METHOD OF CONVERSION, DATED 723–724.

To the venerable and beloved prelate Boniface, Daniel, servant of the people of God.

I rejoice, beloved brother and fellow priest, that you are deserving of the highest prize of virtue. You have approached the hitherto stony and barren hearts of the pagans, trusting in the plenitude of your faith, and have labored untiringly with the plowshare of Gospel preaching, striving by your daily toil to change them into fertile fields. To you may well be applied the Gospel saying: "The voice of one crying in the wilderness," etc. Yet a part of the second prize shall be given, not unfittingly, to those who support so pious and useful a work with what help they can give and supplement the poverty of those laborers with means sufficient to carry on zealously the work of preaching which has already been begun and to raise up new sons to Christ.

And so I have with affectionate good will taken pains to suggest to Your Prudence a few things that may show you how, according to my ideas, you may most readily overcome the resistance of those uncivilized people. Do not begin by arguing with them about the origin of their gods, false as those are, but let them affirm that some of them were begotten by others through the intercourse of male with female, so that you may at least prove that gods and goddesses born after the manner of men are men and not gods and, since they did not exist before, must have had a beginning.

Then, when they have been compelled to learn that their gods had a beginning since some were begotten by others, they must be asked in the same way whether they believe that the world had a beginning or was always in existence without beginning. If it had a beginning, who created it? Certainly they can find no place where begotten gods could dwell before the universe was made. I mean by "universe" not merely this visible earth and sky, but the whole vast extent of space, and this the heathen too can imagine in their thoughts. But if they argue that the world always existed without beginnings, you should strive to refute this and to convince them by many documents and arguments. Ask your opponents who governed the world before the gods were born, who was the ruler? How could they bring under their dominion or subject to their law a universe that had always existed before them? And whence, or from whom or when, was the first god or goddess set up or begotten? Now, do they imagine that gods and goddesses still go on begetting others? Or, if they are no longer begetting, when or why did they cease from intercourse and births? And if they are still producing offspring, then the number of gods must already be infinite. Among so many and different gods, mortal men cannot know which is the most powerful, and one should be extremely careful not to offend that most powerful one.

Do they think the gods are to be worshiped for the sake of temporal and immediate good or for future eternal blessedness? If for temporal things, let them tell in what respect the heathen are better off than Christians. What gain do the heathen suppose accrues to their gods from their sacrifices, since the gods already possess everything? Or why do the gods leave it in the power of their subjects to say what kind of tribute shall be paid? If they are lacking in such things, why do they not themselves choose more valuable ones? If they have plenty, then there is no need to suppose that the gods can be pleased with such offerings of victims.

These and many similar things which it would take long to enumerate you ought to put before them, not offensively or so as to anger them, but calmly and with great moderation. At intervals you should compare their superstitions with our Christian doctrines, touching upon them from the flank, as it were, so that the pagans, thrown into confusion rather than angered, may be ashamed of their absurd ideas and may understand that their infamous ceremonies and fables are well known to us.

This point is also to be made: if the gods are all-powerful, beneficent, and just, they not only reward their worshipers but punish those who reject them. If, then, they do this in temporal matters, how is it that they spare us Christians who are turning almost the whole earth away from their worship and overthrowing their idols? And while these, that is, the Christians, possess lands rich in oil and wine and abounding in other resources, they have left to those, that is, the pagans, lands stiff with cold where their gods, driven out of the world, are falsely supposed to rule. They are also frequently to be reminded of the supremacy of the Christian world, in comparison with which they themselves, very few in number, are still involved in their ancient errors.

If they boast that the rule of the gods over those peoples has been, as it were, lawful from the beginning, show them that the whole world was once given over to idol-worship, until by the grace of Christ and through the knowledge of one God, its Almighty Founder and Ruler, it was enlightened, brought to life, and reconciled to God. For what is the daily baptism of the children of believing Christians but purification of each one from the uncleanness and guilt in which the whole world was once involved?

I have been glad to call these matters to your attention, my brother, out of my affection for you, though I suffer from bodily infirmities so that I may well say with the Psalmist: "I know, Oh Lord, that thy judgments are right and that thou in faithfulness hast afflicted me." Wherefore I earnestly pray Your Reverence and all those who serve Christ in spirit to make supplication for me that the Lord Who gave me to drink of the wine of remorse, may be swift in mercy, that He who was just in condemnation may graciously pardon, and by His mercy enable me to sing in gratitude the words of the Prophet: "In the multitude of my thoughts within me thy comforts delight my soul."

I pray for your welfare in Christ, my very dear colleague, and beg you to bear me in mind.

C. A LETTER WRITTEN BY BONIFACE IN WHICH HE GIVES ADVICE TO ABBESS BUGGA REGARDING HER PILGRIMAGE TO ROME, DATED PRE-738.

To the beloved lady, Abbess Bugga, sister and dearest of all women in Christ, Boniface, a humble and unworthy bishop, wishes eternal salvation in Christ.

I desire you to know, dearest sister, that in the matter about which you wrote asking advice of me, unworthy though I am, I dare neither forbid your pilgrimage on my own responsibility nor rashly persuade you to it. I will only say how the matter appears to me. If, for the sake of rest and divine contemplation, you have laid aside the care for the servants and maids of God and for the monastic life which you once had, how could you now subject yourself with labor and wearing anxiety to the words and wishes of men of this world? It would seem to me better, if you can in no way have freedom and a quiet mind at home on account of worldly men, that you should obtain freedom of contemplation by means of a pilgrimage, if you so desire and are able, as our sister Wiethburga did. She has written me that she has found at the shrine of St. Peter the kind of quiet life which she had long sought in vain. With regard to your wishes, she sent me word, since I had written to her about you, that you would do better to wait until the rebellious assaults and threats of the Saracens who have recently appeared about Rome should have subsided. God willing, she will then send you an invitation. To me also this seems the best plan. Make ready what you will need for the journey, wait for word from her, and then act as God's grace shall command.

In regard to the writings which you have requested of me, you must excuse my remissness, for I have been prevented by pressure of work and by my continual travels from completing the book you ask for. When I have finished it, I shall see that it is sent to you.

In return for the gifts and garments you have sent me, I offer my grateful prayers to God that he may give you a reward with the angels and the archangels in the highest heavens. I exhort you, then, in God's name, my very dear sister—nay mother and most sweet lady—to pray earnestly for me, since for my sins I am wearied with many sorrows and am far more disturbed by anxiety of mind than by the labor of my body. May you rest assured that the long-tried friendship between us shall never be found wanting.

Farewell in Christ.

Reading 2
The Coronation of Pepin the Short, 751

The abbey of Lorsch in southern Germany, like many other abbeys across Christendom, compiled brief, year-by-year records of events that seemed particularly important. These records, known as annals, reflect the perspectives and biases of their respective monasteries. The events they include might range from eclipses, storms, and the births of two-headed cows to matters of major political importance such as the one recorded here.

By 751 the Merovingian dynasty of Frankish kings had become impoverished and politically impotent. Actual power was exercised by the chief official of the royal household, the *Major Domus*. This office was in the hereditary control of a great Frankish aristocratic family known later as the "Carolingians." Pepin the Short, the Carolingian *Major Domus* in 751, hungered for the crown. But the Merovingians, even though powerless, were an ancient and revered royal dynasty, and Pepin therefore needed potent spiritual backing for his coup d'état. Pope Zacharias was harassed by hostile Byzantines and rampaging Lombards and viewed Pepin as a potential military supporter who might rescue the papacy from its predicament. The resulting alliance between the popes and the Carolingians marked a fundamental realignment of the early-medieval political order. And having become king, Pepin had the good sense to abolish the office of *Major Domus*.

In the year [751] of the Lord's incarnation Pepin sent ambassadors to Rome to Pope Zacharias [741–752], to inquire concerning the kings of the Franks who, though they were of the royal line and were called kings, had no power in the kingdom, except that charters and privileges were drawn up in their names. They had absolutely no kingly authority, but did whatever the *Major Domus* of the Franks desired. But on the first day of March in the Campus Martius, according to ancient custom, gifts were offered to these kings by the people, and the king himself sat in the royal seat with the army standing round him and the *Major Domus* in his presence, and he commanded on that day whatever was decreed by the Franks; but on all other days thenceforth he

From *The Lesser Annals of Lorsch*, in *A Sourcebook of Mediaeval History*, ed. F. A. Ogg; New York, American Book Company, 1907, pp. 106–107. Reprinted by permission.

remained quietly at home. Pope Zacharias, therefore, in the exercise of his apostolic authority, replied to their inquiry that it seemed to him better and more expedient that the man who held power in the kingdom should be called king and be king, rather than he who falsely bore the name. Therefore the aforesaid pope commanded the king and people of the Franks that Pepin, who was exercising royal power, should be called king, and should be established on the throne. This was therefore done by the anointing of the holy archbishop Boniface in the city of Soissons. Pepin was proclaimed king, and Childeric, who was falsely called king, was shaved[2] and sent into a monastery.

Reading 3

The Donation of Constantine

King Pepin expressed his gratitude by defeating the Lombards and granting the papacy large portions of central Italy. Since the Lombards had only recently seized this territory from the Byzantine Empire, the Byzantines regarded Pepin's grant as a usurpation of imperial lands. The papacy responded by pointing to the legend, current in Rome, that Constantine I had long ago granted the papacy perpetual dominion over Italy and all the West. The papal court evidently accepted this tale as historically accurate but the documentary proof was lacking. Accordingly, the "Donation of Constantine" was forged, with the intent not of rewriting history but of supplying the missing documentation. Such was the intent of a great number of forged grants throughout the Middle Ages. The "Donation of Constantine" was exposed as a forgery first around A.D. 1000 by court scholars of the Emperor Otto III, and then, more decisively, by the fifteenth-century Italian humanist, Lorenzo Valla. Notice the logical inconsistency in the two references to Constantinople.

In the name of the Holy and Undivided Trinity. The emperor Caesar Flavius Constantinus in Christ . . . to the most holy and blessed Father of fathers, Sylvester, Bishop of the city of Rome and Pope, and to all his successors, who shall forever sit on the throne of Saint Peter until the end of time. . . .

On the first day, then, after receiving the mystery of holy Baptism and after the cure of my body from the filth of leprosy[1] I recognized that there was

---

From *The Medieval World, 300–1300*, ed. Norman Cantor, 2nd ed., New York, 1968, pp. 132–139. Reprinted with permission of Macmillan Publishing Co., Inc.

[1]I.e., his head was shaved. Uncut hair was a mark of royalty among male members of the Merovingian dynasty.

[2]The "Donation" begins with an elaborate statement concerning Constantine's conversion to Christianity and a theological part explaining the Christian Creed. Constantine was believed (incorrectly) to have been miraculously cured of leprosy by Pope Sylvester I.

no other God except the Father and the Son and the Holy Spirit, whom the most blessed Pope Sylvester preaches, Trinity in Unity, Unity in Trinity. For all the gods of the heathen which up to now I have worshipped, have been proved to be demons, the hand-made work of men. That same venerable father told very plainly to us the great power in heaven and earth which our Saviour had committed to the blessed Apostle Peter when, finding him faithful under questioning, he said: "Thou art Peter and upon this rock I will build my Church and the gates of hell shall not prevail against it." Take note, Oh mighty sovereigns, and incline the attention of your heart to what the good Master and Lord gave in addition to His disciple when He said: "And I will give unto you the keys of the kingdom of heaven; whatsoever thou shall bind on earth shall be bound also in heaven and whatsoever thou shall loose on earth shall be loosed also in heaven." It is a very wonderful and glorious thing to bind and loose on earth and to have that sentence of binding and loosing carried out in heaven.

While the blessed Sylvester was preaching these things I understood them and found that I was restored to full health by the beneficence of the same blessed Peter. So we, together with all our satraps and the whole Senate and all the nobles and the whole Roman people which is subject to the glory of our Empire, judged it in the public interest that, because St. Peter was made Vicar of the Son of God on earth, the Pontiffs also, who are the successors of the same Prince of the Apostles, may obtain from us and our Empire greater governmental power than the earthly clemency of our Imperial serenity has so far conceded to them; thus we chose the same Prince of the Apostles and his Vicar to be our powerful patrons with God. And because our Imperial power is earthly, we have decided to honor reverently his most holy Roman Church, and to exalt the most holy See of blessed Peter in glory above our own Empire and earthly throne, ascribing to it power and glorious majesty and strength and Imperial honor.

And we command and decree that he should have primacy over the four principal Sees of Antioch, Alexandria, Constantinople and Jerusalem, as well as over all the Churches of God throughout the whole world; and the Pontiff who occupies at any given moment the See of that same most holy Roman Church shall rank as the highest and chief among all the priests of the whole world and by his decision all things are to be arranged concerning the worship of God or the security of the faith of Christians. For it is just that the holy law should have its center of government at the place where the institutor of the holy laws, our Saviour, commanded blessed Peter to set up the chair of his apostolate, . . .

Let every people and the nations of the Gentiles in all the world rejoice therefore with us; we exhort you all that you return thanks abundantly to our God and Saviour Jesus Christ, because he is God in Heaven above and on earth beneath, Who, visiting us through His holy Apostles made us worthy to receive the holy Sacrament of Baptism and bodily health. In recompense for this we concede to those same holy Apostles, my lords the most blessed Peter and Paul and through them also to blessed Sylvester our father, Supreme Pontiff and Universal Pope of the City of Rome, and to all his successors, the Pontiffs who will preside over the See of blessed Peter until the end of the world, and by this present document we confer, our Imperial palace of the Lateran, which surpasses and excels all palaces in the whole world, then a diadem which is the crown of our head, and at the same time the tiara; also the shoulder covering, that is the strap which is wont to surround our Imperial neck; also the purple cloak and the crimson tunic and all our Imperial garments. They shall also receive the rank of those who preside over the Imperial cavalry. We confer on them also the Imperial scepters and at the same time the spears and standards, also the banners and various Imperial decorations and all the prerogatives of our supreme Imperial position and the glory of our authority.

We decree that those very reverend men, the clerics who serve the most holy Roman Church in various orders, shall have the same dignity, distinction, power and pre-eminence, by the glory of which our Senate is decorated; and we decree that the clergy of the most holy Roman Church shall be adorned as are the soldiers of the Empire. . . . Above all, in addition, we grant to the same our most holy father Sylvester, Bishop of the City of Rome and Pope, and to all the most blessed Pontiffs who shall come after him in succession for ever, for the honor and glory of Christ our God, to add to the numbers in that same great Catholic and Apostolic Church of God any one from our court who shall wish of his own free choice to become a cleric, and to add any to the number of monastic clergy. Let no one presume to act arrogantly in all these matters. . . .

To correspond to our own Empire and so that the supreme Pontifical authority may not be dishonored, but may rather be adorned with glorious power greater than the dignity of any earthly empire, behold, we give to the often-mentioned most holy Pontiff, our father Sylvester, the Universal Pope, not only the above-mentioned palace, but also the city of Rome and all the provinces, districts and cities of Italy and the Western regions, relinquishing them to the authority of himself and his successors as Pontiffs by a definite Imperial grant. We have decided that this should be laid down by this our divine, holy and lawfully framed decree and we grant it on a permanent legal basis to the holy Roman Church.

Therefore we have seen it to be fitting that our Empire and the power of the kingdom should be transferred and translated to the Eastern regions and that in the province of Byzantium in the most suitable place a city should be built in our name and our Empire established there; because it is not just that an earthly Emperor should exercise authority where the government of priests and the Head of the Christian religion have been installed by the heavenly Emperor.

We decree also that all the things, which we have established and approved by this our holy Imperial edict and by other divine decrees shall remain uninjured and unbroken until the end of the world; so, in the presence of the living God, Who ordered us to reign, and in the presence of His terrible judgment, we solemnly warn, by this our Imperial enactment, all our successors as Emperors and all our nobles, the satraps, the most honorable Senate and all people throughout the world, now and in the future and in all times previously subject to our Empire, that none of them will be permitted in any way to oppose or destroy or to take away any of these privileges, which have been conceded by our Imperial decree to the most holy Roman Church and to its Pontiffs.

Reading 4
Einhard's Life of Charlemagne

Einhard was reared in the monastery of Fulda, founded by St. Boniface, and joined Charlemagne's court in the early 790s. He served Charlemagne as an administrative official and knew him well. Einhard wrote his biography a few years after Charlemagne's death (814). As secretary to Charlemagne's son and heir, Louis the Pious, Einhard had easy access to court annals and official records. He also drew on his own intimate knowledge of the great emperor. Modeling his work on *The Lives of the Caesars* by the ancient Roman historian Suetonius, Einhard borrowed a number of descriptive passages from Suetonius' life of Augustus. Later medieval biographers, using a similar methodology, borrowed heavily from Einhard. But Einhard borrowed cautiously and intelligently, and his *Life*, despite its Suetonian echoes and admiring tone, brings us closer to the historical Charlemagne than does any other source. Later biographies portray Charlemagne as a legendary hero performing impossible deeds. The Gascon attack on Charlemagne's rearguard as his army withdrew from Spain was expanded and embroidered in later centuries into the great epic poem, the "Song of Roland."

When [the war in Aquitaine] was ended the Saxon war, which seemed dropped for a time, was taken up again. Never was there a war more prolonged nor more cruel than this, nor one that required greater efforts on the part of the Frankish peoples. For the Saxons, like most of the races that inhabit Germany, are by nature fierce, devoted to the worship of demons and hostile to our religion, and they think it no dishonor to confound and transgress the laws of God and man. There were reasons, too, which might at any time cause a disturbance of the peace. For our boundaries and theirs touch almost everywhere

From *Early Lives of Charlemagne*, ed. and tr. A. J. Grant; London, Chatto & Windus, Ltd., 1922, part I, chaps. 7, 8, 9, 11.

on the open plain, except where in a few places large forests or ranges of mountains are interposed to separate the territories of the two nations by a definite frontier; so that on both sides murder, robbery, and arson were of constant occurrence. The Franks were so irritated by these things that they thought it was time no longer to be satisfied with retaliation but to declare open war against them.

So war was declared, and was fought for thirty years[1] continuously with the greatest fierceness on both sides, but with heavier loss to the Saxons than the Franks. The end might have been reached sooner had it not been for the perfidy of the Saxons. It is hard to say how often they admitted themselves beaten and surrendered as suppliants to King Charles; how often they promised to obey his orders, gave without delay the required hostages, and received the ambassadors that were sent to them. Sometimes they were so cowed and broken that they promised to abandon the worship of devils and willingly to submit themselves to the Christian religion. But though sometimes ready to bow to his commands they were always eager to break their promise, so that it is impossible to say which course seemed to come more natural to them, for from the beginning of the war there was scarcely a year in which they did not both promise and fail to perform.

But the high courage of the King and the constancy of his mind, which remained unshaken by prosperity and adversity, could not be conquered by their changes nor forced by weariness to desist from his undertakings. He never allowed those who offended in this way to go unpunished, but either led an army himself, or sent one under the command of his counts, to chastise their perfidy and inflict a suitable penalty. So that at last, when all who had resisted had been defeated and brought under his power, he took ten thousand of the inhabitants of both banks of the Elbe, with their wives and children, and planted them in many groups in various parts of Germany and Gaul. And at last the war, protracted through so many years, was finished on conditions proposed by the King and accepted by them; they were to abandon the worship of devils, to turn from their national ceremonies, to receive the sacraments of the Christian faith and religion, and then, joined to the Franks, to make one people with them.

In this war, despite its prolongation through so many years, he did not himself meet the enemy in battle more than twice,[2] once near the mountain called Osning, in the district of Detmold, and again at the river Haase, and both these battles were fought in one month, with an interval of only a few

---

[1] The Saxon wars lasted from 772 until 804.

[2] In addition to the two battles mentioned by Einhard, Charlemagne also met the Saxons at a battle near Lübeck in 775 and one at Bochult in 779.

days.[3] In these two battles the enemy were so beaten and cowed that they never again ventured to challenge the King nor to resist his attack unless they were protected by some advantage of ground.

In this war many men of noble birth and high office fell on the side both of the Franks and Saxons. But at last it came to an end in the thirty-third year, though in the meanwhile so many and such serious wars broke out against the Franks in all parts of the world, and were carried on with such skill by the King, that an observer may reasonably doubt whether his endurance of toil or his good fortune deserves the greater admiration. For the war in Italy began two years before the Saxon war [in 770], and though it was prosecuted without intermission no enterprise in any part of the world was dropped, nor was there anywhere a truce in any struggle, however difficult. For this King, the wisest and most high-minded of all who in that age ruled over the nations of the world, never refused to undertake or prosecute any enterprise because of the labor involved, nor withdrew from it through fear of its danger. He understood the true character of each task that he undertook or carried through, and thus was neither broken by adversity nor misled by the false flatteries of good fortune.

While the war with the Saxons was being prosecuted constantly and almost continuously he placed garrisons at suitable places on the frontier, and attacked Spain with the largest military expedition that he could collect. He crossed the Pyrenees, received the surrender of all the towns and fortresses that he attacked, and returned with his army safe and sound, except for a reverse which he experienced through the treason of the Gascons on his return through the passes of the Pyrenees. For while his army was marching in a long line, suiting their formation to the character of the ground and the defiles, the Gascons placed an ambuscade on the top of the mountain—where the density and extent of the woods in the neighborhood rendered it highly suitable for such a purpose—and then rushing down into the valley beneath threw into disorder the last part of the baggage train and also the rearguard which acted as a protection to those in advance. In the battle which followed the Gascons slew their opponents to the last man.[4] Then they seized upon the baggage, and under cover of the night, which was already falling, they scattered with the utmost rapidity in different directions. The Gascons were assisted in this feat by the lightness of their armor and the character of the ground where the affair took place. In this battle Eggihard, who was in charge of the King's table, An-

---

[3] These engagements were fought in 783.

[4] The Gascons, more properly the Basques, engaged the rearguard on 15 August 778 in the Battle of Roncevaux, so-called since the composition of the "Song of Roland" in the late eleventh century.

selm, the count of the Palace, and Roland, lord of the Breton frontier, were killed along with very many others. Nor could this assault be punished at once, for when the deed had been done the enemy so completely disappeared that they left behind them not so much as a rumor of their whereabouts. . . .

Then the Bavarian war broke out suddenly, and was swiftly ended. It was caused by the pride and folly of Tassilo, Duke of Bavaria.[5] For upon the instigation of his wife—who thought that she might revenge through her husband the banishment of her father Desiderius, King of the Lombards—Tassilo made an alliance with the Huns,[6] the eastern neighbors of the Bavarians, and not only refused obedience to King Charles but even dared to challenge him in war. The high courage of the King could not bear his overweening insolence, and he forthwith called a general levy for an attack on Bavaria, and came in person with a great army to the river Lech, which separates Bavaria from Germany. He pitched his camp upon the banks of the river, and determined to make trial of the mind of the Duke before he entered the province. But Duke Tassilo saw no profit either for himself or his people in stubbornness, and threw himself upon the King's mercy. He gave the hostages who were demanded, his own son Theodo among the number, and further promised upon oath that no one should ever persuade him again to fall away from his allegiance to the King. And thus a war which seemed likely to grow into a very great one came to a most swift ending. But Tassilo was subsequently summoned into the King's presence, and was not allowed to return,[7] and the province that he ruled was for the future committed to the administration not of dukes but of counts.

[5]This war took place in 787–788.

[6]More properly the Avars, yet Einhard continually refers to them as the "Huns."

[7]Duke Tassilo was forcibly placed in the monastery at Jumièges.

Reading 5

Charlemagne's General Capitulary for the Missi, Spring, 802

This imperial ordinance (capitulary), issued shortly after Charlemagne's coronation as Roman emperor on Christmas Day 800, provides valuable evidence regarding the administration of the Carolingian realm. It discloses, among other things, the way in which the *missi dominici* were employed, the importance of oaths of loyalty (to the emperor as distinct from the empire), the workings of the Germanic-based legal system, the intimate connection between empire and church, and —by implication —the high incidence of crime and violence within Charlemagne's dominions. What the document does not reveal is the degree to which Charlemagne's commands were actually carried out.

1. Concerning the commission dispatched by our lord the emperor. Our most serene and most Christian lord and emperor, Charles, has selected the most prudent and wise from among his leading men, archbishops and bishops, together with venerable abbots and devòut laymen, and has sent them out into all his kingdom, and bestowed through them on all his subjects the right to live in accordance with a right rule of law. Wherever there is any provision in the law that is other than right or just he has ordered them to inquire most diligently into it and bring it to his notice, it being his desire, with God's help, to rectify it. And let no one dare or be allowed to use his wit and cunning, as many do, to subvert the law as it is laid down or the emperor's justice, whether it concerns God's churches, or poor people and widows and orphans, or any Christian person. Rather should all men live a good and just life in accordance with God's commands, and should with one mind remain and abide each in his appointed place or profession: the clergy should live a life in full accord with the canons without concern for base gain, the monastic orders should keep their life under diligent control, the laity and secular people should make proper use of their laws, refraining from ill-will and deceit, and all should live together in perfect love and peace. And the *missi*[1] themselves, as they wish to have the favor of Almighty God and to preserve it through the loyalty they have promised, are to make diligent inquiry wherever a man claims that someone has done him an injustice; so everywhere, and amongst all men, in God's

From *The Reign of Charlemagne*, ed. H. R. Loyn and J. Percival; London, 1975, pp. 74–79. Reprinted by permission of Edward Arnold, Ltd.

[1]The closest modern equivalent of "missus" or "missi" is "commissioner," but neither it nor "envoy" conveys its full meaning.

holy churches, among poor people, orphans and widows, and throughout the whole people they may administer law and justice in full accordance with the will and the fear of God. And if there be anything which they themselves, together with the counts of the provinces, cannot correct or bring to a just settlement, they should refer it without any hesitation to the emperor's judgment along with their reports. And in no way, whether by some man's flattery or bribery, or by the excuse of blood relationship with someone, or through fear of someone more powerful, should anyone hinder the right and proper course of justice.

2. Concerning the promise of fealty to our lord the emperor. He has given instructions that in all his kingdom all men, both clergy and laity, and each according to his vows and way of life, who before have promised fealty to him as king, should now make the same promise to him as Caesar; and those who until now have not made the promise are all to do so from twelve years old and upwards. And that all should be publicly informed, so that each man may understand how many important matters are contained in that oath—not only, as many have thought until now, the profession of loyalty to our lord the emperor throughout his life, and the undertaking not to bring any enemy into his kingdom for hostile reasons, nor to consent to or be silent about anyone's infidelity towards him, but also that all men may know that the oath has in addition the following meaning within it.

3. First, that everyone on his own behalf should strive to maintain himself in God's holy service, in accordance with God's command and his own pledge, to the best of his ability and intelligence, since our lord the emperor himself is unable to provide the necessary care and discipline to all men individually.

4. Second, that no man, through perjury or any other craft or deceit, or through anyone's flattery or bribery, should in any way withhold or take away or conceal our lord the emperor's serf, or his landmark, or his land, or anything that is his by right of possession; and that no one should conceal the men of his fisc[2] who run away and unlawfully and deceitfully claim to be free men, nor take them away by perjury or any other craft.

5. That no one should presume to commit fraud or theft or any other criminal act against God's holy churches or against widows or orphans or pilgrims; for the lord emperor himself, after God and his saints, has been appointed their protector and defender.

6. That no one should dare neglect a benefice [land granted on condition of service] held of our lord the emperor, and build up his own property from it.

7. That no one should presume to ignore a summons to the host from our lord the emperor, and that no count should be so presumptuous as to dare to

[2]The "fisc" [*fiscus*] is an administrative unit of the royal estates that can be translated "crown lands" or "crown estate," though at times it means, as in this case, the "royal purse."

excuse any of those who ought to go with the host, either on the pretext of kinship or through the enticement of any gift.

8. That no one should presume to subvert in any way any edict or any order of our lord the emperor, nor trifle with his affairs nor hinder nor weaken them, nor act in any other way contrary to his will and his instructions. And that no one should dare to be obstructive about any debt or payment that he owes.

9. That no one in court should make a practice of defending another man in an unlawful manner, by arguing the case weakly through a desire for gain, by hampering a lawful judgment by showing off his skill in pleading, or by presenting a weak case in an attempt to do his client harm. Rather should each man plead for himself, be it a question of tax or debt or some other case, unless he is infirm or unacquainted with pleading; for such men the *missi* or the chief men who are in the court or a judge who knows the case can plead it before the court, or if necessary a man can be provided to plead, who is approved by all parties and has a good knowledge of the case at issue; this, however, should only be done at the convenience of the chief men or *missi* who are present. At all events, it must be done in accordance with justice and the law; and no one should be allowed to impede the course of justice by offering a reward or a fee, by skillful and ill-intentioned flattery, or by the excuse of kinship. And let no one make an unlawful agreement with anyone, but let all men be seriously and willingly prepared to see that justice is done.

25. That the counts and *centenarii*[3] should strive to see that justice is done, and should have as assistants in their duties men in whom they can have full confidence, who will faithfully observe justice and the law, will in no wise oppress the poor, and will not dare, for flattery or a bribe, to conceal in any manner of concealment any thieves, robbers or murderers, adulterers, evil-doers and performers of incantations and auguries, and all other sacrilegious people, but rather will bring them to light, that they may receive correction and punishment according to the law, and that with God's indulgence all these evils may be removed from among our Christian people.

26. That the justices should give right judgment according to the written law, and not according to private opinions.

27. We ordain that no one in all our kingdom, whether rich or poor, should dare to deny hospitality to pilgrims: that is, no one should refuse a roof, a hearth and water to any pilgrims who are traveling the country in the service of God, or to anyone who is journeying for love of God or for the salvation of his soul. And if a man should be willing to offer any further benefit to such people, let him know that God will give him the best reward, as he himself said: "Whoever shall receive one such little child in my name receiveth

---

[3] "Centenarii" were subordinates of a count with administrative and judicial functions within the territorial divisions of a county.

me''; and in another place, ''I was a stranger, and ye took me in'' [Matthew 18.5; 25.35].

28. Concerning the commissions coming from our lord the emperor: The counts and the *centenarii* should, as they are desirous of the favor of our lord the emperor, provide for the *missi* who are sent upon them with all possible attention, that they may go about their duties without any delay; and he has given instructions to all men that it is their duty to make such provision, that they suffer no delay to occur anywhere, and that they help them to go upon their way with all haste, and make such provision for this as our *missi* may require.

29. Concerning those poor men who owe payment of the royal fine and to whom the lord emperor in his mercy has given remission: the counts or the *missi* are not to have the right for their part to bring constraint upon people so excused.

30. Concerning those whom the lord emperor wishes, with Christ's blessing, to have peace and protection in his kingdom, that is, those who have thrown themselves upon his mercy, those who, whether Christians or pagans, have desired to offer any information, or who from poverty or hunger have sought his intervention: let no one dare to bind them in servitude or take possession of them or dispose of them or sell them, but rather let them stay where they themselves choose, and live there under the lord emperor's protection and in his mercy. If anyone should presume to transgress this instruction, let him know that a man so presumptuous as to despise the lord emperor's orders must pay for it with the loss of his life.

31. For those who administer the justice of our lord the emperor let no one dare to devise harm or injury, nor bring any hostility to bear upon them. Anyone who presumes to do so must pay the royal fine; and if he is guilty of a greater offence, the orders are that he be brought to the king's presence.

32. Murder, by which a great multitude of our Christian people perish, we ordain should be shunned and avoided by every possible means; Our Lord himself forbade hatred and enmity among his faithful, and murder even more. How can a man feel confident that he will be at peace with God, when he has killed the son most close to himself? Or who can believe that Christ Our Lord is on his side, when he has murdered his brother? It is, moreover, a great and unacceptable risk with God the Father and Christ the ruler of heaven and earth to arouse the hostility of men. With men, we can escape for a time by hiding, but even so by some chance of fortune we fall into our enemy's hands; but where can a man escape from God, from whom no secrets are hid? What rashness to think to escape his anger! For this reason we have sought, by every kind of precept, to prevent the people entrusted to us for ruling from perishing as a result of this evil; for he who feels no dread at the anger of God should not receive mild and benevolent treatment from us; rather would we wish a man who

had dared to commit the evil act of murder to receive the severest of punishments. Nevertheless, in order that the crime should not increase further, and in order that serious enmity should not arise among Christians when they resort to murders at the persuasion of the devil, the guilty person should immediately set about making amends, and should with all possible speed pay the appropriate recompense to the relatives of the dead man for the evil he has done to them. And this we firmly forbid, that the parents of the dead man should dare in any way to increase the enmity arising from the crime committed, or refuse to allow peace when the request is made; rather, they should accept the word given to them and the compensation offered, and allow perpetual peace, so long as the guilty man does not delay payment of the compensation. And when a man sinks to such a depth of crime as to kill his brother or a relative, he must betake himself immediately to the penance devised for him, and do so as his bishop instructs him and without any compromising. He should strive with God's help to make full amends, and should pay compensation for the dead man according to the law and make his peace in full with his kinsmen; and once the parties have given their word let no one dare to arouse further enmity on the matter. And anyone who scorns to pay the appropriate compensation is to be deprived of his inheritance pending our judgment.

33. We forbid absolutely the crime of incest. If anyone is stained by wicked fornication he must in no circumstances be let off without severe penalty, but rather should be punished for it in such a way that others will be deterred from committing the same offence, that filthiness may be utterly removed from our Christian people, and that the guilty person himself may be fully freed from it through the penance that is prescribed for him by his bishop. The woman concerned should be kept under her parents' supervision subject to our judgment. And if such people are unwilling to agree to the bishop's judgment concerning their improvement they are to be brought to our presence, mindful of that exemplary punishment for incest imposed by Fricco upon a certain nun.

34. That all should be fully and well prepared for whenever our order or announcement may come. And if anyone then maintains that he is not ready and disregards our instructions he is to be brought to the palace—and not he alone, but all those who presume to go against our edict or our orders.

35. That all bishops and their priests should be accorded all honor and respect in their service to God's will. They should not dare to stain themselves or others with incestuous unions. They should not presume to solemnize marriages until the bishops and priests, together with the elders of the people, have carefully inquired to see if there be any blood relationship between the parties, and should only then give their blessing to the marriage. They should avoid drunkenness, shun greediness, and not commit theft; disputes and quarrels and blasphemies, whether in normal company or in a legal sense, should be entirely avoided; rather, they should live in love and unity.

36. That all men should contribute to the full administration of justice by giving their agreement to our *missi*. They should not in any way give their approval to the practice of perjury, which is a most evil crime and must be removed from among our Christian people. And if anyone after this is convicted of perjury he should know that he will lose his right hand; but he is also to be deprived of his inheritance subject to our judgment.

37. That those who commit patricide or fratricide, or who kill an uncle or a father-in-law or any of their kinsmen, and who refuse to obey and consent to the judgment of bishops, priests, and other justices, are for the salvation of their souls and for the carrying out of the lawful judgment to be confined by our *missi* and counts in such custody that they will be safe, and will not pollute the rest of the people, until such time as they are brought to our presence. And in the meantime they are not to have any of their property.

38. The same is to be done with those who are arraigned and punished for unlawful and incestuous unions, and who refuse to mend their ways or submit to their bishops and priests, and who presume to disregard our edict.

39. That no one should dare to steal our beasts in our forests; this we have forbidden already on many occasions, and we now firmly ban it again, that no one should do it any more and should take care to keep the faith which everyone has promised to us and desires to keep. And if any count or *centenarius* or vassal of ours or any of our officials should steal our game he must at all costs be brought to our presence to account for it. As for the rest of the people, anyone who steals the game in this way should in every case pay the appropriate penalty, and under no circumstances should anyone be let off in this matter. And if anyone knows that it has been done by someone else, in accordance with the faith he has promised to us to keep and has now to promise again he should not dare to conceal this.

40. Finally, therefore, from all our decrees we desire it to be known in all our kingdom through our *missi* now sent out: among the clergy, the bishops, abbots, priests, deacons, clerks, and all monks and nuns, that each one in his ministry or profession should keep our edict or decree, and when it is right should of his good will offer thanks to the people, give them help, or if need be correct them in some way. Similarly for the laity, in all places everywhere, if a plea is entered concerning the protection of the holy churches, or of widows or orphans or less powerful people, or concerning the host [army], and is argued on these cases, we wish them to know that they should be obedient to our order and our will, that they maintain observance of our edict, and that in all these matters each man strive to keep himself in God's holy service. This in order that everything should be good and well-ordered for the praise of Almighty God, and that we should give thanks where it is due; that where we believe anything to have gone unpunished we should so strive with all earnestness and willingness to correct it that with God's help we may bring it to correction, to

the eternal reward both of ourselves and of all our faithful people. Similarly concerning the counts and *centenarii*, our officers [*ministerialibus*], we wish all the things above mentioned in our deliberations to be known. So be it.

Reading 6

Charlemagne's Letter to Abbot Baugulf, Late 700s

Although undated, this letter must have been written before Charlemagne's imperial coronation in 800 because he titles himself patrician rather than emperor of the Romans. The letter reflects Charlemagne's policy of using the bishoprics and monasteries of his realm to advance literacy and learning. It also reflects, by implication, the sorry state of learning at the time. Although addressed to Abbot Baugulf of Fulda, the letter is intended for all bishops and abbots—as its conclusion makes clear. One can only hope that they possessed sufficient learning and patience to decipher the tangled sentence that follows the address clause.

Charles, by the grace of God, king of the Franks and Lombards and patrician of the Romans, to Abbot Baugulf and to all the congregation, also to the faithful committed to you, we have directed a loving greeting by our ambassadors in the name of omnipotent God.

Be it known, therefore, to your devotion pleasing to God, that we, together with our faithful, have considered it useful that the bishoprics and monasteries entrusted by the favor of Christ to our control, in addition to the order of monastic life and the intercourse of holy religion, in the culture of letters also ought to be zealous in teaching those who by the gift of God are able to learn, according to the capacity of each individual, so that just as the observance of the rule imparts order and grace to honesty of morals, so also zeal in teaching and learning may do the same for sentences, so that those who desire to please God by living rightly should not neglect to please him also by speaking correctly. For it is written: "Either from thy words thou shalt be justified or from thy words thou shalt be condemned." For although correct conduct may be better than knowledge, nevertheless knowledge precedes conduct. Therefore, each one ought to study what he desires to accomplish, so that so much the more fully the mind may know what ought to be done, as the tongue

From *Translations and Reprints from Original Sources of European History*, ed. and tr. D. C. Munro; Philadelphia, University of Pennsylvania Press, 1897, vol. VI, no. 5, pp. 12–14.

hastens in the praises of omnipotent God without the hindrances of errors. For since errors should be shunned by all men, so much the more ought they to be avoided as far as possible by those who are chosen for this very purpose alone, so that they ought to be the especial servants of truth. For when in the years just passed, letters were often written to us from several monasteries in which it was stated that the brethren who dwelt there offered up in our behalf sacred and pious prayers, we have recognized in most of these letters both correct thoughts and uncouth expressions; because what pious devotion dictated faithfully to the mind, the tongue, uneducated on account of the neglect of study, was not able to express in the letter without error. Whence it happened that we began to fear lest perchance, as the skill in writing was less, so also the wisdom for understanding the Holy Scriptures might be much less than it rightly ought to be. And we all know well that, although errors of speech are dangerous, far more dangerous are errors of the understanding. Therefore, we exhort you not only not to neglect the study of letters, but also with most humble mind, pleasing to God, to study earnestly in order that you may be able more easily and more correctly to penetrate the mysteries of the divine Scriptures. Since, moreover, images, tropes and similar figures are found in the sacred pages, no one doubts that each one in reading these will understand the spiritual sense more quickly if previously he shall have been fully instructed in the mastery of letters. Such men truly are to be chosen for this work as have both the will and the ability to learn and a desire to instruct others. And may this be done with a zeal as great as the earnestness with which we command it. For we desire you to be, as it is fitting that soldiers of the church should be, devout in mind, learned in discourse, chaste in conduct and eloquent in speech, so that whosoever shall seek to see you out of reverence for God, or on account of your reputation for holy conduct, just as he is edified by your appearance, may also be instructed by your wisdom, which he has learned from your reading or singing, and may go away joyfully giving thanks to omnipotent God. Do not neglect, therefore, if you wish to have our favor, to send copies of this letter to all your suffragans and fellow bishops and to all the monasteries.

Reading 7

Dicuil's Book of the Measurement of the Earth

Dicuil, an Irish monk of the late 700s and early 800s, was very likely an instructor at the court school of Charlemagne's son, Louis the Pious (814–840). The "Measurement of the Earth" draws heavily from the work of classical authors, but it also reflects the interest in geography common among Irish scholars of the early Middle Ages. It further suggests the wide range of scholarly interests to be found at the Carolingian court. Like Einhard, Dicuil uses his classical sources with discrimination. His treatise is severely limited by the scarcity and unreliability of available geographical data, but it should put to rest the modern nonsense about medieval scholars believing that the earth was flat.

In Dicuil's time, Viking mariners, without the aid of classical texts, were already undertaking distant voyages that would eventually carry them far out into the Atlantic—to Iceland, Greenland, and North American (see Chapter 4, Reading 6).

1. Having composed my letter on ten questions of the art of grammar, I considered that a book might follow on the measurement of the provinces of the earth, according to the authority of the men whom the holy Emperor Theodosius [379–95] had sent to measure the said provinces; and I desire to indicate their dimensions, supplementing this information on the high authority of Plinius Secundus.[1]

2. But I have two reasons for prefixing the account of the envoys of Theodosius to the words of Plinius Secundus in the order of my writing, as against the chronological order; one that the former, in their last twelve lines, assert that their work has been done more carefully than that of the ancients, and the other, that I saw beforehand that the volumes of the *Natural History* of Plinius Secundus which I had examined, were very much jumbled up by the scribes of recent times.

3. I shall, indeed, devote my attention to correcting, in so far as I can, the reports of the above-mentioned envoys, as they have been composed with fewer mistakes.

[1]Pliny composed his *Natural History* in c. 75 A.D. and with Ptolemy's *Almagest*, recording observations beginning in 127 A.D. and continuing until at least 141 A.D., was one of the most popular scientific treatises of the Middle Ages.

4. But where in the books of Plinius Secundus I find figures which I realize to be undoubtedly corrupt, I shall leave their places vacant for the moment, so that if I do not find trusty copies whoever does find them may correct them. Where I am in doubt as to whether the figures are correct or not, I shall write them down as correct, so that, as I have said, whoever finds the true figures may make the appropriate correction.

5. Discrepancies in the number of miles between Plinius Secundus and the emperor's envoys should occasion no surprise to anyone, since the latter truly testify, as I have said, that they accomplished their work with more care than did the ancients. . . .

The latitude of the earth from south to north makes up less by nearly half, being three thousand three hundred and forty-eight miles. This shows how much the heat has removed on the one hand, and the sea on the other. For I do not think that the earth ceases to be spherical [i.e., at the extreme north and south], or is not spherical at all, but that it is uninhabitable at both extremes and is therefore unknown.[2]

If we measure the longitude given above from the eastern part of India as far as the islands of Cadiz by means of the milesigns, for example by means of the milestones, each marking the end of a mile, the extent will be six thousand six hundred and thirty miles; and the latitude from north to south will be three thousand three hundred and forty-eight, omitting the aforesaid areas where the cold or the heat is unbearable. Here ends the survey of the earth. . . .

Plinius Secundus makes these statements about the Nile in his fifth book: Egypt is situated next to Africa, extending inwards towards the south to where Ethiopia stretches out behind it. The Nile, dividing into a right-hand and a left-hand channel, embraces and forms the bounds of its more low-lying part, the Canopic mouth lying towards Africa, the Pelusiac towards Asia, at an interval of two hundred and seventy miles. Hence some authors have regarded Egypt as an island, this division of the Nile giving the country the shape of a triangle; and therefore many people have called Egypt "Delta" by the name of the Greek letter. . . .

The Nile begins to rise from the time of the new moon which follows the summer solstice. The rise is gradual and moderate while the sun is moving through the Crab, and strongest as it passes through the Lion, and while in the Virgin it subsides at the same rate as that at which it rose. It withdraws, how-

---

[2]In this rather cryptic passage, Dicuil attempts to reconcile the discrepancy between the theoretical diameter of the earth as proposed by Pliny, and later by Ptolemy, and the measurement he has accepted. According to Dicuil, the difference can be accounted for by acknowledging that the extreme points of the earth in the southern and northern hemispheres are uninhabited rather than nonexistent. The interesting point of the passage, however, is the Irish scholar's acceptance of the theory that the earth is spherical and not flat.

ever, entirely within its banks, as Herodotus [fifth-century B.C. Greek historian] states, on the hundredth day, when the sun is in the Scales.

It is regarded as a religious offense for kings or for those in authority to sail on the Nile while it is rising. The rising is observed by means of walls which have measuring-marks. The regular rise is one of sixteen cubits. A less amount of water does not irrigate the whole area, while a larger amount recedes more slowly and so delays operations; the latter takes up the time for sowing because the soil remains wet, the former does not allow sufficient time since the soil is parched; both of these things are carefully reckoned by the province. . . .

Although we read in no authority that a branch of the Nile flows into the Red Sea, yet brother Fidelis asserted this and related it, in my presence, to my teacher Suibne (to whom, under God, I owe any progress that I have made), saying that, for purposes of worship, in the city of Jerusalem, both clerics and laymen . . . sailed in a . . . [the text is corrupt here] . . . as far as the Nile.

Then, after a long sail on the Nile, they saw, like mountains, and admired from a distance, the seven barns built by holy Joseph, according to the number of the years of abundance, four in one place, and three in another.

From here they went to the three barns to admire them and found beside them a lion and eight people, men and women, lying dead. The lion had killed them in his strength, and they had killed him with spears and swords; both places in which the seven barns are built are desert.

After this Brother Fidelis carefully examined the three barns and again was filled with amazement that they were entirely made of stone from their very base to the summit. The barns were square at the base, but rounded at the top; at the very apex they have, as it were, a slender point.

Then the brother whom I have mentioned measured one side of one barn, from corner to corner, as four hundred feet.

Next, embarking on their boats, they sailed along the Nile as far as the entrance of the Red Sea. From this harbor it is a small distance eastwards to the passage of Moses across the Red Sea. He who measured the side of the barn wished to go as far as the harbor where Moses with his people entered the sea, not only to enter the harbor, but in order to see in it the tracks of the chariots and the ruts of Pharaoh's wheels; but the sailors would not oblige. The width of the sea at that place seemed to him to be about six miles.

From thence they made a fast voyage in the western part of the Red Sea, that is, in the gulf which extends far towards the north. That is the sea which prevented the people of Israel, when murmuring in the desert, from being able to return to the land of Egypt.

CHAPTER 4

Ordeal and Survival

The materials in this chapter illustrate how various regions of Western Christendom responded to the breakdown of the Carolingian Empire and the attacks of the Vikings and Hungarians.

When Louis the Pious died in 840, after a reign marred by internal upheavals and Viking raids, his three sons struggled over the division of the Empire (document 1). Their eventual settlement—the Treaty of Verdun of 843—partitioned the Carolingian dominions into a western kingdom (France), an eastern kingdom (Germany), and an unstable middle kingdom stretching from Italy to the Netherlands. Under continued Viking pressure, the kingdom of France broke up into smaller units as the counts and dukes of Carolingian officialdom converted their administrative offices into hereditary lordships and acquired increasing numbers of sworn followers (document 2, A, B, C). These followers—''vassals''—often received lands from their lord in return for their service and loyalty, and sometimes granted portions of these lands to their own oath-bound retainers. This process resulted in a tenurial chain of lord-vassal relationships known as feudalism (document 2, D).

Amid the political confusion and endemic warfare of late-Carolingian Europe there emerged a movement for church reform and social order centering on the Burgundian monastery of Cluny and gradually spreading across Christendom (document 2, E). In England, after a century of Viking raids and conquests, the kings of Wessex managed to reverse the Danish tide (document 3) and, eventually, to unite all England under their rule. Germany, too, saw a revival of royal power under a new, Saxon dynasty whose ablest member, Otto the Great, routed the Hungarians in 955 at the battle of the Lechfeld (document 4). Otto brought northern Italy under his control and was crowned "Roman emperor" in 962—the first of a long line of king-emperors reigning over both Germany and northern Italy. The relative stability that Otto and his successors brought to Italy provided an encouraging environment for the development of Italian commerce and urban life (document 5). Italy's cities were to play a commanding role in the commercial revolution that would transform Europe in the High Middle Ages.

In the course of the eleventh century, the revival of Europe's commerce and political order brought the invasions to an end. The Vikings and Hungarians were themselves Christianized and incorporated into European Civilization. Our final document demonstrates that the seafaring Vikings had much to contribute to Europe's landbound culture—that their activities were by no means limited to death and destruction. With Columbus so deeply etched in our minds, it is too easy to forget that Europe's first discovery of America occurred not in 1492 but toward the end of the early Middle Ages (document 6).

Reading 1
Nithard's Account of the Year 840

Nithard (d. 844) was one of the few lay historians of the early Middle Ages. An illegitimate son of one of Charlemagne's daughters, he was reared and educated at the Carolingian court and subsequently joined the following of King Charles the Bald, the youngest of Louis the Pious's three surviving sons. On Louis' death in 840, Charles and his two royal brothers—Lothair and Louis the German—struggled over the division of the Carolingian Empire. Having fought for Charles the Bald on more than one occasion, Nithard was well placed to report the fraternal struggle but quite unable to mask his own sympathies.

When Lothair [840–855] heard of his father's [Louis the Pious] death, he immediately sent emissaries everywhere, especially all over Francia. They proclaimed that he was coming into the empire which had once been given to him. He promised that he wished to grant everyone the benefices which his father had given and that he would make them even bigger. He gave orders also that oaths of fealty should be exacted from those who were still uncommitted. In addition, he ordered that all should join him as fast as they could; those who were unwilling to appear he threatened with death. He himself advanced slowly since he wanted to find out how the wind was blowing before he crossed the Alps.

Presently, men from everywhere joined him, driven by either greed or fear. When Lothair saw that, his prospects and power made him bold, and he began to scheme about how he might best seize the whole empire. He decided to send an army against Louis [the German] first, since this would not take him out of his way, and to devote himself with all his might to the destruction of Louis' forces. In the meantime he was shrewd enough to send emissaries to Charles [the Bald] in Aquitaine, informing Charles that he was friendly toward him, as their father had demanded and as was proper for one to feel toward a godchild. But he begged him to spare their nephew, Pepin's son [Pepin II of Aquitaine], until he had spoken to him. Having settled this, he turned to the city of Worms.

At that time [June 840] Louis had left part of his army as a garrison in Worms and had gone to meet the Saxons who were in revolt. But after a small skirmish Lothair put the defenders to flight and, crossing the Rhine with his entire army, headed for Frankfurt. Here they suddenly came upon each other,

From *Carolingian Chronicles*, ed. and tr. Bernhard W. Schloz; Ann Arbor, 1970, pp. 141–145, 174. Reprinted by permission of the University of Michigan Press.

Lothair approaching from one side and Louis from the other. After peace had been arranged for the night, they pitched their camps, not exactly in brotherly love, Lothair right at the place where they had met and Louis at the point where the Main flows into the Rhine. Since Louis' opposition was vigorous and his brother was not sure that he could make him give in without a fight, Lothair thought it might be easier to get the better of Charles first. He therefore put off battle with the understanding that he would meet Louis again at the same place on November 11. Unless an agreement could be negotiated beforehand, they would settle by force what each of them was going to get. And so, giving up his initial schemes, Lothair set out to subdue Charles.

At this time [July 840] Charles had come to Bourges to the assembly which Pepin [II] was going to attend, as his men had sworn. When Charles had learned what he could from everybody, he selected as ambassadors Nithard and Adalgar[1] and dispatched them as speedily as possible to Lothair, enjoining and entreating him to remember the oaths they had sworn each other and to preserve what their father had arranged between them. He also reminded him that he, Charles, was his brother and godson. Lothair should have what belonged to him; but should also permit Charles to have without a fight what his father had granted him with Lothair's consent. Charles pledged, if Lothair should do this, that he was willing to be loyal and subject to him, as it is proper to behave toward one's first-born brother. Besides, Charles promised that he would wholeheartedly forgive whatever Lothair had done to him up to that time. He implored him to stop stirring up his people and disturbing the kingdom committed to him by God, and sent word to Lothair that peace and harmony should rule everywhere. This peace he and his people considered most desirable and were willing to preserve. If Lothair did not believe this, Charles promised to give him whatever assurances he wanted.

Lothair pretended to receive this message kindly, but permitted the emissaries to return with greetings only and the reply that he would answer fully through his own envoys. Moreover, he deprived Charles' emissaries of the benefices which his father had given them because they did not want to break their fealty and join him. In this way he unwittingly betrayed his designs against his brother. Meanwhile, all men living between the Meuse and the Seine sent to Charles, asked him to get there before the land was taken over by Lothair, and promised to wait for his arrival. Charles quickly set out with only a few men and marched from Aquitaine to Quierzy. There he received graciously those who had come from the Charbonniere and the land on this side

---

[1]This Nithard is the author of the *Histories* and Adalgar was a count of Charles the Bald's court party.

of it.[2] Beyond the Charbonnière, however, Herefrid, Gislebert, Bovo, and the others duped by Odulf[3] disregarded their sworn fealty and defected.

At the same time [August 840] a messenger coming from Aquitaine announced that Pepin and his partisans wanted to attack Charles' mother. Charles left the Franks at Quierzy by themselves, but ordered them to move his way if his brother should attempt to subdue them before his return. In addition, he dispatched Hugo, Adalhard, Gerard, and Hegilo to Lothair. Repeating everything that he had said before, he entreated Lothair again for God's sake not to subvert Charles' men and further to whittle away at the kingdom which God and his father had given to Charles with Lothair's consent. After making this appeal to Lothair he rushed into Aquitaine, fell upon Pepin and his men, and put them to flight.

Meanwhile [October 840], Lothair was returning from the confrontation with Louis and being joined by every man on this side of the Charbonnière. He thought it best to cross the Meuse and advance as far as the Seine. On his way there Hilduin, abbot of St. Denis, and Gerard, count of the city of Paris, came and met him. They had broken their fealty and defected from Charles. When Pepin, son of Bernard, king of the Lombards, and others saw this treachery, like slaves they also chose to break their word and disregard their oaths rather than give up their holdings for a little while. That is why these men broke faith, followed the example of those we mentioned already, and submitted to Lothair. Then Lothair became bold and crossed the Seine, sending ahead, as he always did, to the inhabitants between the Seine and the Loire men who were to make them defect by threats and promises. He himself followed slowly, as usual, heading for the city of Chartres. When he learned that Theodoric and Eric were on the way with the rest who had decided to join him, he resolved to proceed as far as the Loire, putting his confidence in his great numbers. Charles returned from the pursuit in which he had dispersed Pepin and his followers, and since he had no place where he could safely leave his mother, they both hastily departed for Francia.

In the meantime Charles heard of all these defections and that Lothair was determined to hound him to the death with an immense army, while Pepin on one side and the Bretons on the other had raised arms against him. So he and his men sat down to think about all these troubles. They easily found a simple solution. Since they had nothing left but their lives and their bodies, they chose to die nobly rather than betray and abandon their king.

They headed [in November 840] in Lothair's direction, and both sides thus approached the city of Orlèans. They pitched camps at a distance of bare-

---

[2]This territory constitutes the frontier between Neustria and Austrasia.

[3]Ordulf was the lay-abbot of St.-Josse in northern France.

ly six Gallic miles from each other, and both parties dispatched emissaries. Charles only asked for peace and justice, but Lothair tried to think of a way he could deceive and get the better of Charles without a fight. This scheme came to nothing because of strong resistance on the other side. Then Lothair hoped that his own forces would continue to grow from day to day, and he thought he might be able to conquer his brother more easily when Charles' following had further dwindled.

But he was disappointed in the hope and refrained from battle. The condition of the truce was that Charles should be granted Aquitaine, Septimania, Provence, and ten counties between the Loire and the Seine, with the stipulation that he should be satisfied with them and remain there for the time being until they met again at Attigny on May 8.[4] Lothair promised that he was indeed willing to talk over and settle the interests of both parties by mutual consent. The leaders of Charles' party also realized that the problems at hand were more than they could handle. They feared, if it came to a battle, that they might be hard put to save the king in view of their small numbers, and all of them set great store by his talents. So they consented to the stipulations if only Lothair from now on would be as loyal a friend to Charles as a brother should be, permit him to hold peacefully the lands he had allotted to him, and in the meantime also refrain from hostilities against Louis. Otherwise, they should be absolved from the oath they had sworn.

By this device they both rescued their king from danger and soon freed themselves from an oath. For those who had sworn this had not yet left the house when Lothair tried to seduce some of them from Charles and by the next day in fact he received a few defectors. He immediately sent into the lands which he had assigned to his brother, to stir up trouble so that they would not submit to Charles. Then he moved on in order to receive homage from those coming to him out of Provence and tried to think of ways to overcome Louis by force or deception. . . .

From this history, everyone may gather how mad it is to neglect the common good and to follow only private and selfish desires, since both sins insult the Creator, so much in fact that He turns even the elements against the madness of the sinner. I shall easily prove this by examples still known to almost everyone. In the times of Charles the Great [d. 814] of good memory, who died almost thirty years ago, peace and concord ruled everywhere because our people were treading the one proper way, the way of the common welfare, and thus the way of God. But now since each goes his separate way, dissension and struggle abound. Once there was abundance and happiness everywhere, now everywhere there is want and sadness. Once even the elements smiled on every-

---

[4]Of the lands assigned to Charles at Worms in 839, one-third, which included Burgundy, were now left out.

thing and now they threaten, as Scripture which was left to us as the gift of God, testifies: "And the world will wage war against the madness."

Reading 2

Select Feudal Documents

The following sources illustrate the evolution of lord-vassal relationships and hereditary tenures from pre-Carolingian to post-Carolingian times. The element of reciprocal rights and obligations between lord and vassal is particularly evident in the letter of Fulbert bishop of Chartres (1102–28), a celebrated scholar and school master. Reciprocity also characterized the relationships between aristocratic benefactors and the religious houses that they founded; monks were normally expected to serve their benefactors with prayers for their souls and, often, with knights enfeoffed on the monastic lands. Duke William of Aquitaine, when he founded the abbey of Cluny in 909, granted it far greater privileges and liberties than were customary at the time, thereby providing the precondition for Cluny's subsequent role as a generator of ecclesiastical reform across Western Christendom.

A. A SEVENTH CENTURY FRANKISH FORMULA OF COMMENDATION.

To that magnificent lord [blank], I, [blank]. Since it is known familiarly to all how little I have whence to feed and clothe myself, I have therefore petitioned your piety, and your good will has decreed to me that I should hand myself over or commend myself to your guardianship, which I have thereupon done; that is to say in this way, that you should aid and succor me as well with food as with clothing, according as I shall be able to serve you and deserve it.

And so long as I shall live I ought to provide service and honor to you, suitably to my free condition; and I shall not during the time of my life have the ability to withdraw from your power or guardianship; but must remain during the days of my life under your power or defense. Wherefore it is proper that if either of us shall wish to withdraw himself from these agreements, he

A. "Frankish commendation," from *Translations and Reprints of Original Sources of European History*, ed. and tr. E. P. Cheyney; Philadelphia, 1897, vol. 4, no. 3, pp. 3–4. B. "Capitulary of Mersen," from *ibid.*, p. 5. C. "Capitulary of Quierzy," from *ibid.*, p. 14. D. Letter of Fulbert of Chartres, from *ibid.*, p. 23–24. E. Foundation Charter of Cluny, from *The Tenth Century*, ed. R. S. Lopez; New York, Holt, Rinehart & Winston, 1959, pp. 14–15; by permission.

shall pay [blank] shillings to the other party, and this agreement shall remain unbroken.

B. THE CAPITULARY OF MERSEN OF 847

We [Emperor Lothair and Kings Lewis the German and Charles the Bald] will moreover that each free man in our realms shall choose a lord, from us or our faithful, such a one as he wishes.

We command moreover that no man shall leave his lord without just cause, nor should any one receive him, except in such a way as was customary in the time of our predecessors.

And we wish you to know that we want to grant right to our faithful subjects and we do not wish to do anything to them against reason. Similarly we admonish you and the rest of our faithful subjects that you grant right to your men and do not act against reason toward them.

And we will that the man of each one of us in whosesoever kingdom he is, shall go with his lord against the enemy, or in his other needs unless there shall have been (as may there not be) such an invasion of the kingdom as is called a *landwer*, so that the whole people of that kingdom shall go together to repel it.

C. FROM CHARLES THE BALD'S CAPITULARY OF QUIERZY OF 877

If a count of this kingdom, whose son is with us, shall die, our son with the rest of our faithful shall appoint some one of the nearest relatives of the same count, who, along with the officials of his province and with the bishop in whose diocese the same province is, shall administer that province until announcement is made to us, so that we may honor his son who is with us with his honors.

If, however, he had a minor son, this same son, along with the officials of that province and with the bishop in whose diocese it is, shall make provision for the same province until the notice of the death of the same count shall come to us, that his son may be honored, by our concession, with his honors.

If, however, he had no son, our son along with the rest of the faithful, shall take charge, who, along with the officials of the same province and with the proper bishop shall make provision for the same province until our order may be made in regard to it. Therefore, let him not be angry who shall provide for the province if we give the same province to another whom it pleases us, rather than to him who has so far provided for it.

Similarly also shall this be done concerning our vassals. And we will and command that as well the bishops as the abbots and the counts, and any others of our faithful also, shall study to preserve this toward their men.

D. A LETTER OF BISHOP FULBERT OF CHARTRES, DATED 1020, TO DUKE WILLIAM V OF AQUITAINE CONCERNING VASSALS AND LORDS

To William most glorious duke of the Aquitanians, Bishop Fulbert the favor of his prayers.

Asked to write something concerning the form of fealty, I have noted briefly for you on the authority of books the things which follow. He who swears fealty to his lord ought always to have these six things in memory; what is harmless, safe, honorable, useful, easy, practicable. Harmless, that is to say that he should not be injurious to his lord in his body; safe, that he should not be injurious to him in his secrets or in the defenses through which he is able to be secure; honorable, that he should not be injurious to him in his justice or in other matters that pertain to his honor; useful, that he should not be injurious to him in his possessions; easy or practicable, that that good which his lord is able to do easily, he make not difficult, nor that which is practicable he make impossible to him.

However, that the faithful vassal should avoid these injuries is proper, but not for this does he deserve his holding; for it is not sufficient to abstain from evil, unless what is good is done also. It remains, therefore, that in the same six things mentioned above he should faithfully counsel and aid his lord, if he wishes to be looked upon as worthy of his benefice and to be safe concerning the fealty which he has sworn.

The lord also ought to act toward his faithful vassal reciprocally in all these things. And if he does not do this he will be justly considered guilty of bad faith, just as the former, if he should be detected in the avoidance of or the doing of or the consenting to them, would be perfidious and perjured. . . .

E. THE FOUNDATION CHARTER OF THE ABBEY OF CLUNY, DATED 909

It is clear to all men of sane mind that the providence of God so decrees for any rich man that he may be able to deserve everlasting rewards by means of the goods he transitorily possesses, if he uses them well. . . .

And I, William, count [of Auvergne] and duke [of Aquitaine] by the gift of God, carefully pondering this, and desiring to provide for my own salvation while it is permissible for me, have considered it proper, nay, most necessary, that from the goods which have been temporarily conferred upon me, I am to give a small portion for the gain of my soul. . . . And in order to make this deed not a temporary but lasting one, I am to support at my own expense a congregation of monks, trusting and hoping that even though I myself am unable to despise all things, nevertheless, by taking charge of despisers of the world whom I deem to be righteous, "I may receive the reward of the righteous" [Matthew X, 41].

Therefore, . . . I hand over from my own domains to the holy apostles, Peter and Paul, the following goods legally held by me: the vill of Cluny with the court and demesne manor, and the chapel in honor of Saint Mary, mother of God, and of Saint Peter, prince of the apostles, together with all the goods pertaining to it, namely, the vills, the chapels, the serfs of both sexes, the vines, the fields, the meadows, the waters and their courses, the mills, the entrances and exits, what is cultivated and what is not, all in their entirety. . . . [I give all this] with this understanding, that a regular monastery be constructed in Cluny in honor of the holy apostles Peter and Paul, and that there the monks shall congregate and live according to the rule of the blessed Benedict. . . .

And let the monks, as well as all the aforesaid possessions, be under the power and authority of the Abbot Bernon [d. 926], who shall regularly preside over them, as long as he lives, according to his knowledge and ability. But after his death, the same monks are to have power and permission to elect as abbot and rector any one of their order whom they will choose, in keeping with the will of God and the rule promulgated by Saint Benedict, so that they may not be impeded from making a canonical election by our opposition or that of any other power. Every five years, then, the aforesaid monks are to pay ten shillings to the church of the apostles for their lights. . . . We further will that every day they perform works of mercy toward the poor, the needy, the stranger and the pilgrim. . . .

The same monks there congregated are to be subject neither to our sway nor to that of our relatives, nor to the splendor of the royal greatness, nor to that of any earthly power. And I warn and beseech, through God and all His saints, and by the terrible Day of Judgment, that no one of the secular princes, no count whatever, no bishop at all, nor the pontiff of the aforesaid Roman See, is to invade the property of these servants of God, or alienate it, or impair it, or give it as a benefice to any one, or appoint any prelate over them against their will. . . . And I beseech you, Oh Peter and Paul, holy apostles and glorious princes of the earth, and you, Pontiff of the pontiffs of the apostolic see, that . . . you remove from the community of the holy church of God and of life eternal the robbers and invaders and alienators of these goods. . . .

Reading 3

The Anglo-Saxon Chronicle on the Viking Invasions of England and King Alfred's Early Wars

The *Anglo-Saxon Chronicle* is an unusual and diabolically complex document. Unlike most of our sources, it was written not in Latin but in the Old English vernacular, a distant ancestor of modern English and indecipherable without special training. From the 890s onward, copies of the *Anglo-Saxon Chronicle* were circulated to a number of English monasteries, at a few of which they were kept up to date more or less year by year. Thus, the so-called "Chronicle" is actually a series of interrelated annals varying in content between one manuscript and another. The "Parker Version," translated here, is the oldest of them. All its year-entries through 891 were transcribed in a single hand by an anonymous monk who was probably writing at Winchester, the chief city of the kingdom of Wessex. The entries after 891 occur in a variety of hands, suggesting that the writers were contemporary with the events described. But the annals translated here run from about 789 to 878, and the monk who transcribed them must therefore have been depend-· ing in part on earlier sources, now lost. His point of view is suggested by the fact that he was writing toward the end of the reign of Alfred the Great and probably at Alfred's capital.

789. In this year . . . three [of the Norsemen's] ships came [to Portland, Dorset] for the first time; and then the reeve rode there and tried to force them to go to the king's manor because he did not know who they were; and they slew him. These ships were the first of the Danes that attacked the English.

836. In this year King Ecgbert fought with thirty-five ships' crews at Carhampton, and great slaughter was made there, and the Danes had possession of the place of slaughter. . . .

838. In this year a large hostile army came into west Wales [Cornwall], and [the Britons] joined forces with them and continued to fight against King Ecgbert of Wessex. When the king heard this, he and his levies fought against them at Hingston Down and there put to flight both the Britons and the Danes.

840. In this year the ealdorman[1] Wulfheard fought against thirty-three ships' crews at Southampton and he made great slaughter there and won a vic-

From *Two of the Anglo-Saxon Chronicles Parallel*, ed. Charles Plummer and John Earle; Oxford, The Clarendon Press, 1899, vol. 1, pp. 54, 62–76. Tr. Marc Anthony Meyer.

[1]The ealdorman is a leading man of high birth found throughout the Anglo-Saxon kingdoms, and the English equivalent of the continental "count."

tory. And Wulfheard died that same year. And in the same year, Ealdorman Æthelhelm with the Dorset levies fought against the Danish host at Portland, and for a long time put the host to flight; but the Danes had possession of the place of battle and killed the ealdorman.

851. In this year Ealdorman Ceorl with the Devonshire levies fought against the heathens at Wicga's Hill and great slaughter was made there, and he won the victory. And that same year King Athelstan and Ealdorman Ealhhere annihilated a great army at Sandwich in Kent and seized nine ships and scattered the rest. And for the first time the heathens pitched a winter camp [in England]. And then in the following year [852], three hundred and fifty ships came to the mouth of the River Thames and attacked Canterbury and London, and the heathens put to flight King Beorhtwulf of Mercia and his army. Then they went south, crossing the Thames into Surrey, and King Æthelwulf and his son Æthelbald and the West Saxon army fought against them at *Acleah*, and there the greatest slaughter was made of the heathen army of which we have heard until the present day, and the West Saxons won the battle.

860. In this year King Æthelbald died and his body lies at Sherborne; and then his brother Æthelbert succeeded to the whole kingdom and maintained it in good peace and great tranquility. And in his days a great heathen army landed and attacked Winchester [the capital town of Wessex], and Ealdorman Osric and the Hampshire levies and Ealdorman Æthelwulf and the men of Berkshire fought against the enemy host, put them to flight and had possession of the place of slaughter. And King Æthelbert ruled for five years and his body lies at Sherborne.

865. In this year the heathen army camped on the Isle of Thanet and made peace with the men of Kent, and the Kentishmen promised them money in return for that peace. And under the shelter of that peace and promise of money, the heathen army covertly traveled at night and devastated all of eastern Kent. In this year [866], Æthelred, King Æthelbert's brother, succeeded to the West Saxon kingdom. And in that same year, a great hostile army [known as the "Great Danish Army"] came to the land of the English and set up winter quarters in East Anglia, crossing the mouth of the Humber to York in Northumbria [in 867], where there was great discord among those people. They had rejected their king, Osbert, and had accepted Ælla as king, a man without a proper claim to rule. Only late in the year, when they began to make war on the heathens, did they gather a great army and move to attack them at York. They stormed the city [on 21 or 23 March 867] and some of them got inside, but the Northumbrians were very soundly defeated—some inside and some outside—and both kings were killed and the rest of the Northumbrians made peace with the enemy host. . . .

870. In this year the heathen army rode across Mercia into East Anglia

and set up winter quarters at Thetford; and that winter King Edmund[2] fought against them, but the Danes were victorious and killed the king and subdued the whole kingdom. . . .

871. In this year the enemy army came to Reading [a royal residence] in Wessex, and after three nights two jarls[3] rode up-country. Then Ealdorman Æthelwulf met them at Englefield and fought against them and won the victory. Then after four nights, King Æthelred and his brother Alfred [the Great] led a great army to Reading and fought against the enemy, and great slaughter was made on both sides, and Ealdorman Æthelwulf was killed and the Danes had possession of the place of slaughter. And after four nights King Æthelred and his brother Alfred fought at Ashdown against the whole heathen army which was in two companies: in one was Bagsecg and Halfdan [son of Ragnar Lothbrok], and in the other the jarls. And there King Æthelred fought against the company of the heathen kings, whence King Bagsecg was slain. And Alfred, the king's brother, fought against the company of the jarls, and Jarls Sidroc the Elder and Sidroc the Younger, and Jarls Osbearn, Fraena, and Harald were slain. Both companies were put to flight and many thousands were killed and fighting continued until nightfall. And two weeks later, King Æthelred and his brother Alfred fought against the enemy host at Basing, and there the Danes won a victory. And after two months, King Æthelred and his brother Alfred fought at *Meretun* against the enemy who, again, were in two companies; and the [English] levies put both to flight and until late in the day were victorious. There was much bloodshed on both sides; but afterwards the Danes held the place of slaughter. And Bishop Heahmund was killed there along with many other good men. And after this fight, a great summer host[4] came. And then, after Easter [15 April], King Æthelred died, having ruled for five years; and his body lies at Wimborne.

Then his brother Alfred, son of Æthelwulf, succeeded to the West Saxon kingdom. And one month later, King Alfred, with a small force, fought against the whole heathen army at Wilton, and for a long while during the day fought off the host; but then the Danes had possession of the battlefield. And during this year, nine pitched battles were fought against the enemy army in

[2]King Edmund is said to have refused to share his Christian kingdom with the heathen Vikings, and they tied him to a tree and shot him with arrows and cut off his head. His cult spread quickly, and his body was enshrined at Bury, where in 1020 a monastery was founded and dedicated to St. Edmund, King and Martyr.

[3]The jarl or chieftain was a Scandinavian warrior who had gathered a band of other warriors around himself and united his area of country.

[4]A Scandinavian army that did not remain in England over the winter and came primarily for plunder and raiding.

this kingdom south of the Thames besides the many small encounters that King Alfred, the king's brother, and a single ealdorman and king's thegns[5] rode on which were not counted. And during this year, nine jarls and one king were killed; and in this year the West Saxons made peace with the Viking host.

874. In this year the heathens went from Lindsey to Repton [in Northumbria] and constructed a winter camp there, and they drove King Burgred [of Mercia] across the sea twenty-two years after he succeeded to the kingdom; and they conquered the whole kingdom. And the king traveled to Rome and settled there, and his body lies in the church of Saint Mary in the English school.[6] And in the same year, the heathens gave the kingdom of Mercia to a foolish king's thegn, and he swore oaths and gave hostages to them so that at all times the kingdom would be held ready for them whenever they needed it, and he would hold himself in readiness and, with his followers, would serve the needs of the enemy army in all things.

876. In this year the Viking host stole away inland into Wareham and eluded the West Saxon levies, and the king concluded a peace with the heathen army, and they swore oaths to him on the sacred ring[7] which before they would not do for any nation, that they would immediately depart from the kingdom. And the enemy army stole away from the West Saxon levies by night under shelter of this pact and, provided with horses, the enemy got to Exeter. And in this year Halfdan distributed the land of the Northumbrians [among his followers] and they engaged in ploughing and tilling for themselves.

878. In this year the heathen army stole away inland to Chippenham in the middle of winter over Twelfth Night and attacked and occupied the land of the West Saxons and drove a great part of the people overseas and, with the exception of King Alfred, conquered the greater part of those people who remained. And with a small company the king went with extreme difficulty through the woods [of Selwood] and into defensible positions in the swamps [of Somerset]. And during this same winter a brother of Ivar [the Boneless] and Halfdan was in the kingdom of Wessex, in Devonshire, with twenty-three ships and was slain there and eight hundred men with him and forty men of his retinue. And the Easter after this [23 March], King Alfred with a small force built a stronghold at Athelney and with the men of that part of Somerset nearest to it continued fighting against the heathens. Then in the seventh week after Easter

---

[5]Free warriors of the king to whom he often granted land and other privileges. A thegn is the English equivalent of the continental knight.

[6]The English "school"—not really a school at all but a quarter of the city—was located on the Vatican Hill and was frequented by churchmen, nuns and monks, pilgrims, and others who had business in Rome.

[7]The sacred ring was worn by the chief at assemblies and otherwise kept in the inner sanctuary of the heathen temple.

he rode to Egbert's stone to the east of Selwood and there met all the men of Somerset, Wiltshire and that part of Hampshire which was on this side of the sea [west of Southampton Water]; and they gladly received him. After one night he journeyed from that camp to Iley Oak and after another to Edington, and there fought against the whole heathen army, and put it to flight and pursued it up to the stronghold [at Chippenham] and laid seige there for fourteen nights. And then the host gave him preliminary hostages and great oaths that they would leave his kingdom and vowed as well that their king would receive baptism; and they fulfilled that promise in this way. After three weeks the king, Guthrum, one of thirty very honorable men in the host, came to him at Allen, which is near Athelney. King Alfred stood sponsor for him there and [some time afterwards] the loosening of the baptismal fillet[8] was performed at Wedmore, where for twelve days Guthrum stayed with the king, who honored him and his companions with gifts.

Reading 4

Widukind of Corvey's "Deeds of the Saxons" concerning Otto the Great's Victory at the Battle of the Lechfeld, 955

Widukind, a monk of the Saxon abbey of Corvey, was well trained in the Roman classics. He began writing his "Deeds of the Saxons" during the reign of Otto I "the Great" (936–973), the second of the Saxon kings of Germany and, after 962, "emperor of the Romans." Widukind was thus contemporary or nearly contemporary with the events he described. His outlook was shaped by his own kinship to the Saxon royal family and by the fact that his abbey was a royal foundation. He dedicated his history to Otto I's daughter with the express purpose of intensifying her admiration for the exploits of her family. Otto emerges in the pages of Widukind as an heroic warrior in the ancient tradition of imperial Rome. The excerpt translated here, an account of Otto's decisive victory over the Hungarians, is inflated in tone but trustworthy in detail.

From *The Rise of the First Reich*, ed. Boyd H. Hill, Jr.; New York, John Wiley & Sons, Inc., 1969, pp. 15–18. Reprinted by permission.

[8]White baptismal robes and a white band of cloth bound around the head and anointed with the chrism were worn for eight days after the baptism ceremony.

Having returned to Saxony around the first of July Otto met Hungarian legates who were apparently visiting him on account of ancient fealty and favor. In fact, however, it seemed to some that they had come in order to ascertain the outcome of the civil war [in Bavaria].

They stayed with him for some days, and he dismissed them in peace after having parceled out some small gifts. Subsequently he heard from messengers sent by his brother [Henry], the duke of the Bavarians: "The Hungarians have spread out and invaded your territory; they are determined to go to war with you." When the king heard this, he advanced to meet the enemy undaunted by the previous conflict. Only a very few of the Saxons were with him because he had been pressing for a war against the Slavs. When the camp had been set up within the city of Augsburg, an army of Franks and Bavarians came to his aid. Duke Conrad [the Red, former duke of Lotharingia] also hurried to the camp with a strong force of cavalry; his arrival encouraged the soldiers, who now did not wish to delay the battle. Conrad was dear to his companions both at home and in the field, for he was by nature bold of mind and what is rare in the brave, he was also a man of good judgment. Whenever he ran against the enemy as a horseman or a foot-soldier, he was an irresistible warrior.

Scouting forces of both sides ascertained that the two armies were not far distant from each other. Otto's forces were ordered to fast and to be ready for war on the next day [10 August 955]. At the first rays of dawn the troops received and accepted the protection of their commander and then promised him their service. And after they had sworn an oath to one another, they raised their standards and proceeded from camp, about eight legions in all.[1]

The army was led through rugged terrain so that the enemy would not have an opportunity to shoot arrows at them. The Bavarians formed the first, second and third legions, which Duke Henry's subordinates were in charge of, for the dying Henry [d. 1 November 955] was absent as a result of the last campaign. The Franks constituted the fourth legion, under the command of Duke Conrad.

In the fifth and largest legion, called the "royal," was the prince himself in the midst of a thousand hand-picked youthful soldiers, and before him the victorious Archangel [Michael], thickly surrounded by troops. The Swabians made up the sixth and seventh legions; they were commanded by Burchard, whom the king's brother's daughter had married.[2] In the eighth were the Bohemians, a thousand strong, whose expertise was supply. They were in last place, presumably the safest.

---

[1] A legion consisted of at least 1000 men. Widukind is here deliberately employing an archaic, Roman term.

[2] Burchard III, Duke of Swabia (954–73), married Hedwig, daughter of Henry, Duke of Bavaria (947–55), who was a brother of King Otto I.

But events turned out otherwise than expected, for the Hungarians did not delay at all but crossed the river Lech and surrounded the army while harassing the last legion with arrows. With a loud shout they attacked, killed or captured most of the eighth legion, and having taken possession of the baggage, they compelled the other soldiers of that legion to flee.

Similarly they attacked the seventh and sixth legions and put many of them to flight. When the king discovered that the battle was still ahead of him and that the rear columns were already in danger, he sent Duke Conrad back with the fourth legion, who pulled out the captives, cast out the booty, and drove the plundering columns of the enemy forward. The enemy were surrounded on all sides, and Duke Conrad returned to the king with the standards of victory. It is somewhat strange that veteran soldiers who were accustomed to the glory of victory had delayed fighting, whereas Duke Conrad held a triumph with troops who were new and virtually ignorant of waging war. . . .

When the king saw that the whole burden of the fight was now in front he spoke in order to encourage his comrades. "It is up to us in this emergency, as you yourselves see, my soldiers, not to tolerate the enemy at a distance but meet them face to face. For up to now I have made glorious use of your energetic hands and unconquerable weapons everywhere outside my own soil and *imperium*. Shall I now turn my back on my land and realm? We are surpassed, I know, by numbers, but not by courage or arms. For we know that for the most part they are devoid of all armor, and what is a greater solace to us, they are deprived of the help of God. Their audacity is like a wall of defense, but we have the hope of divine protection. Now it would shame almost all the rulers of Europe to give in to the enemy. If the end lies near, my soldiers, it is better that we die gloriously in battle than be beaten by the enemy and enslaved or strung up like animals. I would say more, my soldiers, if I could augment your courage or boldness by words. Now let's open this conference with swords rather than with tongues."

And when he had finished speaking, he seized his shield and the Holy Lance,[3] and being the first to turn his horse to the enemy he was a most valiant warrior and excellent commander. At first the bolder of the enemy resisted, but then as they saw their companions being routed, and stunned at being surrounded by us, they were ultimately killed.

Some of those remaining whose horses were tired out entered nearby villages, and being surrounded by soldiers were burned up along with the buildings. Others swam the nearby river, and when they could not get a foothold on the farther bank, they were swallowed up by the river and perished. On that day the [Hungarian] camp was invaded and all the captives were set free. On

[3]The Holy Lance, which supposedly contained in its shaft one of the nails of the Cross of Christ, became a symbol of rule among the Germans even as late as World War II.

the second and third day the remaining Hungarians from the neighboring cities were virtually annihilated so that hardly any of them got away; but the victory over such a cruel tribe was not of course won without bloodshed to our side.

Duke Conrad was fighting hard, and on fire with purpose and with the heat of the sun, which was oppressive that day, he loosened the bonds of his cuirass to take a breath of air and was killed by an arrow in the throat. On the king's command his body was picked up and honorably transported to Worms. This man, famous for greatness of mind and body, was interred there with the weeping and wailing of all Franks.

Three leaders of the Hungarians were captured, and being presented to Duke Henry they died as they deserved by hanging.

The king having been made glorious by his army was hailed as father of his country and *Imperator*[4] in a celebrated triumph. Then he decreed that God and His Holy Mother be honored and praised in every church. Amidst dancing and joy he returned victorious to Saxony and was lovingly received by his people, for such a great royal victory had not been celebrated in the 200 years before the reign of Otto.

Reading 5

An Account of the Lombard Kingdom in the Late Tenth Century

In this passage an anonymous Pavian writer of the early eleventh century looks back at the flourishing state of the Lombard kingdom and its capital at Pavia several decades earlier, not long after Otto I had absorbed the kingdom into his empire. Otto and his successors were usually content to rule northern Italy gently and from a distance, but by contributing to its political stability they encouraged the growing vitality of its commerce. Like Einhard and many other medieval writers, our anonymous author seems to have modeled his description on another source, the nearly contemporary *Book of the Prefect* relating to Constantinople. Nevertheless, the account of Lombard Italy abounds in factual information that can almost certainly be trusted.

Merchants entering the kingdom used to pay the 10 per cent tax [*decima*] on all merchandise at the customs houses and at the beginning of the roads

From the *Instituta regalia et ministeria camere regnum Longobardum*, in *The Tenth Century*, ed. R. S. Lopez; New York, Holt, Rinehart & Winston, 1959, pp. 15–17. By permission.

[4]"Imperator" means both victorious field commander and emperor, and in this case the former is meant.

subject to the king[1]. . . . All persons coming from beyond the mountains into Lombardy are obligated to pay the *decima* on horses, male and female slaves, woolen, linen, and hemp cloth, tin, and swords. On all merchandise they are obligated to give the *decima* to the delegate of the treasurer. But everything that pilgrims bound for Rome take with them for personal expenses is to be passed without payment of the *decima*. . . .

And the nation of the Angles and Saxons, who came and used to come with their merchandise and wares, when they saw their trunks and sacks being emptied at the gates, grew angry and started rows with the employees of the treasury. Abusive words were exchanged and, moreover, very often the parties inflicted wounds upon one another. But in order to cut short such great evils and to remove all danger, the king of the Angles and Saxons and the king of the Lombards agreed together as follows: The nation of the Angles and Saxons is no longer to be subject to the *decima*. And in return for this the king of the Angles and Saxons and their nation are expected and obligated to send to the king's palace in Pavia and to the king's treasury, every third year, fifty pounds of refined silver, two large and handsome greyhounds, hairy or furred, in chains, with collars covered with gilded plates sealed or enameled with the arms of the king, two excellent embossed shields, two excellent lances, and two excellent swords wrought and tested. And to the master of the treasury they are obligated to give two large coats of miniver[2] and two pounds of refined silver. And they are to receive a passport from the master of the treasury, that they may not suffer any annoyance as they come and return home.

And the duke of the Venetians, together with his Venetians, is obligated to give every year in the king's palace in Pavia fifty pounds of Venetian deniers. These deniers are of one ounce each, equally good as the Pavian deniers in regard to weight and silver content. And to the master of the treasury the duke is obligated to give one excellent silk cloak on account of the rights belonging to the king of the Lombards. And that nation [of the Venetians] does not plow, sow, or gather vintage. This tribute is called pact, and by it the nation of the Venetians are allowed to buy grain and wine in every marketplace and to make their purchases in Pavia, and they are not to suffer any annoyance.

Many wealthy Venetian merchants used to come to Pavia with their merchandise, and they paid to the monastery of Saint Martin, which is called Outgate, the fortieth shilling on all merchandise. When the prominent Venetians come to Pavia, each of them is obligated to give to the master of the treasury every year one pound of pepper, one pound of cinnamon, one pound of galangal, and one pound of ginger; and to the wife of the master of the treasury, an

[1] At this period, the king of Italy and the German emperor were the same person.

[2] Miniver was a white fur used mainly for robes of state.

ivory comb and a mirror and a set of accessories, or twenty shillings of good Pavian deniers.

Likewise the men of Salerno, Gaeta, and Amalfi used to come to Pavia with abundant merchandise. And they used to give to the treasury in the king's palace the fortieth shilling, and to the wife of the treasurer they gave individually spices and accessories just as did the Venetians.

And the great and honorable and very wealthy merchants of Pavia have always received from the hand of the emperor the most honorable credentials, so that they suffer no harm or annoyance in any way, wherever they may be, whether in a market or traveling by water or by land. And whoever acts contrary to this is obligated to pay a thousand gold *mancusi* into the king's treasury.

And the mystery [guild] of the mint of Pavia is obligated to have nine noble and wealthy masters above all the other moneyers, who are to supervise and to direct all other moneyers jointly with the master of the treasury, so that no deniers be ever struck that be inferior to those they always have struck in regard to weight and silver content, to wit, ten of twelve. And these nine masters are obligated to pay for the rent of the mint twelve pounds of Pavian deniers into the king's treasury every year and four pounds of the same to the count palatine of Pavia. If a mint master discover a forger, they are to act in this way: jointly with the count of Pavia and the master of the treasury, they are under obligation to have the right hand of the forger cut off and to turn over his entire property to the king's treasury. . . .

And there are all the gold washers who send their accounts to the treasury in Pavia, and must never sell gold to anyone else but the sworn moneyers, and are obligated to deliver it to them and to the treasurer. And the latter are obligated to buy all that gold obtained from the rivers. . . .

And there are in Pavia fishermen, who are obligated to have a master from the best members of the whole mystery. And they are obligated to keep sixty boats, and to give for every boat two deniers on the first day of each month. And these two monthly deniers they are obligated to give to their master . . . and to make sure that whenever the king is in Pavia, fish is purchased with those deniers or their own fish is brought to him in the most honorable manner. And they are obligated to give fish every Friday to the master of the treasury.

There also are in Pavia twelve tanners preparing leather, with twelve junior members. And they are obligated to prepare every year twelve excellent ox-skins and to give them to the royal treasury, in order that no other man be allowed to prepare leather. And let whoever acts contrary to this pay a hundred Pavian shillings into the royal treasury. And whenever a tanner first enters the mystery to become one of these senior tanners, he is obligated to give four pounds, one half to royal treasury and the other half to the other tanners.

There also are other mysteries. All shipmen and boatmen are obligated to furnish two good men as masters under the authority of the treasurer in Pavia. Whenever the king is in Pavia, these men are obligated to go with the ships. And these two masters are obligated to outfit two large vessels, one for the king and one for the queen, and to build a house with planks, and to cover it well. As for the pilots, let them have one vessel, so that the others may be safe on the water; and they are entitled, together with their juniors, to receive every day their expenses from the king's court.

And there was in Pavia the mystery of the soapmakers, who used to make soap and to give every year on the steelyard a hundred pounds of soap to the royal treasury and ten pounds to the treasurer, in order that no one else be entitled to make soap in Pavia. . . .

And concerning all these mysteries you should know this: that no man is entitled to perform their functions unless he is a member. And should another man perform them, he is obligated to pay the *bannum* [fine] into the king's treasury and to swear that he will no longer do so. Nor ought any merchant to conclude his business in any market, unless he is a Pavian merchant. And let any one acting contrary to this pay the *bannum*. . . .

Reading 6

The "Greenland Saga" concerning the Discovery of North America

The Icelandic sagas mark the pinnacle of medieval Norse literature. The "Greenland Saga," like others of its kind, is based on actual historical events. But as poetic celebrations of heroic deeds, transmitted orally for several generations before being transcribed, the sagas tend to coat historical facts with a crust of legend. The voyage described here took place around A.D. 1000; the saga was probably first committed to writing in the later 1100s. Our oldest surviving text, in the *Flateyjarbok* of the later 1300s, is based on earlier texts that have since perished.

Some time later, Bjarni Herjolfsson sailed from Greenland to Norway and visited Earl Eirik,[1] who received him well. Bjarni told the earl about his voyage and the lands he had sighted. People thought he had shown great lack

From the *Graenlendiga Saga*, in *The Vineland Sagas: The Norse Discovery of America*, ed. and tr. Magnus Magnusson and Hermann Palsson; London, Penguin Classics, 1965, pp. 54–58. Copyright Magnus Magnusson and Hermann Palsson, 1965. Reprinted by permission of Penguin Books, Ltd.

[1] Earl Eirik Hakonarson ruled over Norway from 1000 to 1014.

of curiosity, since he could tell them nothing about these countries, and he was criticized for this. Bjarni was made a retainer at the earl's court, and went back to Greenland the following summer.

There was now great talk of discovering new countries. Leif, the son of Eirik the Red of Brattahlid, went to see Bjarni Herjolfsson and bought his ship from him, and engaged a crew of thirty-five.

Leif asked his father Eirik to lead this expedition too, but Eirik was rather reluctant: he said he was getting old, and could endure hardships less easily than he used to. Leif replied that Eirik would still command more luck than any of his kinsmen. And in the end, Eirik let Leif have his way.

As soon as they were ready, Eirik rode off to the ship which was only a short distance away. But the horse he was riding stumbled and he was thrown, injuring his leg. "I am not meant to discover more countries than this one we now live in," said Eirik. "This is as far as we go together."

Eirik returned to Brattahlid, but Leif went aboard the ship with his crew of thirty-five. Among them was a Southerner called Tyrkir.[2]

They made their ship ready and put out to sea. The first landfall they made was the country that Bjarni had sighted last. They sailed right up to the shore and cast anchor, then lowered a boat and landed. There was no grass to be seen, and the hinterland was covered with great glaciers, and between glaciers and shore the land was like one great slab of rock. It seemed to them a worthless country.

Then Leif said, "Now we have done better than Bjarni where this country is concerned—we at least have set foot on it. I shall give this country a name and call it *Helluland*."[3]

They returned to their ship and put to sea, and sighted a second land. Once again they sailed right up to it and cast anchor, lowered a boat and went ashore. This country was flat and wooded, with white sandy beaches wherever they went; and the land sloped gently down to the sea. Leif said, "This country shall be named after its natural resources: it shall be called *Markland*."[4]

They hurried back to their ship as quickly as possible and sailed away to sea in a north-east wind for two days until they sighted land again. They sailed towards it and came to an island which lay to the north of it.

---

[2] "Southerner" refers to someone from central or southern Europe; Tyrkir appears to have been a German.

[3] Bjarni Herjolfsson's last landfall on his way back to Greenland from his accidental sighting of America, a glaciated rock-bound country, and Leif's first landfall on his way to find Bjarni's countries. *Helluland* can only be the southeast coast of Baffin Island or some northerly part of the coast of Labrador.

[4] *Markland* was a heavily wooded country between *Helluland* and *Vinland*, named by Leif on his voyage and probably the southeast coast of Labrador or perhaps Newfoundland.

They went ashore and looked about them. The weather was fine. There was dew on the grass, and the first thing they did was to get some of it on their hands and put it to their lips, and to them it seemed the sweetest thing they had ever tasted. Then they went back to their ship and sailed into the sound that lay between the island and the headland jutting out to the north.

They steered a westerly course round the headland. There were extensive shallows there and at low tide their ship was left high and dry, with the sea almost out of sight. But they were so impatient to land that they could not bear to wait for the rising tide to float the ship; they ran ashore to a place where a river flowed out of a lake. As soon as the tide had refloated the ship they took a boat and rowed out to it and brought it up the river into the lake, where they anchored it. They carried their hammocks ashore and put up booths. Then they decided to winter there, and built some large houses.

There was no lack of salmon in the river or the lake, bigger salmon than they had ever seen. The country seemed to them so kind that no winter fodder would be needed for livestock: there was never any frost all winter and the grass hardly withered at all.

In this country, night and day were of more even length than in either Greenland or Iceland: on the shortest day of the year, the sun was already up by 9 a.m., and did not set until after 3 p.m.[5]

When they had finished building their houses, Leif said to his companions, ''Now I want to divide our company into two parties and have the country explored; half of the company are to remain here at the houses while the other half go exploring—but they must not go so far that they cannot return the same evening, and they are not to become separated.''

They carried out these instructions for a time. Leif himself took turns at going out with the exploring party and staying behind at the base.

Leif was tall and strong and very impressive in appearance. He was a shrewd man and always moderate in his behaviour.

One evening news came that someone was missing: it was Tyrkir the Southerner. Leif was very displeased at this, for Tyrkir had been with the family for a long time, and when Leif was a child had been devoted to him. Leif rebuked his men severely, and got ready to make a search with twelve men.

They had gone only a short distance from the houses when Tyrkir came walking towards them, and they gave him a warm welcome. Leif quickly realized that Tyrkir was in excellent humor.

Tyrkir had a prominent forehead and shifty eyes, and not much more of a face besides; he was short and puny-looking but very clever with his hands.

---

[5]This statement indicates that the location of *Vinland* must have been south of latitude fifty and north of latitude forty—anywhere between the Gulf of St. Lawrence and New Jersey.

Leif said to him, "Why are you so late, foster-father? How did you get separated from your companions?"

At first Tyrkir spoke for a long time in German, rolling his eyes in all directions and pulling faces, and no one could understand what he was saying. After a while he spoke in Icelandic. "I did not go much farther than you," he said. "I have some news. I found vines and grapes."[6]

"Is that true, foster-father?" asked Leif.

"Of course it is true," he replied. "Where I was born there were plenty of vines and grapes."

They slept for the rest of the night, and next morning Leif said to his men, "Now we have two tasks on our hands. On alternate days we must gather grapes and cut vines, and then fell trees, to make a cargo for my ship."

This was done. It is said that the tow-boat was filled with grapes. They took on a full cargo of timber; and in the spring they made ready to leave and sailed away. Leif named the country after its natural qualities and called it *Vinland.*[7]

---

[6]Many later explorers of the New England region commented on the wild grapes they found growing there. Grapes have been known to grow wild on the east coast as far north as Passamaquoddy Bay.

[7]Literally, "Wine-land." With the compound *Vin-land*, compare the Icelandic term *vinber*, "grapes" (literally "wine-berries"). In order to explain away the absence of grapes in certain parts of North America which have been suggested as the site of *Vinland*, some scholars have argued that the first element in the name is not *vín* ("wine") but *vin*, meaning "fertile land," or "oasis."

Part Two
THE HIGH MIDDLE AGES

The period from about 1050 to 1300 has been called the High Middle Ages because it represented, in important respects, the zenith of medieval culture. Europe transformed itself during these years from an embattled, agrarian culture to an expanding and increasingly urbanized civilization. The papacy reached the height of its power in the course of its protracted struggle with the Holy Roman Empire. The English and French monarchies evolved toward early-modern states, with bureaucracies, official archives, a growing sense of national identity, and, in England, the beginnings of Parliament. This was the age of Europe's first universities, where students flocked to study the liberal arts and sometimes advanced into graduate-level studies in philosophy and theology, medicine and law.

Historians have traditionally regarded this period as an age of faith, pointing to the building of the great cathedrals, the power of the papacy, and the proliferation of new religious orders—Cistercians, Dominicans, Franciscans, and many more. But the splendor of this religious culture was made possible by a great commercial revival. The overall balance of trade shifted in Europe's favor, and cities rose and flourished in its river valleys—the Rhine, Rhone, Loire, Seine, Po, Arno, Thames, and countless others. Warriors and Crusaders expanded Europe's territorial frontiers in all directions, reconquering most of Spain from the Muslims, establishing new principalities on the eastern shores of the Mediterranean, pushing northeastward along the Baltic coast, and carving out a prosperous new kingdom in southern Italy and Sicily at the expense of Byzantium and Islam.

Some of these territories were eventually lost, and in subsequent centuries Europe would be threatened once again by the advance of hostile armies. But despite that, the changes that Western Christendom experienced during the High Middle Ages proved to be decisive. It had become a civilization of cities and commerce, of sophisticated states and flourishing universities—and so it would remain.

CHAPTER 5

New Frontiers: Economic, Territorial, Religious

Emerging from a world of peasants, clerics, and landholding warriors, the townspeople of the High Middle Ages were obliged to secure from their lords or princes the privileges essential to their new vocation (documents 1 and 2). These privileges, whether won by negotiation or rebellion, mark the birth of a new class, the burghers or bourgeoisie, whose wealth and power would grow across the centuries. The towns achieved a corporate status—the right to operate their own courts, collect their own taxes, and pay their lords' dues in a lump sum. Within the towns, smaller corporate bodies, the guilds, bound their members to regulations governing the production, quality, and prices of the goods they manufactured (document 3).

The towns were centers not only of commerce and manufacturing but of intellectual and cultural change as well. Urban wealth funded the building of cathedrals, parish churches, and hospitals, and the launching of crusades. The conquests of warriors and crusaders, in turn, opened new markets and drew new cities into Europe's expanding commercial network. The relationship between urban wealth and crusading zeal was nowhere more evident than in the Fourth Crusade, manned by north-European knights and financed by Venice (document 4).

Systematic habits of mind, reflecting the business mentality of town dwellers and the growing emphasis on logic in the schools, affected every phase of high-medieval civilization. The management of Church, kingdoms, principalities, and fiefs became steadily more orderly and more elaborate. The Fourth Lateran Council (1215), convened by Pope Innocent III, was a landmark in the application of system and order to the international Church (document 5). But these values found equal expression in the well-regulated wilderness abbeys of the new Cistercian Order. The Cistercians have been described as applying logical organization to the spiritual life, rejecting disorder and unnecessary display and stripping monasticism down to its essentials. The great Cistercian abbot St. Bernard of Clairvaux was not the slightest bit embarrassed to scold powerful churchmen who fell short of his austere, spiritually functional ideal (document 6).

Francis of Assisi, the most beloved saint of the High Middle Ages, was not a systematizer. The Franciscan Rule of 1223 reflects an effort by the Church to provide the Order with a logical structure alien to Francis himself (document 7). But Francis was a townsman, and he and his followers placed strong emphasis on preaching and serving in the towns. The intense urban piety that inspired them also gave rise to the first major heretical movements since late antiquity. The Albigensians and Waldensians, although condemned by the papacy, flourished in the towns of southern Europe (documents 8 and 9). They posed a serious threat to the religious unity of Western Christendom until, in the course of the thirteenth century, they were suppressed by the Albigensian Crusade and the Inquisition.

Reading 1

The Customs of Newcastle-upon-Tyne

This document typifies a great many royal charters granting privileges to towns, but it is not itself a charter. It is a list, compiled during the reign of Henry II (1154–89), of the customs that the Newcastle townspeople (burgesses) enjoyed under Henry II's grandfather, Henry I (1100–35). If Henry I conceded these privileges to Newcastle in a charter, it has been lost.

These are the laws and customs which the burgesses of Newcastle-upon-Tyne had in the time of Henry, king of England, and which they still have by right:

The burgesses may distrain foreigners [i.e., seize their goods in pledge for debts or damages] within their market and without, and within their houses and without, and within their borough and without, and they may do this without the permission of the reeve [royal official], unless the [royal] courts are being held within the borough, or unless they are in the field on army service [for the king], or are doing castle-guard. But a burgess may not distrain on another burgess without the permission of the reeve.

If a burgess shall lend anything in the borough to someone dwelling outside, the debtor shall pay back the debt if he admit it, or otherwise do right in the court of the borough.

Pleas which arise in the borough shall there be held and concluded except those which belong to the king's crown.

If a burgess shall be sued in respect of any plaint he shall not plead outside the borough except for defect of court; nor need he answer, except at a stated time and place, unless he has already made a foolish answer, or unless the case concerns matters pertaining to the crown.

If a ship comes to the Tyne and wishes to unload, it shall be permitted to the burgesses to purchase what they please. And if a dispute arises between a burgess and a merchant, it shall be settled before the third tide.

Whatever merchandise a ship brings by sea must be brought to the land; except salt and herring which must be sold on board ship.

If anyone has held land in burgage for a year and a day justly and without challenge, he need not answer any claimant, unless the claimant is outside the kingdom of England, or unless he be a boy not having the power of pleading.

If a burgess have a son in his house and at his table, his son shall have the same liberty as his father.

From *English Historical Documents, Volume II, 1042–1189*, ed. D.C. Douglas and G.W. Greenaway; Oxford, Oxford University Press, 1953, pp. 970–971. Reprinted by permission.

If a villein come to reside in the borough, and shall remain as a burgess in the borough for a year and a day, he shall thereafter always remain there, unless there was a previous agreement between him and his lord for him to remain there for a certain time.

If a burgess sues anyone concerning anything, he cannot force the burgess to trial by battle, but the burgess must defend himself by his oath, except in a charge of treason when the burgess must defend himself by battle. Nor shall a burgess offer battle against a villein unless he has first quitted his burgage.

No merchant except a burgess can buy wool or hides or other merchandise outside the town, nor shall he buy them within the town except from burgesses.

If a burgess incurs forfeiture he shall give 6 oras to the reeve.

In the borough there is no "merchet" nor "heriot" nor "bloodwite" nor "stengesdint."[1]

Any burgess may have his own oven and handmill if he wishes, saving always the rights of the king's oven.

If a woman incur a forfeiture concerning bread or ale, none shall concern himself with it except the reeve. If she offend twice she shall be punished by the forfeiture. If she offend thrice justice shall take its course.

No one except a burgess may buy cloth for dyeing or make or cut it.

A burgess can give or sell his land as he wishes, and go where he will, freely and quietly unless his claim to the land is challenged.

Reading 2

The Peace of Constance

In 1183, Emperor Frederick Barbarossa and his son granted a series of privileges to the Lombard cities of northern Italy. These cities were united in a military alliance, the Lombard League, which had waged war successfully against the forces of the Holy Roman Empire. Compare the privileges that the Lombard cities wrung from Barbarossa with those that Henry I had granted to Newcastle, voluntarily and presumably for a stiff price.

From *A Source Book for Mediaeval History*, ed. O.J. Thatcher and E.H. McNeal; New York, Charles Scribner's Sons, 1905, pp., 199–202.

[1]These are specific fines which relate to marriage, inheritance, crimes of assault with bloodshed and without.

In the name of the holy and undivided Trinity. Frederick, by divine mercy emperor of the Romans, Augustus, and Henry VI, his son, king of the Romans, Augustus. . . .

1. We, Frederick, emperor of the Romans, and our son Henry, king of the Romans, hereby grant to you, the cities, territories, and persons of the league, the regalia[1] and other rights within and without the cities, as you have been accustomed to hold them; that is each member of the league shall have the same rights as the city of Verona has had in the past or has now.

2. The members of the league shall exercise freely and without interference from us all the rights which they have exercised of old.

3. These are the rights which are guaranteed to you: the *fodrum,*[2] forests, pastures, bridges, streams, mills, fortifications of the cities, criminal and civil jurisdiction, and all other rights which concern the welfare of the city.

4. The regalia which are not to be granted to the members of the league shall be determined in the following manner: in the case of each city, certain men shall be chosen for this purpose from both the bishopric and the city; these men shall be of good repute, capable of deciding these questions, and such as are not prejudiced against either party. Acting with the bishop of the diocese, they shall swear to inquire into the questions of the regalia and to set aside those that by right belong to us. If, however, the cities do not wish to submit to this inquisition, they shall pay to us an annual tribute of 2000 marks in silver as compensation for our regalia. If this sum seems excessive, it may be reduced.

5. If anyone appeals to us in regard to matters which are by this treaty admitted to be under your jurisdiction, we agree not to hear such an appeal.

6. The bishops, churches, cities, and other persons, clerical and lay, shall retain possession of the property or rights which have been granted to them before this war by us or by our predecessors, the above concessions excepted. The accustomed dues for such holdings shall be paid to us, but not the tax.

7. Such possessions as we have granted to members of the league, inside or outside of cities, shall not be included among those regalia for which taxes are to be paid to us.

8. All privileges, gifts, and concessions made in the time of the war by us or our representatives to the prejudice or injury of the cities, territories, or members of the league are to be null and void.

9. Consuls of cities where the bishop holds the position of count from the king or emperor shall receive their office from the bishop, if this has been the

[1] Royal rights.

[2] Forage tax.

custom before. In all other cities the consuls shall receive their office from us, in the following manner: after they have been elected by the city they shall be invested with office by our representative in the city or bishopric, unless we are ourselves in Lombardy, in which case they shall be invested by us. At the end of every five years each city shall send its representative to us to receive the investiture.

10. This arrangement shall be observed by our successor, and all such investitures shall be free.

11. After our death, the cities shall receive investiture in the same way from our son and from his successors.

12. The emperor shall have the right of hearing appeals in cases involving more than 25 pounds, saving the right of the church of Brescia to hear appeals. The appellant shall not, however, be compelled to come to Germany, but he shall appeal to the representative of the emperor in the city or bishopric. This representative shall examine the case fairly and shall give judgment according to the laws and customs of that city. The decision shall be given within two months from the time of appeal, unless the case has been deferred by reason of some legal hindrance or by the consent of both parties.

13. The consuls of cities shall take the oath of allegiance to the emperor before they are invested with office.

14. Our vassals shall receive investiture from us and shall take the vassal's oath of fidelity. All other persons between the ages of 15 and 70 shall take the ordinary oath of fidelity to the emperor unless there be some good reason why this oath should be remitted.

15. Vassals who have failed to receive investiture from us or to render the services due for their fiefs, during the war or the truce, shall not on this account lose their fiefs.

16. Lands held by *libelli* and *precariæ*[3] shall be held according to the customs of each city, the feudal law of Frederick I to the contrary notwithstanding.

17. All injuries, losses, and damages which we or our followers have sustained from the league or any of its members or allies are hereby pardoned, and all such transgressors are hereby received back into our favor.

18. We will not remain longer than is necessary in any city or bishopric.

19. It shall be permitted to the cities to erect fortifications within or without their boundaries.

20. It shall be permitted to the league to maintain its organization as it now is or to renew it as often as it desires.

---

[3]Two specific forms of land tenure.

Reading 3
Guild Regulations for the Shearers of Arras

These regulations, issued in 1236 for the cloth cutters in the Flemish textile center of Arras, could be applied with only minor modifications to countless guilds throughout Europe. Notice that the guild is both a commercial organization and a religious brotherhood.

This is the first ordinance of the shearers, who were founded in the name of the Fraternity of God and St. Julien, with the agreement and consent of those who were at the time mayor and aldermen.

1. Whoever would engage in the trade of a shearer shall be in the Confraternity of St. Julien, and shall pay all the dues, and observe the decrees made by the brethren.

2. That is to say: first, that whoever is a master shearer shall pay 14 solidi to the Fraternity. And there may not be more than one master shearer working in a house. And he shall be a master shearer all the year, and have arms for the need of the town.

3. And a journeyman shall pay 5 solidi to the Fraternity.

4. And whoever wishes to learn the trade shall be the son of a burgess or he shall live in the town for a year and a day; and he shall serve three years to learn this trade.

5. And he shall give to his master 3 *muids*[1] for his bed and board; and he ought to bring the first *muid* to his master at the beginning of his apprenticeship, and another *muid* a year from that day, and a third *muid* at the beginning of the third year.

6. And no one may be a master of this trade of shearer if he has not lived a year and a day in the town, in order that it may be known whether or not he comes from a good place.

8. And if masters, or journeymen, or apprentices, stay in the town to do their work they owe 40 solidi, if they have done this without the permission of the aldermen of Arras.

9. And whoever does work on Saturday afternoon, or on the Eve of the Feast of Our Lady, or after Vespers on the Eve of the Feast of St. Julien, and

From *A Source Book for Medieval Economic History*, ed. Roy C. Cave and Herbert H. Coulson; New York, Bilbo & Tannen, Inc., 1965; pp. 250–252. Reprinted by permission.

[1]Payment expressed in terms of a liquid measure. ("One muid equals approximately 52 liters"—Cave and Coulson).

completes the day by working, shall pay, if he be a master, 12 denarii, and if he be a journeyman, 6 denarii. And whoever works in the four days of Christmas, or in the eight days of Easter, or in the eight days of Pentecost, owes 5 solidi.

11. And an apprentice owes to the Fraternity for his apprenticeship 5 solidi.

12. And whoever puts the cloth of another in pledge shall pay 10 solidi to the Fraternity, and he shall not work at the trade for a year and a day.

13. And whoever does work in defiance of the mayor and aldermen shall pay 5 solidi.

14. And if a master flee outside the town with another's cloth and a journeyman aids him to flee, if he does not tell the mayor and aldermen, the master shall pay 20 solidi to the Fraternity and the journeyman 10 solidi: and they shall not work at the trade for a year and a day.

16. And those who are fed at the expense of the city shall be put to work first. And he who slights them for strangers owes 5 solidi: but if the stranger be put to work he cannot be removed as long as the master wishes to keep him. . . . And when a master does not work hard he pays 5 solidi, and a journeyman 2 solidi.

18. And after the half year the mayor and aldermen shall fix such wages as he ought to have.

19. And whatever journeyman shall carry off from his master, or from his fellow man, or from a burgess of the town, anything for which complaint is made, shall pay 5 solidi.

20. And whoever maligns the mayor and aldermen, that is while on the business of the Fraternity, shall pay 5 solidi.

22. And no one who is not a shearer may be a master, in order that the work may be done in the best way, and no draper may cut cloth in his house, if it be not his own work, except he be a shearer, because drapers cannot be masters.

23. And if a draper or a merchant has work to do in his house, he may take such workmen as he wishes into his house, so long as the work be done in his house. And he who infringes this shall give 5 solidi to the Fraternity.

25. And each master ought to have his arms when he is summoned. And if he has not he should pay 20 solidi.

26–30. (Other army regulations)

31. And whatever brother has finished cloth in his house and does not inform the mayor and aldermen, and it be found in his house, whatever he may say, shall forfeit 10 solidi to the Fraternity.

32. And if a master does not give a journeyman such wage as is his due, then he shall pay 5 solidi.

33. And he who overlooks the forfeits of this Fraternity, if he does not wish to pay them when the mayor and aldermen summon him either for the army or the district, then he owes 10 solidi, and he shall not work at the trade until he has paid. Every forfeit of 5 solidi, and the fines which the mayor and aldermen command, shall be written down. All the fines of the Fraternity ought to go for the purchase of arms and for the needs of the Fraternity.

34. And whatever brother of this Fraternity shall betray his confrere for others shall not work at the trade for a year and a day.

35. And whatever brother of this Fraternity perjures himself shall not work at the trade for forty days. And if he does so he shall pay 10 solidi if he be a master, but if he be a journeyman let him pay 5 solidi.

36. And should a master of this Fraternity die and leave a male heir he may learn the trade anywhere where there is no apprentice.

37. And no apprentice shall cut to the selvage for half a year, and this is to obtain good work. And no master or journeyman may cut by himself because no one can measure cloth well alone. And whoever infringes this rule shall pay 5 solidi to the Fraternity for each offense.

38. Any brother whatsoever who lays hands on, or does wrong to, the mayor and aldermen of this Fraternity, as long as they work for the city and the Fraternity, shall not work at his trade in the city for a year and a day.
And if he should do so, let him be banished from the town for a year and a day, saving the appeal to Monseigneur the King and his Castellan.

39. And the brethren of this Fraternity, and the mayor and aldermen shall not forbid any brother to give law and do right and justice to all when it is demanded of them, or when someone claims from them. And he who infringes this shall not have the help of the aldermen at all.

Reading 4
The Fourth Crusade: Villehardouin's Account of the Capture of Zara

Geoffrey de Villehardouin, marshal of Champagne, was one of the organizers and leaders of the Fourth Crusade (1201–04), which aimed at Jerusalem but was diverted by various circumstances, first to Zara, then to Constantinople. Villehardouin's *Conquest of Constantinople*, from which our excerpt is

From *Villehardouin and de Joinville's Memoirs of the Crusades*, tr. Sir Frank Marzials; London, Everyman's Library, and New York, E. P. Dutton, 1908, pp. 1–2, 4–9, 12–27. Reprinted by permission.

drawn, is the earliest surviving historical prose narrative to be written in French. Attentive to military detail, it has the freshness of an eyewitness account. It also goes to some lengths to justify the strange misdirections of a crusade in which its author participated and from which he profited. Villehardouin became the marshal of the Latin Empire of Constantinople and hereditary lord of the Greek principality of Acaia.

Be it known to you that eleven hundred and ninety-seven years after the Incarnation of our Lord Jesus Christ, in the time of Innocent Pope of Rome, and Philip King of France, and Richard King of England, there was in France a holy man named Fulk of Neuilly—which Neuilly is between Lagni-sur-Marne and Paris—and he was a priest and held the cure of the village. And this said Fulk began to speak of God throughout the Isle-de-France, and the other countries round about; and you must know that by him the Lord wrought many miracles.

Be it known to you further, that the fame of this holy man so spread, that it reached the Pope of Rome, Innocent; and the Pope sent to France, and ordered the right worthy man to preach the cross [the Crusade] by his authority. And afterwards the Pope sent a cardinal of his, Master Peter of Capua, who himself had taken the cross, to proclaim the Indulgence of which I now tell you, viz, that all who should take the cross and serve in the host for one year, would be delivered from all the sins they had committed, and acknowledged in confession. And because this indulgence was so great, the hearts of men were much moved, and many took the cross for the greatness of the pardon. . . .

[The barons who took the cross appointed six envoys, to whom] the business in hand was fully committed, all the barons delivering to them valid charters, with seals attached, to the effect that they would undertake to maintain and carry out whatever conventions and agreements the envoys might enter into, in all sea ports, and whithersoever else the envoys might fare.

Thus were the six envoys dispatched, as you have been told; and they took counsel among themselves, and this was their conclusion: that in Venice they might expect to find a greater number of vessels than in any other port. So they journeyed day by day, till they came thither in the first week of Lent [February 1201].

The Doge[1] of Venice, whose name was Henry Dandolo, and who was very wise and very valiant, did them great honour, both he and the other folk, and entertained them right willingly, marvelling, however, when the envoys had delivered their letters, what might be the matter of import that had brought them to that country. For the letters were letters of credence only, and declared

---

[1]Chief magistrate of Venice.

no more than that the bearers were to be accredited as if they were the counts in person, and that the said counts would make good whatever the six envoys should undertake.

So the Doge replied: "Signors, I have seen your letters; well do we know that of men uncrowned your lords are the greatest, and they advise us to put faith in what you tell us, and that they will maintain whatsoever you undertake. Now, therefore, speak, and let us know what is your pleasure."

And the envoys answered: "Sire, we would that you should assemble your council; and before your council we will declare the wishes of our lords; and let this be tomorrow, if it so pleases you." And the Doge replied asking for respite till the fourth day, when he would assemble his council, so that the envoys might state their requirements.

The envoys waited then till the fourth day as had been appointed them, and entered the palace, which was passing rich and beautiful; and found the Doge and his council in a chamber. There they delivered their message after this manner: "Sire, we come to thee on the part of the high barons of France, who have taken the sign of the cross to avenge the shame done to Jesus Christ, and to reconquer Jerusalem, if so be that God will suffer it. And because they know that no people have such great power to help them as you and your people, therefore we pray you by God that you take pity on the land oversea, and the shame of Christ, and use diligence that our lords have ships for transport and battle."

"And after what manner should we use diligence?" said the Doge. "After all manners that you may advise and propose," rejoined the envoys, "in so far as what you propose may be within our means." "Certes," said the Doge, "it is a great thing that your lords require of us, and well it seems that they have in view a high enterprise. We will give you our answer eight days from today. And marvel not if the term be long, for it is meet that so great a matter be fully pondered."

When the term appointed by the Doge was ended, the envoys returned to the palace. Many were the words then spoken which I cannot now rehearse. But this was the conclusion of that parliament: "Signors," said the Doge, "we will tell you the conclusions at which we have arrived, if so be that we can induce our great council and the commons of the land to allow of them; and you, on your part, must consult and see if you can accept them and carry them through.

"We will build transports to carry four thousand five hundred horses, and nine thousand squires, and ships for four thousand five hundred knights, and twenty thousand sergeants of foot. And we will agree also to purvey food for these horses and people during nine months. This is what we undertake to do at the least, on condition that you pay us for each horse four marks, and for each man two marks.

"And the covenants we are now explaining to you, we undertake to keep, wheresoever we may be, for a year, reckoning from the day on which we sail from the port of Venice in the service of God and of Christendom. Now the sum total of the expenses above named amounts to 85,000 marks.

"And this will we do moreover. For the love of God, we will add to the fleet fifty armed galleys on condition that, so long as we act in company, of all conquests in land or money, whether at sea or on dry ground, we shall have the half, and you the other half. Now consult together to see if you, on your parts, can accept and fulfil these covenants."

The envoys then departed, and said that they would consult together and give their answer on the morrow. They consulted, and talked together that night, and agreed to accept the terms offered. So the next day they appeared before the Doge, and said: "Sire, we are ready to ratify this covenant." The Doge thereon said he would speak of the matter to his people, and, as he found them affected, so would he let the envoys know the issue.

On the morning of the third day, the Doge, who was very wise and valiant, assembled his great council, and the council was of forty men of the wisest that were in the land. And the Doge, by his wisdom and wit, that were very clear and very good, brought them to agreement and approval. Thus he wrought with them; and then with a hundred others, then two hundred, then a thousand, so that at last all consented and approved. Then he assembled well ten thousand of the people in the church of St. Mark, the most beautiful church that there is, and bade them hear a mass of the Holy Ghost, and pray to God for counsel on the request and messages that had been addressed to them. And the people did so right willingly.

When mass has been said, the Doge desired the envoys to humbly ask the people to assent to the proposed covenant. The envoys came into the church. Curiously were they looked upon by many who had not before had sight of them.

Geoffrey of Villehardouin, the Marshal of Champagne, by will and consent of the other envoys, acted as spokesman and said unto them: "Lords, the barons of France, most high and puissant, have sent us to you; and they cry to you for mercy, that you take pity on Jerusalem, which is in bondage to the Turks, and that, for God's sake, you help to avenge the shame of Christ Jesus. And for this end they have elected to come to you, because they know full well that there is none other people having so great power on the seas, as you and your people. And they commanded us to fall at your feet, and not to rise till you consent to take pity on the Holy Land which is beyond the seas."

Then the six envoys knelt at the feet of the people, weeping many tears. And the Doge and all the others bust into tears of pity and compassion, and cried with one voice, and lifted up their hand, saying: "We consent, we consent!'' Then was there so great a noise and tumult that it seemed as if the earth itself were falling to pieces.

And when this great tumult and passion of pity—greater did never any man see—were appeased, the good Doge of Venice, who was very wise and valiant, went up into the reading-desk, and spoke to the people, and said to them: "Signors, behold the honour that God has done you; for the best people in the world have set aside all other people, and chosen you to join them in so high an enterprise as the deliverance of our Lord!''

All the good and beautiful words that the Doge then spoke, I cannot repeat to you. But the end of the matter was, that the covenants were to be made on the following day; and made they were, and devised accordingly. When they were concluded, it was notified to the council that we should go to Babylon (Cairo), because the Turks could better be destroyed in Babylon than in any other land; but to the folk at large it was only told that we were bound to go overseas. We were then in Lent (March 1201), and by St. John's Day, in the following year—which would be twelve hundred and two years after the Incarnation of Jesus Christ—the barons and pilgrims were to be in Venice, and the ships ready against their coming.

When the treaties were duly indited and sealed, they were brought to the Doge in the grand palace, where had been assembled the great and the little council. And when the Doge delivered the treaties to the envoys, he knelt greatly weeping, and swore on holy relics faithfully to observe the conditions thereof, and so did all his council, which numbered fifty-six persons. And the envoys, on their side, swore to observe the treaties, and in all good faith to maintain their oaths and the oaths of their lords; and be it known to you that for great pity many a tear was there shed. And forthwith were messengers sent to Rome, to the Pope Innocent, that he might confirm this covenant—the which he did right willingly.

Then did the envoys borrow five thousand marks of silver and gave them to the Doge so that the building of the ships might be begun. And taking leave to return to their own land, they journeyed day by day till they came to Placentia in Lombardy. There they parted. Geoffrey, the Marshal of Champagne and Alard Maquereau went straight to France, and the others went to Genoa and Pisa to learn what help might there be had for the land oversea. . . .

After Easter and towards Whitsuntide (June 1202) began the pilgrims to leave their own country. And you must know that at their departure many were the tears shed for pity and sorrow, by their own people and by their friends. So they journeyed through Burgundy, and by the mountains of Mont-Joux (? Jura) by Mont Cenis, and through Lombardy, and began to assemble at Venice, where they were lodged on an island which is called St. Nicholas in the port. . . .

Thus did Count Lewis and the other barons wend their way to Venice; and they were there received with feasting and joyfully, and took lodging in the Island of St. Nicholas with those who had come before. Goodly was the host, and right worthy were the men. Never did man see goodlier or worthier. And the Venetians held a market, rich and abundant, of all things needful for horses and men. And the fleet they had got ready was so goodly and fine that never did Christian man see one goodlier or finer; as well galleys as transports, and sufficient for at least three times as many men as were in the host.

Ah! the grievous harm and loss when those who should have come thither sailed instead from other ports! Right well, if they had kept their tryst, would Christendom have been exalted, and the land of the Turks abased! The Venetians had fulfilled all their undertakings, and above measure, and they now summoned the barons and counts to fulfil theirs and make payment, since they were ready to start.

The cost of each man's passage was now levied throughout the host; and there were people enough who said they could not pay for their passage, and the barons took from them such moneys as they had. So each man paid what he could. When the barons had thus claimed the cost of the passages, and when the payments had been collected, the moneys came to less than the sum due—yea, by more than one half.

Then the barons met together and said: "Lords, the Venetians have well fulfilled all their undertakings, and above measure. But we cannot fulfil ours in paying for our passages, seeing we are too few in number; and this is the fault of those who have journeyed by other ports. For God's sake therefore let each contribute all that he has, so that we may fulfil our covenant; for better is it that we should give all that we have, than lose what we have already paid, and prove false to our covenants; for if this host remains here, the rescue of the land oversea comes to naught."

Great was then the dissension among the main part of the barons and the other folk, and they said: "We have paid for our passages, and if they will take us, we shall go willingly; but if not, we shall inquire and look for other means of passage." And they spoke thus because they wished that the host should fall to pieces and each return to his own land. But the other party said, "Much rather would we give all that we have and go penniless with the host, than that the host should fall to pieces and fail; for God will doubtless repay us when it so pleases Him."

Then the Count of Flanders began to give all that he had and all that he could borrow, and so did Count Lewis, and the Marquis, and the Count of Saint-Paul, and those who were of their party. Then might you have seen many a fine vessel of gold and silver borne in payment to the palace of the Doge. And when all had been brought together, there was still wanting, of the sum required, 34,000 marks of silver. Then those who had kept back their possessions and not brought them into the common stock, were right glad, for they thought now surely the host must fail and go to pieces. But God, who advises those who have been ill–advised, would not so suffer it.

Then the Doge spoke to his people, and said unto them: "Signors, these people cannot pay more; and in so far as they have paid at all, we have benefited by an agreement which they cannot now fulfil. But our right to keep this money would not everywhere be acknowledged; and if we so kept it we should be greatly blamed, both us and our land. Let us therefore offer them terms.

"The King of Hungary has taken from us Zara in Sclavonia, which is one of the strongest places in the world; and never shall we recover it with all the power that we possess, save with the help of these people. Let us therefore ask them to help us to reconquer it, and we will remit the payment of the debt of 34,000 marks of silver, until such time as it shall please God to allow us to gain the moneys by conquest, we and they together." Thus was agreement made. Much was it contested by those who wished that the host should be broken up. Nevertheless the agreement was accepted and ratified.

Then, on a Sunday, was assemblage held in the church of St. Mark. It was a very high festival, and the people of the land were there, and the most part of the barons and pilgrims.

Before the beginning of High Mass, the Doge of Venice, who bore the name of Henry Dandolo, went up into the reading-desk, and spoke to the people, and said to them: "Signors, you are associated with the most worthy people in the world, and for the highest enterprise ever undertaken; and I am a man old and feeble, who should have need of rest, and I am sick in body; but I see that no one could command and lead you like myself, who am your lord. If you will consent that I take the sign of the cross to guard and direct you, and that my son remain in my place to guard the land, then shall I go to live or die with you and with the pilgrims."

And when they had heard him, they cried with one voice: "We pray you by God that you consent, and do it, and that you come with us!"

Very great was then the pity and compassion on the part of the people of the land and of the pilgrims; and many were the tears shed, because that worthy and good man would have had so much reason to remain behind, for he was an old man, and albeit his eyes were unclouded, yet he saw naught, having lost his sight through a wound in the head. He was of a great heart. Ah! how little like him were those who had gone to other ports to escape the danger.

Thus he came down from the reading-desk, and went before the altar, and knelt upon his knees greatly weeping. And they sewed the cross onto a great cotton hat, which he wore, in front, because he wished that all men should see it. And the Venetians began to take the cross in great numbers, a great multitude, for up to that day very few had taken the cross. Our pilgrims had much joy in the cross that the Doge took and were greatly moved, because of the wisdom and the valour that were in him.

Thus did the Doge take the cross, as you have heard. Then the Venetians began to deliver the ships, the galleys, and the transports to the barons, for departure; but so much time had already been spent since the appointed term, that September drew near (1202). . . .

Then were the ships and transports apportioned by the barons. Ah, God! what fine war-horses were put therein. And when the ships were fulfilled with arms and provisions, and knights and sergeants, the shields were ranged round the bulwarks and castles of the ships, and the banners displayed, many and fair.

And be it known to you that the vessels carried more than three hundred petraries and mangonels,[2] and all such engines as are needed for the taking of cities, in great plenty. Never did finer fleet sail from any port. And this was in the octave of the Feast of St. Remigius (October) in the year of the Incarnation of Jesus Christ twelve hundred and two. Thus did they sail from the port of Venice, as you have been told.

On the Eve of St. Martin (10th November) they came before Zara in Sclavonia, and beheld the city enclosed by high walls and high towers; and vainly would you have sought for a fairer city, or one of greater strength, or richer. And when the pilgrims saw it, they marvelled greatly, and said one to another, "How could such a city be taken by force, save by the help of God himself?"

The first ships that came before the city cast anchor, and waited for the others; and in the morning the day was very fine and very clear, and all the galleys came up with the transports, and the other ships which were behind; and they took the port by force and broke the chain that defended it and was very strong and well-wrought; and they landed in such sort that the port was between them and the town. Then might you have seen many a knight and many a sergeant swarming out of the ships, and taking from the transports many a good war-horse, and many a rich tent and many a pavilion. Thus did the host encamp. And Zara was besieged on St. Martin's Day (11th November 1202). . . .

Then rose the abbot of Vaux, of the order of the Cistercians, and said to them: "Lords, I forbid you, on the part of the Pope of Rome, to attack this city; for those within it are Christians, and you are pilgrims." When the Doge heard this, he was very wroth, and much disturbed, and he said to the counts and barons: "Signors, I had this city, by their own agreement, at my mercy, and your people have broken that agreement; you have covenanted to help me to conquer it, and I summon you to do so."

---

[2]Military machines constructed on the principle of the catapult.

Whereon the counts and barons all spoke at once, together with those who were of their party, and said: "Great is the outrage of those who have caused this agreement to be broken, and never a day has passed that they have not tried to break up the host. Now we are shamed if we do not help to take the city." And they came to the Doge, and said: "Sire, we will help you to take the city in despite of those who would let and hinder us."

Thus, was the decision taken. The next morning the host encamped before the gates of the city, and set up their petraries and mangonels, and other engines of war, which they had in plenty, and on the side of the sea they raised ladders from their ships. Then they began to throw stones at the walls of the city and at the towers. So did the assault last for about five days. Then were the sappers set to mine one of the towers, and began to sap the wall. When those within the city saw this, they proposed an agreement, such as they had before refused by the advice of those who wished to break up the host.

Thus did the city surrender to the mercy of the Doge, on condition only that all lives should be spared. Then came the Doge to the counts and barons, and said to them: "Signors, we have taken this city by the grace of God, and your own. It is now winter, and we cannot stir hence till Eastertide; for we should find no market in any other place; and this city is very rich, and well furnished with all supplies. Let us therefore divide it in the midst, and we will take one half, and you the other."

As he had spoken, so was it done. The Venetians took the part of the city towards the port, where were the ships, and the Franks took the other part. There were quarters assigned to each, according as was right and convenient. And the host raised the camp, and went to lodge in the city.

On the third day after they were all lodged, there befell a great misadventure in the host, at about the hour of vespers; for there began a fray, exceeding fell and fierce, between the Venetians and the Franks, and they ran to arms from all sides. And the fray was so fierce that there were but few streets in which battle did not rage with swords and lances and cross-bows and darts; and many people were killed and wounded.

But the Venetians could not abide the combat, and they began to suffer great losses. Then the men of mark, who did not want this evil to befall, came fully armed into the strife, and began to separate the combatants; and when they had separated them in one place, they began again in another. This lasted the better part of the night. Nevertheless with great labour and endurance at last they were separated. And be it known to you that this was the greatest misfortune that ever befell a host, and little did it lack that the host was not lost utterly. But God would not suffer it.

Great was the loss on either side. There was slain a high lord of Flanders, whose name was Giles of Landas: he was struck in the eye, and with that stroke he died in the fray; and many another of whom less was spoken. The

Doge of Venice and the barons laboured much, during the whole of that week, to appease the fray, and they laboured so effectually that peace was made. God be thanked therefor.

Reading 5

Canons from the Fourth Lateran Council

In 1215 Pope Innocent III presided over a universal council of the Church at his Lateran basilica in Rome. More than 1200 prelates attended, including the Patriarchs of Jerusalem and recently conquered Constantinople, along with envoys from all the kingdoms and major principalities of Christendom. The canons (decrees) of the Fourth Lateran Council reflect the efforts of the high-medieval papacy to reform, systematize, and standardize religious practice throughout Europe. Among other things, clerical dress was regularized; bishops were ordered to preach regularly and to maintain schools; priests were forbidden to participate in judicial ordeals and to charge fees for performing sacraments; lay people were commanded to do penance and receive the eucharist at least once a year.

The excerpts below illustrate the Church's concern over the spread of the Albigensian and Waldensian heresies, with their denial of papal authority and of the priesthood's exclusive power to perform the sacrament of the eucharist. Notice the emphasis on combating heresy by force, through the Albigensian Crusade (then in full gallop) and accompanying judicial proceedings. The Church's response to heresy bears some similarity to the response of modern states to treason.

CANON 1

[The first two paragraphs repeat the Orthodox, Nicene doctrine of the Holy Trinity]. . . . There is one Universal Church of the faithful, outside of which there is absolutely no salvation. In which there is the same priest and sacrifice, Jesus Christ, whose body and blood are truly contained in the sacrament of the altar under the forms of bread and wine; the bread being changed (*transsubstantiatis*) by divine power into the body, and the wine into the blood, so that to realize the mystery of unity we may receive of Him what He

From *Disciplinary Decrees of the General Councils*, ed. and tr. H.J. Schroeder; St. Louis, B. Herder Book Co., 1937, pp. 238–239, 242–244.

has received of us. And this sacrament no one can effect except the priest who has been duly ordained in accordance with the keys of the Church, which Jesus Christ Himself gave to the Apostles and their successors.

But the sacrament of baptism, which by the invocation of each Person of the Trinity, namely, of the Father, Son, and Holy Ghost, is effected in water, duly conferred on children and adults in the form prescribed by the Church by anyone whatsoever, leads to salvation. And should anyone after the reception of baptism have fallen into sin, by true repentance he can always be restored. Not only virgins and those practicing chastity, but also those united in marriage, through the right faith and through works pleasing to God, can merit eternal salvation.

CANON 3

We excommunicate and anathematize every heresy that raises itself against the holy, orthodox and Catholic faith which we have above explained; condemning all heretics under whatever names they may be known, for while they have different faces, they are nevertheless bound to each other by their tails, since in all of them vanity is a common element. Those condemned, being handed over to the secular rulers or their bailiffs, let them be abandoned, to be punished with due justice, clerics being first degraded from their orders. As to the property of the condemned, if they are laymen, let it be confiscated; if clerics, let it be applied to the churches from which they received revenues. But those who are only suspected, due consideration being given to the nature of the suspicion and the character of the person, unless they prove their innocence by a proper defense, let them be anathematized and avoided by all until they have made suitable satisfaction; but if they have been under excommunication for one year, then let them be condemned as heretics. Secular authorities, whatever office they may hold, shall be admonished and induced and if necessary compelled by ecclesiastical censure, that as they wish to be esteemed and numbered among the faithful, so for the defense of the faith they ought publicly to take an oath that they will strive in good faith and to the best of their ability to exterminate in the territories subject to their jurisdiction all heretics pointed out by the Church; so that whenever anyone shall have assumed authority, whether spiritual or temporal, let him be bound to confirm this decree by oath. But if a temporal ruler, after having been requested and admonished by the Church, should neglect to cleanse his territory of this heretical foulness, let him be excommunicated by the metropolitan and the other bishops of the province. If he refuses to make satisfaction within a year, let the matter be made known to the supreme pontiff, that he may declare the ruler's vassals absolved from their allegiance and may offer the territory to be ruled by Catholics, who on the extermination of the heretics may possess it without hindrance and preserve it in the purity of faith; the right, however, of the chief ruler is to be respected so long as he offers no obstacle in this matter and permits freedom of action. The same law is to be observed in regard to those who have no chief rulers (that is, are independent). Catholics who have girded themselves with the cross for the extermination of the heretics, shall enjoy the indulgences and privileges granted to those who go in defense of the Holy Land.

We decree that those who give credence to the teachings of the heretics, as well as those who receive, defend, and patronize them, are excommunicated; and we firmly declare that after any one of them has been branded with excommunication, if he has deliberately failed to make satisfaction within a year, let him incur *ipso jure* the stigma of infamy and let him not be admitted to public offices or deliberations, and let him not take part in the election of others to such offices or use his right to give testimony in a court of law. Let him also be intestable, that he may not have the free exercise of making a will, and let him be deprived of the right of inheritance. Let no one be urged to give an account to him in any matter, but let him be urged to give an account to others. If perchance he be a judge, let his decisions have no force, nor let any cause be brought to his attention. If he be an advocate, let his assistance by no means be sought. If a notary, let the instruments drawn up by him be considered worthless, for, the author being condemned, let them enjoy a similar fate. In all similar cases we command that the same be observed. If, however, he be a cleric, let him be deposed from every office and benefice, that the greater the fault the graver may be the punishment inflicted.

If any refuse to avoid such after they have been ostracized by the Church, let them be excommunicated till they have made suitable satisfaction. Clerics shall not give the sacraments of the Church to such pestilential people, nor shall they presume to give them Christian burial, or to receive their alms or offerings; otherwise they shall be deprived of their office, to which they may not be restored without a special indult of the Apostolic See. Similarly, all regulars, on whom also this punishment may be imposed, let their privileges be nullified in that diocese in which they have presumed to perpetrate such excesses.

But since some, under "the appearance of godliness, but denying the power thereof," as the Apostle says (II Tim. 3:5), arrogate to themselves the authority to preach, as the same Apostle says: "How shall they preach unless they be sent?" (Rom. 10:15), all those prohibited or not sent, who, without the authority of the Apostolic See or of the Catholic bishop of the locality, shall presume to usurp the office of preaching either publicly or privately, shall be excommunicated and unless they amend, and the sooner the better, they shall be visited with a further suitable penalty. We add, moreover, that every archbishop or bishop should himself or through his archdeacon or some other suitable persons, twice or at least once a year make the rounds of his diocese in which report has it that heretics dwell, and there compel three or more men of good character or, if it should be deemed advisable, the entire neighborhood, to swear that if anyone know of the presence there of heretics or others holding secret assemblies, or differing from the common way of the faithful in faith and morals, they will make them known to the bishop. The latter shall then call together before him those accused, who, if they do not purge themselves of the matter of which they are accused, or if after the rejection of their error they lapse into their former wickedness, shall be canonically punished. But if any of them by damnable obstinacy should disapprove of the oath and should perchance be unwilling to swear, from this very fact let them be regarded as heretics.

We wish, therefore, and in virtue of obedience strictly command, that to carry out these instructions effectively the bishops exercise throughout their dioceses a scrupulous vigilance if they wish to escape canonical punishment. If from sufficient evidence it is apparent that a bishop is negligent or remiss in cleansing his diocese of the ferment of heretical wickedness, let him be deposed from the episcopal office and let another, who will and can confound heretical depravity, be substituted.

Reading 6
Letter of St. Bernard to Abbot Suger

Nearly 500 letters by the great Cistercian abbot Bernard of Clairvaux (1090–1153) have survived. He is writing here, in 1127, to one of the most powerful churchmen in France, Suger (1081–1151), abbot of the royal monastery of Saint Denis near Paris and adviser of King Louis VI. Bernard's florid style, exaggerated in tone and bristling with biblical quotations and allusions, echoes the epistolatory conventions of his age. The boldness with which he addresses powerful non-Cistercians such as Suger reflects Bernard's self-image as the conscience of Christendom.

The churchman whom Bernard condemns in the latter paragraphs of the letter was Stephen of Garlande, the chief official of Louis VI's household, who held concurrently the offices of royal steward, archdeacon of Notre Dame Cathedral in Paris, and dean of the Cathedral of Orléans. Although Bernard regards Stephen's service to church and kingdom as a detestable impropriety, the use of prelates as royal officials was common at the time.

From *The Letters of St. Bernard of Clairvaux*, tr. B.S. James; Chicago, Henry Regnery Co., 1953, pp. 110–118, *passim*. Reprinted by permission of Search Books, Ltd., London.

Stephen fell from power shortly thereafter, a victim not of Bernard's disapproval but of the hostility of Louis VI's queen.

The good news of what God has done in your soul has gone forth in our land encouraging all the good people who hear it. To be sure all those who fear God and have heard of it are amazed and full of joy at this great and sudden change of the right arm of the Most High. Everywhere "your soul is praised in the Lord and the meek hear and rejoice." Even those who have not known you, but have only heard how great has been the change from what you were to what you are, marvel and praise God in you. But what increases both the wonder and the joy alike is that you should have fulfilled what is written in the Scriptures, "Let everyone who hears this say: Come," and, "What I have said to you under cover of darkness you are to utter in the light of day; what has been whispered in your ears you are to proclaim on the house-tops," by endeavouring to spread amongst your monks the counsel of salvation which possesses your soul. In this you have acted like a resolute soldier, or rather like a devoted and strong captain who, when he sees his men in flight and slaughtered on all sides by the swords of the enemy, would be ashamed to survive them and scorn to save his own life by flight, even if he could. He stands fast in battle, he fights stoutly, and he runs hither and thither between the lines amongst the blood-stained swords trying with sword and voice to dishearten the enemy and encourage his own men. He is always on the spot where he discovers the enemy are breaking through and his men being hewn down. Where anyone is being hard-pressed and overcome he is always there to assist him, being all the more ready to die for each one in that he despairs of saving all. And, while he is trying little by little to stem and stop the advance of the enemy, it often happens that by his valour he snatches a victory for his own men from the confusion of the enemy, all the more welcome for being unexpected. They in their turn now put to flight those from whom they fled, and overcome those whom hitherto they have barely been able to stave off from vanquishing them, so that those who were lately all but victims now exult as victors. . . .

Who suggested this perfection to you? I must confess that although I much desired to hear such things of you, yet I hardly dared hope that I ever would. Who would have believed that with one jump, so to speak, you would attain the summits of virtue, the pinnacle of merit? But God forbid that I should measure the immensity of God's love by the narrow limits of my own capacity for faith and hope. He can do whatsoever he wills. He can hasten the working of his grace and lighten the burden of his commands. It was your fault, not those of your monks, that good and zealous people censured. It was against you and not against the whole community that they murmured. In fact, it was you whom they held responsible. If you had corrected yourself, there would have been nothing left to criticize. If you, I say, had changed your

ways, soon all the tumult would have died down, all the talk would have subsided. As for myself, the whole and only thing that upset me was the pomp and
splendour with which you travelled. This seemed to me to savour of arrogance.
If you had been content to put off your haughtiness and put away your splendid attire, the resentment of everyone would easily have died down. But you
have done more than satisfy your critics, you have earned their praise,
although this sudden change of so many great things should be deemed more
the work of God than of yourself. In heaven the conversion of one sinner
arouses great joy, but what about the conversion of a whole community, and a
community such as yours?

From early times yours was a noble abbey of royal dignity.[1] It served the
palace and the armies of the king. Without any deception or delay it rendered
to Caesar his dues, but not with equal enthusiasm what was due to God. I
speak of what I have heard, not of what I have seen. They say the cloister of
the monastery was often crowded with soldiers, that business was done there,
that it echoed to the sound of men wrangling, and that sometimes women were
to be found there. In all this hubbub how could anyone have attended to
heavenly, divine, and spiritual things? But now everything is very different.
God is invoked there, continence is cultivated, discipline maintained, spiritual
reading encouraged, for the silence is now unbroken, and the hush from all the
din of secular affairs invites the mind to heavenly thoughts. Furthermore the
labour of continence, the rigour of discipline, is relieved by the sweet tones of
hymns and psalms. Shame for the past encourages the austerity of this new
way of life. The men who pluck the fruit of a good conscience are inspired by a
desire which shall not be frustrated, and a hope which shall not be confounded. Fear of future judgment gives place to a loving practice of brotherly
charity, for "Love has no room for fear." The variety of holy observances
keeps at bay tedium and *acidie*.[2] I have recalled all this for the honour and
glory of God, who is the author of it all, but not without yourself as his col-
laborator in all things. He could have done it all without you, but he preferred
that you should share in his work, so that you might also share the glory. Our
Saviour rebuked certain persons for making his house a den of thieves. And so
without any doubt he will commend one who applies himself to saving a holy
thing from dogs, and pearls from swine; whose efforts and zeal have restored
what was little better than a workshop of Vulcan to being a sanctuary of
prayer and spiritual pursuits, what was a synagogue of Satan to its former use.

I have certainly not recalled all these past evils so as to taunt or shame
anyone, but so as to make the new glories appear all the more important and
comely by comparing them to the old infamy. Recent good things show up to

The abbey of Saint Denis was closely tied to the kings of France, and was founded, at least
according to tradition, by the early Merovingians.

[2]"A traditional term for a state of spiritual aridity"—note by Bruno S. James.

all the better advantage when compared with former evils. We recognize like things by comparing them with like, but contrary things compared either please or displease the more. Join black things to white and the comparison will show up each colour the better. When ugly things are set against beautiful things, the beautiful seem more beautiful and the ugly seem more ugly. But so as to avoid any occasion for confusion or offence let me repeat to you also what the Apostle said: "This is what you were once, but now you have been washed clean, now you have been sanctified." The house of God is no longer open to seculars, the merely curious find no admittance to the holy places. There is no longer any idle gossiping, and the usual chatter of boys and girls is no longer heard there. According to the words, "Here stand I and these children the Lord has given me," the place is free and open only to the children of Christ and is kept with becoming care and reverence only for the divine praises and sacred functions. How the martyrs, a great number of whom ennoble the place with their relics, must hear with joy the songs of these children, to whom they will reply with no less affectionate exuberance, "Praise the Lord, ye children, praise ye the name of the Lord"; and again, "A psalm, a psalm for our God, a psalm, a psalm for our king."

Now the vaults of the great abbey that once resounded to the hubbub of secular business echo only to spiritual canticles. Now breasts are bruised by the hands that beat upon them, and knees by the stones on which they kneel, and from the altars ascend vows and devout prayers. Now one can see cheeks furrowed with tears of repentance and hear the murmur of weeping and sighs. What can better please the citizens of heaven than this, what sight can be more welcome to the King of heaven than this sacrifice of praise with which he is now honoured here? Oh if only we could have our eyes opened to see what Eliseus by his prayers revealed to his servant! Without doubt we would see "how before us go chieftains, and minstrels with them." We would see with what attention and with what elation they assist in our singing, stand by us when we pray, join with us when we meditate, watch over us when we rest, and guide those of us who preside over and care for others. The powers of heaven know who are their fellow citizens, they earnestly delight over, comfort, instruct, protect, and care for in everything those who take the heritage of salvation. Although, being absent, I cannot see with my own eyes these things which you have done, yet I count myself happy even to have heard of them. But you, my brethren, I esteem still more happy, for to you it has been given to perform them. And more blessed than all is he whom the Author of all good has deigned to give the leadership in these things. On this great privilege I especially congratulate you my dear friend, for it is due to you that all these wonderful things have happened.

Perhaps you are embarrassed by my praises? You should not be. What I have said has nothing in common with the flattery of those who "call good evil and evil good," so that they betray whomsoever they praise. Theirs is a smooth but treacherous praise by which "the sinner is praised in the desires of his soul." Whatever kind of favour mine may be, it certainly proceeds from charity and, so far as I can see, it does not exceed the bounds of truth. He is safely applauded who is only applauded in the Lord, that is to say in truth. I have not called evil good, on the contrary I have called evil what was evil. I am all the more bound to lift up my voice and praise the good when I see it for having boldly denounced former evils or else, were I to cry out against what is evil and say nothing about what is good, I would prove myself a mere backbiter and not a reformer, one who would rather carp at evil than remedy it. The righteous man admonishes lovingly, the sinner praises wickedly. The former admonishes evil that he may remedy it, the latter praises that he may conceal what calls for remedy. You need have no anxiety that your head will be anointed with the oil of sinners as it used to be, by those who fear the Lord. I praise you because I consider you have done what is deserving of praise. I certainly do not flatter you; I am only fulfilling what you sing in the psalm: "They that fear thee shall see me, and shall be glad, because I have greatly hoped in thy works"; and again: "This wisdom of his shall be praised on all sides." How many who used to abhor your folly now praise your wisdom! . . .

Two unheard-of and detestable improprieties have arisen in the Church lately. If you will pardon my saying so, one of these was the arrogance of your way of life. But this, by the grace of God, is now mended to the glory of his name, to your everlasting reward, and to the edification of all of us. God can also bring it about that we will soon be consoled by the mending of this other matter. I fear to mention this hateful novelty in public, but I am loath to let it pass in silence. My grief urges me to speak, but fear binds my tongue. My fear is only lest I offend anyone by speaking openly of what is disturbing me, for the truth can sometimes breed hatred. But I hear the truth that breeds this sort of hatred comforting me with the words, "It must needs be that scandals come," and I do not consider that what follows applies to me at all: "But woe to the man through whom it comes." When scandal comes through vices being denounced, it comes through those who do what is blameworthy and not through those who blame it. And I do not set myself up as being more circumspect or more discreet than he who said: "It is better that there should be a scandal than that truth should be compromised." Although I do not know what good it would do if I did keep silent about what all the world is talking, if I alone were to try and cover up that foul thing the stench of which is in everyone's nostrils. I dare not hold my own nose against such a bad smell.

And who would not be indignant, who would not deplore, even if only in secret, that a man should against the Gospel both serve God as a deacon and Mammon as a minister of state, that he should be so loaded with ecclesiastical honours as to seem hardly inferior to the bishops, while being at the same time so involved in military affairs as to take precedence over the commanders of the army? I ask you what sort of monster is this that being a cleric wishes to be thought a soldier as well, and succeeds in being neither? It is an abuse of both conditions that a deacon should serve the table of a king and that a servant of the king should minister at the holy mysteries of the altar. Who would not be astonished, or rather disgusted, that one and the same person should, arrayed in armour, lead soldiers into battle and, clothed in alb and stole, pronounce the Gospel in the church, should at one time give the signal for battle on the bugle and at another inform the people of the commands of the bishop. Unless perhaps something worse is true, namely that the man is ashamed of the Gospel in which the Vessel of Election gloried, is embarrassed at being seen as a cleric, and thinks it more honourable to be thought a soldier, preferring the court to the church, the table of the king to the altar of Christ, the cup of demons to the chalice of the Lord. This seems to be the more probable, in that although he holds many preferments from the Church, despite the unwilling toleration of the canons for such a number of offices being held by one man, yet they say he is more proud of the one name by which he is known in the palace than of all his other titles. Although he is archdeacon, deacon, and provost in many churches yet none of these titles gives him so much pleasure as Seneschal to his Majesty the King. What a novel and odious perversity it is that a man should think it more becoming to be known as a retainer of another man than a servant of God and consider it more dignified to be called an official of a king of this world than of the King of heaven. A man that puts the army before his clerical state, secular business before the Church, certainly proves that he prefers human things to divine and earthly to heavenly things. Is it more dignified to be called Seneschal than Deacon or Archdeacon? It is, but for a layman not for a deacon.

What a strange and blind sort of ambition this man has! He prefers the depths to the heights, a dung-hill to the pleasant places in which his lot has been cast, and he pours scorn on the desirable land. He completely confuses two different states of life, that of a minister of God and that of a minister of the king; and he abuses with great nicety both of them by choosing the honours, but not the labour of the army in the one, and the revenues, but not the service of religion in the other. Who cannot understand that the kingdom, just as much as religion, is disgraced by this, for it is just as unbecoming to the majesty of the king that hardy men should be commanded by a cleric, as it is to the state of a deacon that he should take the king's money to fight. What king would choose to have an unwarlike cleric at the head of his army rather than one of his most intrepid soldiers? And what cleric would consider it anything but unworthy of his state to be under obedience to a layman? His very tonsure more becomes the kingly state than the condition of a retainer, and on the other hand it is not on psalms so much as arms that the throne depends. Certainly if perhaps, as sometimes happens, the one gains where the other loses so that, namely, the abasement of the king makes for the honour of the cleric or the derogation of the cleric adds something to the honour of the king, as for instance when some noble woman by marrying a man of humble birth lessens her dignity while raising his; if, I say, this is the case and from such a state of affairs either the king or the cleric gains something, the evil of it might somehow be tolerated. But as it is the loss of both has been to the advantage of neither, the dignity of both has suffered since it ill beomes a cleric to be called to be the seneschal of the king, just as much as it ill becomes the king to have in that position of government anyone but a strong and brave man. It is indeed very strange that either power should allow such a state of affairs, that the Church should not reject the military deacon and that the court should not expel its clerical chief.

I had intended and probably ought to have denounced this state of affairs more sharply than I have done, but the limits of a letter indicate an end. And I have spared a man whom report speaks of as your friend chiefly because I fear to offend you. I would not have a man your friend who is not true. If you persist in regarding him as your friend, prove yourself a true friend to him by doing what you can to make him a friend of the truth. True friendship is only possible between two who are united in the love of truth. And, if he will not yield to you in this, do you hold fast to what you have got and join the head to the tail of the offering. By the grace of God you have received a robe of many colours, see that it covers you for it is no use beginning a work if you do not persevere to the end. Let my letter end with this warning to you to make a good end of what you have begun.

Reading 7

The Rule of St. Francis, 1223

St. Francis (1181–1226), son of a cloth merchant of the Italian hillside town of Assisi, founded a religious order that differed significantly from traditional Benedictine monasticism. His followers, the Friars Minor (Lesser Brothers) were bound to both individual and corporate poverty. Instead of being cloistered in a monastery, they worked and preached in the outside world, particularly in cities. In 1210 Francis won the provisional approval of Pope Innocent III for his brief, simple Rule consisting of carefully chosen quotations from the Bible. The Franciscan Order grew so swiftly during the following

From *A Source Book for Mediaeval History*, ed. O.J. Thatcher and E.H. McNeal; New York, 1905, pp. 498–504.

decade that the original Rule of 1210 no longer sufficed. The more elaborate
Rule of 1223, issued in Francis's name, was prepared by others under the
authorization of Innocent's successor, Pope Honorius III. It preserves Francis's basic ideals but frames them in a much more coherent organizational
structure with appropriate jurisdictional safeguards. The document should
be read with an effort to untangle the original ideals from the later structure.

1.   This is the rule and life of the Minor Brothers, namely, to observe the
holy gospel of our Lord Jesus Christ by living in obedience, in poverty, and in
chastity. Brother Francis promises obedience and reverence to Pope Honorius
and to his successors who shall be canonically elected, and to the Roman
Church. The other brothers are bound to obey brother Francis, and his successors.

2. If any, wishing to adopt this life, come to our brothers [to ask admis-
sion], they shall be sent to the provincial ministers, who alone have the right to
receive others into the order. The provincial ministers shall carefully examine
them in the catholic faith and the sacraments of the church. And if they believe
all these and faithfully confess them and promise to observe them to the end of
life, and if they have no wives, or if they have wives, and the wives have either
already entered a monastery, or have received permission to do so, and they
have already taken the vow of chastity with the permission of the bishop of the
diocese [in which they live], and their wives are of such an age that no suspicion can rise against them, let the provincial ministers repeat to them the word
of the holy gospel, to go and sell all their goods and give to the poor [Matt.
19:21]. But if they are not able to do so, their good will is sufficient for them.
And the brothers and provincial ministers shall not be solicitous about the
temporal possessions of those who wish to enter the order; but let them do
with their possessions whatever the Lord may put into their minds to do.
Nevertheless, if they ask the advice of the brothers, the provincial ministers
may send them to God-fearing men, at whose advice they may give their
possessions to the poor. Then the ministers shall give them the dress of a
novice, namely: two robes without a hood, a girdle, trousers, a hood with a
cape reaching to the girdle. But the ministers may add to these if they think it
necessary. After the year of probation is ended they shall be received into obedience [that is, into the order], by promising to observe this rule and life
forever. And according to the command of the pope they shall never be permitted to leave the order and give up this life and form of religion. For according to the holy gospel no one who puts his hand to the plough and looks
back is fit for the kingdom of God [Luke 9:62]. And after they have promised
obedience, those who wish may have one robe with a hood and one without a
hood. Those who must may wear shoes, and all the brothers shall wear common clothes, and they shall have God's blessing if they patch them with coarse

cloth and pieces of other kinds of cloth. But I warn and exhort them not to despise nor judge other men who wear fine and gay clothing, and have delicious foods and drinks. But rather let each one judge and despise himself.

3. The clerical brothers shall perform the divine office according to the rite of the holy Roman church, except the psalter, from which they may have breviaries. The lay brothers shall say 24 Paternosters at matins, 5 at lauds, 7 each at primes, terces, sexts, and nones, 12 at vespers, 7 at completorium, and prayers for the dead. And they shall fast from All Saints' day [November 1] to Christmas. They may observe or not, as they choose, the holy Lent which begins at epiphany [January 6] and lasts for 40 days, and which our Lord consecrated by his holy fasts. Those who keep it shall be blessed of the Lord, but those who do not wish to keep it are not bound to do so. But they shall all observe the other Lent [that is, from Ash Wednesday to Easter]. The rest of the time the brothers are bound to fast only on Fridays. But in times of manifest necessity they shall not fast. But I counsel, warn, and exhort my brothers in the Lord Jesus Christ that when they go out into the world they shall not be quarrelsome or contentious, nor judge others. But they shall be gentle, peaceable, and kind, mild and humble, and virtuous in speech, as is becoming to all. They shall not ride on horseback unless compelled by manifest necessity or infirmity to do so. When they enter a house they shall say, "Peace be to this house." According to the holy gospel, they may eat of whatever food is set before them.

4. I strictly forbid all the brothers to accept money or property either in person or through another. Nevertheless, for the needs of the sick, and for clothing the other brothers, the ministers and guardians may, as they see that necessity requires, provide through spiritual friends, according to the locality, season, and the degree of cold which may be expected in the region where they live. But, as has been said, they shall never receive money or property.

5. Those brothers to whom the Lord has given the ability to work shall work faithfully and devotedly, so that idleness, which is the enemy of the soul, may be excluded and not extinguish the spirit of prayer and devotion to which all temporal things should be subservient. As the price of their labors they may receive things that are necessary for themselves and the brothers, but not money or property. And they shall humbly receive what is given them, as is becoming to the servants of God and to those who practise the most holy poverty.

6. The brothers shall have nothing of their own, neither house, nor land, nor anything, but as pilgrims and strangers in this world, serving the Lord in poverty and humility, let them confidently go asking alms. Nor let them be ashamed of this, for the Lord made himself poor for us in this world. This is that highest pitch of poverty which has made you, my dearest brothers, heirs and kings of the kingdom of heaven, which has made you poor in goods, and

exalted you in virtues. Let this be your portion, which leads into the land of the living. Cling wholly to this, my most beloved brothers, and you shall wish to have in this world nothing else than the name of the Lord Jesus Christ. And wherever they are, if they find brothers, let them show themselves to be of the same household, and each one may securely make known to the other his need. For if a mother loves and nourishes her child, how much more diligently should one nourish and love one's spiritual brother? And if any of them fall ill, the other brothers should serve them as they would wish to be served.

7. If any brother is tempted by the devil and commits a mortal sin, he should go as quickly as possible to the provincial minister, as the brothers have determined that recourse shall be had to the provincial ministers for such sins. If the provincial minister is a priest, he shall mercifully prescribe the penance for him. If he is not a priest, he shall, as may seem best to him, have some priest of the order prescribe the penance. And they shall guard against being angry or irritated about it, because anger and irritation hinder love in themselves and in others.

8. All the brothers must have one of their number as their general minister and servant of the whole brotherhood, and they must obey him. At his death the provincial ministers and guardians shall elect his successor at the chapter held at Pentecost, at which time all the provincial ministers must always come together at whatever place the general minister may order. And this chapter must be held once every three years, or more or less frequently, as the general minister may think best. And if at any time it shall be clear to the provincial ministers and guardians that the general minister is not able to perform the duties of his office and does not serve the best interests of the brothers, the aforesaid brothers, to whom the right of election is given, must, in the name of the Lord, elect another as general minister. After the chapter at Pentecost, the provincial ministers and guardians may, each in his own province, if it seems best to them, once in the same year convoke the brothers to a provincial chapter.

9. If a bishop forbids the brothers to preach in his diocese, they shall obey him. And no brother shall preach to the people unless the general minister of the brotherhood has examined and approved him and given him the right to preach. I also warn the brothers that in their sermons their words shall be chaste and well chosen for the profit and edification of the people. They shall speak to them of vices and virtues, punishment and glory, with brevity of speech, because the Lord made the word shortened over the earth [Rom. 9:28].

10. The ministers and servants shall visit and admonish their brothers and humbly and lovingly correct them. They shall not put any command upon them that would be against their soul and this rule. And the brothers who are subject must remember that for God's sake they have given up their own wills. Wherefore I command them to obey their ministers in all the things which they

have promised the Lord to observe and which shall not be contrary to their souls and this rule. And whenever brothers know and recognize that they cannot observe this rule, let them go to their ministers, and the ministers shall lovingly and kindly receive them and treat them in such a way that the brothers may speak to them freely and treat them as lords speak to, and treat, their servants. For the ministers ought to be the servants of all the brothers. I warn and exhort the brothers in the Lord Jesus Christ to guard against all arrogance, pride, envy, avarice, care, and solicitude for this world, detraction, and murmuring. And those who cannot read need not be anxious to learn. But above all things let them desire to have the spirit of the Lord and his holy works, to pray always to God with a pure heart, and to have humility, and patience in persecution and in infirmity, and to love those who persecute us and reproach us and blame us. For the Lord says, "Love your enemies and pray for those who persecute and speak evil of you" [cf. Matt. 5:44]. "Blessed are they who suffer persecution for righteousness' sake, for theirs is the kingdom of heaven" [Matt. 5:10]. He that endureth to the end shall be saved [Matt. 10:22].

11. I strictly forbid all the brothers to have any association or conversation with women that may cause suspicion. And let them not enter nunneries, except those which the pope has given them special permission to enter. Let them not be intimate friends of men or women, lest on this account scandal arise among the brothers or about brothers.

12. If any of the brothers shall be divinely inspired to go among Saracens and other infidels they must get the permission to go from their provincial minister, who shall give his consent only to those who he sees are suitable to be sent. In addition, I command the ministers to ask the pope to assign them a cardinal of the holy Roman church, who shall be the guide, protector, and corrector of the brotherhood, in order that being always in subjection and at the feet of the holy church, and steadfast in the catholic faith, they may observe poverty, humility, and the holy gospel of our Lord Jesus Christ, as we have firmly promised to do. Let no man dare act contrary to this confirmation.

Reading 8

An Account of the Albigensian Heresy

This account, written between 1208 and 1213, antedates the Fourth Lateran Council by only a few years and helps explain the Council's severely anti-Albigensian stance. Although it is more nearly a diatribe than an objective work of investigative reporting, it does make clear that, by Catholic standards, the Albigensian (or Cathar) beliefs were quite exotic. Blending Christian ideas with the religious dualism of ancient Persia, the Albigensians appear to have been not only anti-Catholic but anti-Semitic as well.

The question remains, to what extent can a document of this sort be trusted? Could one trust an analysis of the United States government appearing in *Pravda*? Or a discussion of Catholic doctrine written by an Albigensian? The answer is not simple. Perhaps one might expect such hostile testimony to be more or less accurate in its general outline but selective or deceptive in detail. To what degree does the following document provide a believable picture?

The group of heretics inhabiting our region, that is to say, the dioceses of Narbonne, Béziers, Carcassonne, Toulouse, Albi, Rodez, Cahors, Agen, and Périgueux [all in Southern France], believe and have the effrontery to say that there are two gods, that is, a good God and a strange god, using the text of Jeremiah: "As you have forsaken me," He said, "and served a strange god in your own land, so you shall serve strangers in a land not your own." The present world and all that is visible therein, they declare, were created and made by the malign god, for they show by whatever arguments they can command that these are evil. Of the world they say that it is "wholly seated in wickedness," and that "a good tree cannot bring forth evil fruit, neither can an evil tree bring forth good fruit." They hold that all good things came from the good God and from the evil one all evil things. The Mosaic law, they say, was imparted by the evil god, for they cite from the words of the Apostle, "The Law is one of sin and death" and "worketh wrath." They declare that when Christ gave the bread to His disciples, He told them, "Take ye and eat," and, touching Himself with His hand, said, "This is my body"; wherefore they do not believe that anyone consecrates the Host. They speak slightingly of marriage of the flesh because Christ said, "Whoever shall look on a woman," and so on. They reject baptism of children performed with actual water because children do not have faith, for which they cite the Gospel, "He that believeth

From *Heresies of the High Middle Ages*, ed. Walter L. Wakefield and Austin P. Evans; New York, Columbia University Press, 1969, pp. 231–235. Reprinted by permission.

not shall be condemned.'' They do not believe in the resurrection of the bodies of this world, for Paul said, ''Flesh and blood cannot possess the kingdom of God.'' Whatever is ritually observed in the Church Universal they call vain and absurd, for they hold that doctrine to be a thing of men and without basis, whereby one worships God in vain.

In their secret meetings their elders recount that the wicked god first fashioned his creatures and at the beginning of his act of creation, made four beings, two male and two female, a lion and a bee-eater, an eagle and a spirit. The good God took from him the spirit and the eagle and with them He produced the things which He made. After a long time, the malign god, enraged by his spoliation, sent a certain son of his, whom they call Melchizedek, Seir, or Lucifer, with a great and splendid host of men and women to the court of the good God, to find whether guile might not avenge his father for his own. And on beholding him, distinguished in beauty and intelligence, the good God appointed him prince, priest, and steward over His own people, and through him gave a testament to the people of Israel. In the absence of the Lord, he beguiled the people into disbelief of the truth, promising them that much more, better, and delightful things than those which they had in their own land would be given them in his. They yielded to his blandishments, spurning their God and the testament given them. He bore away some of them and scattered them throughout his realms. The more noble, a designation which these people took to themselves, he sent into this world, which they call the last lake, the farthest earth, and the deepest hell. He sent the souls, so they say, leaving the bodies prostrate in the desert, abandoned by the spirits, for as John says in the Apocalypse, ''The great dragon, that old serpent, devil and Satan, struck with his tail the third part of the stars and dashed them to earth.'' Such, they say, are ''the sheep which are lost of the house of Israel,'' to whom Christ was sent, as He himself says in the Gospel: ''The Son of man is come to seek and to save that which was lost''; and also, ''The Son of man came not to destroy souls but to save.'' That Seir, as they assert, was the father of the lawgiver, for which they cite in the Law: ''The Lord came from Sinai, and from Seir he was born to us''; and in Ezechiel, ''Son of man, set thy face against Mount Seir, and prophesy concerning it, and say to it: Behold, Mount Seir, and I will make thee desolate and waste. I will destroy thy cities and thou shalt be desolate; and thou shalt know that I am the Lord, because thou hast been an everlasting enemy and hast shut up the children of Israel in the hands of the sword.'' Also, they say that the malign god exists without beginning or end, and rules as many and as extensive lands, heavens, people, and creatures as the good God. The present world, they say, will never pass away or be depopulated. They have the daring to assert that the Blessed Mary, mother of Christ, was not of this world. For they say in their secret meetings that Christ, in whom they hope for salvation, was not in this world except in a spiritual sense within the body of Paul, citing Paul himself: "Do you seek a proof of Christ that speaketh in me?" For they say that Paul, "sold under sin," brought the Scriptures into this world and was held prisoner, that he might reveal the ministry of Christ.

For they believe that Christ was born in the "land of the living," of Joseph and Mary, whom they say were Adam and Eve; there He suffered and rose again; thence He ascended to His Father; there He did and said all that was recorded of Him in the New Testament. With this testament, and with His disciples, His father and mother, He passed through seven realms, and thence freed His people. In that land of the living, they believe, there are cities and outside them castles, villages and woodlands, meadows, pastures, sweet water and salt, beasts of the forest and domestic animals, dogs and birds for the hunt, gold and silver, utensils of various kinds, and furniture. They also say that everyone shall have his wife there and sometimes a mistress. They shall eat and drink, play and sleep, and do all things just as they do in the world of the present. And all will be, as they say, well pleasing to God when "the saints shall rejoice in glory; they shall be joyful in their beds," and when they shall have "two-edged swords in their hands to execute vengeance upon the nations," and when the children of Zion shall praise His name in choir and with the timbrel, for "this glory will be to all his saints." For God himself, they say, has two wives, Collam and Colibam, and from them He engendered sons and daughters, as do humans. On the basis of this belief, some of them hold there is no sin in man and woman kissing and embracing each other, or even lying together for intercourse, nor can one sin in doing so for payment.

They also believe that when the soul leaves the human body, it passes to another body, either of a human or of a beast, unless the person shall have died while under their instruction. If, however, he shall have died while continuing steadfast among them, they say that the soul goes to a new earth, prepared by God for all the souls that are to be saved, where it finds clothing, that is, the body prepared for it by its own father and mother. There all await the general resurrection which they shall experience, so they say, in the land of the living, with all their inheritance which they shall recover by force of arms. For they say that until then they shall possess that land of the malign spirit and shall make use of the clothing of the sheep, and shall eat the good things of the earth, and shall not depart thence until all Israel is saved. Also they teach in their secret meetings that Mary Magdalen was the wife of Christ. She was the Samaritan woman to whom He said, "Call thy husband." She was the woman taken in adultery, whom Christ set free lest the Jews stone her, and she was with Him in three places, in the temple, at the well, and in the garden. After the Resurrection, He appeared first to her. They say that John the Baptist is one of the chief malign spirits.

Reading 9

An Account of the Waldensian Heresy

The same questions should be asked of this source as of the previous one. The author, Rainier Sacconi, was an inquisitor, and his testimony can therefore be expected to be both well informed and unsympathetic. Compare the canon of the Fourth Lateran Council relating to the priest's role in the consecration of the eucharist.

The doctrines described here were first promulgated in the later twelfth century by a townsman of Lyons (southern France) named Pierre Valdes or "Peter Waldo." He and his followers are customarily called "Waldensians" by modern historians but were known at the time as the "Poor Men of Lyons." Which of the two doctrines, Waldensian or Albigensian, came closest to anticipating modern Protestant beliefs?

We have said enough of the heresy of the Cathars. Now let us turn to that of the *Leonistae*, or Poor Men of Lyons. They are divided into two parts, the Poor Men from North of the Alps [*Pauperes Ultramontani*] and the Poor Men of Lombardy, the latter being descended from the former.

The first, the Poor Men from across the Alps, say that the New Testament prohibits all swearing as mortal sin. They also reject secular justice, on the ground that kings, princes and potentates ought not to punish evil-doers. They say that an ordinary layman may consecrate the body of the Lord, and I believe that they apply this to women as well for they have never denied it to me. They allege that the Roman Church is not the Church of Jesus Christ.

The Poor Men of Lombardy agree with the others about swearing and secular justice. On the eucharist they are even worse, holding that it may be consecrated by any man who is not in mortal sin. They say that the Roman Church is a church of evil, the beast and harlot which are found in the Book of Revelations, and that it is no sin to eat meat during Lent or on Friday against the precept of the Church, if it is done without offence to others.

They also say that the Church of Christ remained in bishops and other prelates until St. Sylvester, and failed in him, until they themselves restored it, though they do say there have always been some who have feared God and been saved. They believe that children can be saved without baptism.

This work was faithfully compiled by Brother Rainier in A.D. 1250. Deo Gratias.

From *The Birth of Popular Heresy*, ed. and tr. R. I. Moore (Documents of Medieval History Series); London, Edward Arnold Ltd., 1975, pp. 144–145. Reprinted by permission.

6

The Quest for Stability: Papacy and Empire; England and France

In the mid-eleventh century, as the High Middle Ages dawned, the papacy was just beginning to emerge as an international force, whereas the kings of Germany (Holy Roman emperors) were at the height of their power. Emperor Henry III (1039–1056) appointed popes as readily as he appointed the bishops of his own German kingdom. But with Henry III's premature death, reformers at the papal court took advantage of a weak imperial regency government to assert papal independence from imperial control (document 1A). Subsequently, the fiery reformer Gregory VII (pope: 1073-1085), gripped by the ideal of a papal monarchy asserting its authority over kings, princes, and bishops, struggled fiercely against Henry III's son and successor, Henry IV (documents 1B–1E). Gregory was determined to abolish the traditional royal/imperial privilege of appointing bishops and abbots at will, and Henry IV was equally determined to preserve it. The resulting papal-imperial conflict, known as the Investiture Controversy, was finally resolved in the Concordat of Worms of 1122 (document 1F). But the power of the international papacy continued to grow. In 1213, for example, Pope Innocent III accepted the submission of King John and the overlordship of England (document 2). During the decades following Innocent III's death, however, papal authority was gradually overshadowed by the growing power of England and France. The papal bull *Unam Sanctam*, issued by Pope Boniface VIII in 1302, set forth the high-medieval theory of papal monarchy in the strongest possible terms (document 3), but it also marked a widening gulf between the claims of the papacy and its declining powers.

Royal authority had been growing in England since the Norman Conquest of 1066, when William the Conqueror established tight control of the realm (document 4). Under William's great-grandson, King Henry II (1154-1189), the power of the royal courts was extended significantly (document 5). But in the reign of King John (1199-1216) a baronial reaction compelled the monarchy to recognize the traditional rights of the feudal nobility and other free Englishmen in *Magna Carta* (the Great Charter: document 6). The effort to compel the monarchy to respect customs and laws found further expression in the Provisions of Oxford, wrung by dissident barons from John's son, Henry III, in 1258 (document 7). Parliament was given a major role in the Provisions of Oxford, and although the Provisions themselves did not long endure, Parliament continued to grow in importance as England edged toward limited monarchy.

In France royal power grew more slowly, but during the reign of King Philip Augustus (1180–1223) the monarchy won direct control over much of France and developed highly effective administrative machinery (document 8). Whereas England was viewed increasingly as a regime in which the king governed through Parliament—a "Community of the Realm"—France was developing gradually toward the absolute monarchy of early-modern times. During the long, beneficent reign of St. Louis IX (1226–1270), the French came more and more to accept the rule of a holy and beloved king, who ruled in the interests of his subjects but with few constitutional limitations (documents 9A and 9B). Under St. Louis' grandson, Philip IV, the monarchy became rather less holy and rather more absolute (document 10).

By the end of the High Middle Ages, the English and French monarchies had alike developed strong administrative institutions. But with respect to constitutional limitations on royal power, they were drifting apart.

Reading 1

Documents of the Investiture Controversy, 1059–1122.

A. THE PAPAL ELECTION DECREE OF 1059

Despite a characteristically medieval effort to seek historical precedents for their act, Pope Nicholas II and his reform cardinals revolutionized the papal election process. Traditionally, popes had been selected either by the king/emperor or by factions among the Roman nobility. But the reformers were determined to terminate lay control of ecclesiastical appointments, and they began at the top. Henry IV was still a child in 1059, but the reformers correctly anticipated that the German imperial court would bitterly oppose this papal declaration of independence. They address the problem in clauses 5 and 6.

In the name of the Lord God, our Saviour Jesus Christ, in the 1059th year from his incarnation, in the month of April, in the 12th indiction, in the presence of the holy gospels, the most reverend and blessed apostolic pope Nicholas presiding in the Lateran patriarchal basilica which is called the church of Constantine, . . .

Fortified by the authority of our predecessors and the other holy fathers, we decide and declare:

1. On the death of a pontiff of the universal Roman church, first, the cardinal bishops, with the most diligent consideration, shall elect a successor; then they shall call in the other cardinal clergy [to ratify their choice], and finally the rest of the clergy and the people shall express their consent to the new election.

2. In order that the disease of venality may not have any opportunity to spread, the devout clergy shall be the leaders in electing the pontiff, and the others shall acquiesce. And surely this order of election is right and lawful, if we consider either the rules or the practice of various fathers, or if we recall that decree of our predecessor, St. Leo, for he says: "By no means can it be allowed that those should be ranked as bishops who have not been elected by the clergy, and demanded by the people, and consecrated by their fellow-bishops of the province with the consent of the metropolitan." But since the apostolic seat is above all the churches in the earth, and therefore can have no metropolitan over it, without doubt the cardinal bishops perform in it the of-

From *A Source Book for Mediaeval History*, ed. O.J. Thatcher and E.H. McNeal; New York, Charles Scribner's Sons, 1905, pp. 128–131, 136–138, 151–156, 164–166.

fice of the metropolitan, in that they advance the elected prelate to the apostolic dignity [that is, choose, consecrate, and enthrone him].

3. The pope shall be elected from the church in Rome, if a suitable person can be found in it, but if not, he is to be taken from another church.

4. In the papal election—in accordance with the right which we have already conceded to Henry and to those of his successors who may obtain the same right from the apostolic see—due honor and reverence shall be shown our beloved son, Henry, king and emperor elect [that is, the rights of Henry shall be respected].

5. But if the wickedness of depraved and iniquitous men shall so prevail that a pure, genuine, and free election cannot be held in this city, the cardinal bishops with the clergy and a few laymen shall have the right to elect the pontiff wherever they shall deem most fitting.

6. But if after an election any disturbance of war or any malicious attempt of men shall prevail so that he who is elected cannot be enthroned according to custom in the papal chair, the pope elect shall nevertheless exercise the right of ruling the holy Roman church, and of disposing of all its revenues, as we know St. Gregory did before his consecration.

But if anyone, actuated by rebellion or presumption or any other motive, shall be elected or ordained or enthroned in a manner contrary to this our decree, promulgated by the authority of the synod, he with his counsellors, supporters, and followers shall be expelled from the holy church of God by the authority of God and the holy apostles Peter and Paul, and shall be subjected to perpetual anathema as Antichrist and the enemy and destroyer of all Christianity; nor shall he ever be granted a further hearing in the case, but he shall be deposed without appeal from every ecclesiastical rank which he may have held formerly. Whoever shall adhere to him or shall show him any reverence as if he were pope, or shall aid him in any way, shall be subject to like sentence. Moreover, if any rash person shall oppose this our decree and shall try to confound and disturb the Roman church by his presumption contrary to this decree, let him be cursed with perpetual anathema and excommunication, and let him be numbered with the wicked who shall not arise on the day of judgment. Let him feel upon him the weight of the wrath of God the Father, the Son, and the Holy Spirit, and let him experience in this life and the next the anger of the holy apostles, Peter and Paul, whose church he has presumed to confound. Let his habitation be desolate and let none dwell in his tents [Ps. 69:25]. Let his children be orphans and his wife a widow. Let him be driven forth and let his sons beg and be cast out from their habitations. Let the usurer take all his substance and let others reap the fruit of his labors. Let the whole earth fight against him and let all the elements be hostile to him, and let the powers of all the saints in heaven confound him and show upon him in this life their evident vengeance. But may the grace of omnipotent God protect those who observe this decree and free them from the bonds of all their sins by the authority of the holy apostles Peter and Paul.''

B. THE DICTATUS PAPAE OF GREGORY VII

These twenty-seven points were compiled at the papal court around 1075 at the instigation of Pope Gregory VII. The *Dictatus Papae* (dictates of the pope) were not made public, but were probably intended as a guide to papal lawyers. Few of the claims were new, yet together they constitute a silent manifesto for the Gregorian idea of papal monarchy. Gregory VII took these claims very seriously and made them the basis of his international policy. A careful reading will explain why Gregory's opponents included bishops as well as kings.

1. That the Roman church was established by God alone.
2. That the Roman pontiff alone is rightly called universal.
3. That he alone has the power to depose and reinstate bishops.
4. That his legate, even if he be of lower ecclesiastical rank, presides over bishops in council, and has the power to give sentence of deposition against them.
5. That the pope has the power to depose those who are absent [i.e., without giving them a hearing].
6. That, among other things, we ought not to remain in the same house with those whom he has excommunicated.
7. That he alone has the right, according to the necessity of the occasion, to make new laws, to create new bishoprics, to make a monastery of a chapter of canons, and vice versa, and either to divide a rich bishopric or to unite several poor ones.
8. That he alone may use the imperial insignia.
9. That all princes shall kiss the foot of the pope alone.
10. That his name alone is to be recited in the churches.
11. That the name applied to him belongs to him alone.
12. That he has the power to depose emperors.
13. That he has the right to transfer bishops from one see to another when it becomes necessary.
14. That he has the right to ordain as a cleric anyone from any part of the church whatsoever.
15. That anyone ordained by him may rule [as bishop] over another church, but cannot serve [as priest] in it, and that such a cleric may not receive a higher rank from any other bishop.
16. That no general synod may be called without his order.
17. That no action of a synod and no book shall be regarded as canonical without his authority.

18. That his decree can be annulled by no one, and that he can annul the decrees of anyone.

19. That he can be judged by no one.

20. That no one shall dare to condemn a person who has appealed to the apostolic seat.

21. That the important cases of any church whatsoever shall be referred to the Roman church [that is, to the pope].

22. That the Roman church has never erred and will never err to all eternity, according to the testimony of the holy scriptures.

23. That the Roman pontiff who has been canonically ordained is made holy by the merits of St. Peter, according to the testimony of St. Ennodius, bishop of Pavia, which is confirmed by many of the holy fathers, as is shown by the decrees of the blessed pope Symmachus.

24. That by his command or permission subjects may accuse their rulers.

25. That he can depose and reinstate bishops without the calling of a synod.

26. That no one can be regarded as catholic who does not agree with the Roman church.

27. That he has the power to absolve subjects from their oath of fidelity to wicked rulers.

C. THE DECREE AGAINST LAY INVESTITURE

"Investiture" was the formal installation ceremony in which new prelates were given the insignia of their offices. An incoming bishop or abbot would receive a ring and a staff, symbolic of his "marriage" to the Church and his role as shepherd of his flock. It had long been customary for churchmen to receive their investiture from lay lords. Bishops and abbots were normally invested by their territorial princes—counts, dukes, kings, or the Holy Roman emperor. The papal reform party condemned this practice as the key symbolic expression of lay control over ecclesiastical appointments. Lay investiture was first prohibited at the Roman Lenten Synod of 1059, which also promulgated the Papal Election Decree. For a time the investiture issue was largely ignored and forgotten. But Gregory VII issued a second investiture ban at a Roman synod in 1075, and subsequent papal synods legislated against the practice repeatedly. The following document, a product of Gregory VII's synod of 1078, is probably quite similar to the investiture decree of 1075, which no longer survives.

Since we know that investitures have been made by laymen in many places, contrary to the decrees of the holy fathers, and that very many disturbances injurious to the Christian religion have thereby arisen in the church, we therefore decree: that no clergyman shall receive investiture of a bishopric, monastery, or church from the hand of the emperor, or the king, or any lay person, man or woman. And if anyone has ventured to receive such investiture, let him know that it is annulled by apostolic authority, and that he is subject to excommunication until he has made due reparation.

D. THE DEPOSITION OF GREGORY VII BY HENRY IV

The Holy Roman emperors depended heavily on the support of powerful and loyal bishops. Accordingly, Gregory VII's energetic opposition to the appointment of churchmen by laymen earned him the fierce opposition of Henry IV and his hand-picked bishops. When Gregory suspended some of them, Henry responded by convening a synod at Worms in January 1076, and dispatching a letter to Gregory under his prepapal name, Hildebrand.

Henry, king not by usurpation, but by the holy ordination of God, to Hildebrand, not pope, but false monk.

This is the salutation which you deserve, for you have never held any office in the church without making it a source of confusion and a curse to Christian men instead of an honor and a blessing. To mention only the most obvious cases out of many, you have not only dared to touch the Lord's anointed, the archbishops, bishops, and priests; but you have scorned them and abused them, as if they were ignorant servants not fit to know what their master was doing. This you have done to gain favor with the vulgar crowd. You have declared that the bishops know nothing and that you know everything; but if you have such great wisdom you have used it not to build but to destroy. Therefore we believe that St. Gregory, whose name you have presumed to take, had you in mind when he said: "The heart of the prelate is puffed up by the abundance of subjects, and he thinks himself more powerful than all others." All this we have endured because of our respect for the papal office, but you have mistaken our humility for fear, and have dared to make an attack upon the royal and imperial authority which we received from God. You have even threatened to take it away, as if we had received it from you, and as if the empire and kingdom were in your disposal and not in the disposal of God. Our Lord Jesus Christ has called us to the government of the empire, but he never called you to the rule of the church. This is the way you have gained advancement in the church: through craft you have obtained wealth; through wealth you have obtained favor; through favor, the power of the sword; and through the power of the sword, the papal seat, which is the seat of peace; and then from the seat of peace you have expelled peace. For you have incited subjects to rebel against their prelates by teaching them to despise the bishops, their rightful rulers. You have given to laymen the authority over priests, whereby they condemn and depose those whom the bishops have put over them to teach them. You have attacked me, who, unworthy as I am, have yet been anointed to rule among the anointed of God, and who, according to the teaching of the fathers, can be judged by no one save God alone, and can be deposed for no crime except infidelity. For the holy fathers in the time of the apostate Julian did not presume to pronounce sentence of deposition against him, but left him to be judged and condemned by God. St. Peter himself said: "Fear God, honor the king" [1 Pet. 2:17]. But you, who fear not God, have dishonored me, whom He hath established. St. Paul, who said that even an angel from heaven should be accursed who taught any other than the true doctrine, did not make an exception in your favor, to permit you to teach false doctrines. For he says: "But though we, or an angel from heaven, preach any other gospel unto you than that which we have preached unto you, let him be accursed" [Gal. 1:8]. Come down, then, from that apostolic seat which you have obtained by violence; for you have been declared accursed by St. Paul for your false doctrines and have been condemned by us and our bishops for your evil rule. Let another ascend the throne of St. Peter, one who will not use religion as a cloak of violence, but will teach the life-giving doctrine of that prince of the apostles. I, Henry, king by the grace of God, with all my bishops, say unto you: "Come down, come down, and be accursed through all the ages."

E. THE DEPOSITION OF HENRY IV BY GREGORY VII

Gregory responded at the Roman Synod of February 1076 by exercising one of the papal prerogatives that he had claimed in the *Dictatus Papae* (clause 12). He reminded his readers, in the form of a prayer, that the papacy derives its power from the authority granted by Jesus to the Apostle Peter, the first pope and Rome's patron saint.

St. Peter, prince of the apostles, incline thine ear unto me, I beseech thee, and hear me, thy servant, whom thou hast nourished from mine infancy and hast delivered from mine enemies that hate me for my fidelity to thee. Thou art my witness, as are also my mistress, the mother of God, and St. Paul thy brother, and all the other saints, that thy holy Roman church called me to its government against my own will, and that I did not gain thy throne by violence; that I would rather have ended my days in exile than have obtained thy place by fraud or for worldly ambition. It is not by my efforts, but by thy grace, that I am set to rule over the Christian world which was specially intrusted to thee by Christ. It is by thy grace and as thy representative that God has given to me the power to bind and to loose in heaven and in earth. Confident of my integrity and authority, I now declare in the name of omnipotent God, the Father, Son, and Holy Spirit, that Henry, son of the emperor Henry, is deprived of his kingdom of Germany and Italy; I do this by thy authority and in defence of the honor of thy church, because he has rebelled against it. He who attempts to destroy the honor of the church should be deprived of such honor as he may have held. He has refused to obey as a Christian should, he has not returned to God from whom he had wandered, he has had dealings with excommunicated persons, he has done many iniquities, he has despised the warnings which, as thou art witness, I sent to him for his salvation, he has cut himself off from thy church, and has attempted to rend it asunder; therefore, by thy authority, I place him under the curse. It is in thy name that I curse him, that all people may know that thou art Peter, and upon thy rock the Son of the living God has built his church, and the gates of hell shall not prevail against it.

F. THE CONCORDAT OF WORMS

After dragging on for several decades, the Investiture Controversy was settled in 1122 by a compromise between Pope Calixtus II (1119–1124) and Emperor Henry V (1106–1125), Henry IV's son and heir. The settlement drew a distinction between a prelate's spiritual and secular authority: the former was conferred by investiture with ring and staff, the latter by receipt of the "regalia"—a scepter symbolizing territorial lordship. The Concordat of Worms was followed by a generation of peace between empire and papacy.

1. Calixtus, bishop, servant of the servants of God, to his beloved son, Henry, by the grace of God emperor of the Romans, Augustus.

We hereby grant that in Germany the elections of the bishops and abbots who hold directly from the crown shall be held in your presence, such elections to be conducted canonically and without simony or other illegality. In the case of disputed elections you shall have the right to decide between the parties, after consulting with the archbishop of the province and his fellow-bishops. You shall confer the regalia of the office upon the bishop or abbot elect by giving him the scepter, and this shall be done freely without exacting any payment from him; the bishop or abbot elect on his part shall perform all the duties that go with the holding of the regalia.

In other parts of the empire the bishops shall receive the regalia from you in the same manner within six months of their consecration, and shall in like manner perform all the duties that go with them. The undoubted rights of the Roman church, however, are not to be regarded as prejudiced by this concession. If at any time you shall have occasion to complain of the carrying out of these provisions, I will undertake to satisfy your grievances as far as shall be consistent with my office. Finally, I hereby make a true and lasting peace with you and with all of your followers, including those who supported you in the recent controversy.

2. In the name of the holy and undivided Trinity.

For the love of God and his holy church and of Pope Calixtus, and for the salvation of my soul, I, Henry, by the grace of God, emperor of the Romans, Augustus, hereby surrender to God and his apostles, Sts. Peter and Paul, and to the holy Catholic church, all investiture by ring and staff. I agree that elections and consecrations shall be conducted canonically and shall be free from all interference. I surrender also the possessions and regalia of St. Peter which have been seized by me during this quarrel, or by my father in his lifetime, and which are now in my possession, and I promise to aid the church to recover such as are held by any other persons. I restore also the possessions of all other churches and princes, clerical or secular, which have been taken away during the course of this quarrel, which I have, and promise to aid them to recover such as are held by any other persons.

Finally, I make true and lasting peace with Pope Calixtus and with the holy Roman church and with all who are or have ever been of his party. I will aid the Roman church whenever my help is asked, and will do justice in all matters in regard to which the church may have occasion to make complaint.

All these things have been done with the consent and advice of the princes whose names are written below: Adelbert, archbishop of Mainz; Frederick, archbishop of Cologne, etc.

Reading 2

King John's Fealty to Pope Innocent III, 1213

This document is the act of a cornered king. John had been wrestling with Innocent III for seven years over a disputed succession to the archbishopric of Canterbury. By 1213 Innocent was threatening to depose John, and the king of France, Philip Augustus, was proposing to invade England.

Philip Augustus had conquered most of John's French dominions a decade earlier. John's claims to be duke of Normandy and count of Anjou are hollow ones. But in 1213 John was making final arrangements for a military campaign to recover the lost territories. Having more than enough enemies to contend with, he took the prudent course of surrendering to Innocent III—giving in to him on the issue of the Canterbury succession and granting him the overlordship of England and Ireland. This last idea seems to have been John's, not Innocent's, but Innocent cheerfully agreed. He was already overlord of Poland, Sicily, Denmark, Sweden, and Aragon. John's

From *Church and State through the Centuries*, ed. Sidney Z. Ehler and John B. Morrall; New York, Bilbo & Tannen, Inc., 1967, pp. 74–76. Reprinted by permission.

subsequent continental campaign ended in failure, but England remained officially a papal vassal state for the next century and a half.

John, by the grace of God king of England, lord of Ireland, duke of Normandy and Aquitaine, count of Anjou, to all faithful Christians who shall see this present charter, greeting.

We wish it to be known to you all through this our charter, bearing our seal, that since we have offended God and our Mother the Holy Church in many things and therefore are notoriously in great need of the Divine mercy and since we can not offer to God and to the Church anything worthy and fitting to satisfy duly God and the Church unless we humble ourselves and our realms:

We, willing to humble ourselves for Him Who humbled Himself for us even to death, inspired by the grace of the Holy Spirit and not induced by violence or coerced by fear, but acting by our spontaneous good will and by the common counsel of our barons, offer and freely concede to God and His Holy Apostles Peter and Paul and to our Mother the Holy Church, to our lord Pope Innocent and to his Catholic successors, the whole kingdom of England and the whole kingdom of Ireland with all their rights and appurtenances, for the remission of our sins and of the sins of all the members of our family, living or dead; and receiving them and holding them, from now onwards, from God and the Roman Church as a vassal, we now do and swear fealty to the aforesaid our lord Pope Innocent, to his Catholic successors and to the Roman Church in the presence of this prudent man Pandulf, subdeacon and one of the household of the lord Pope, according to the form as annexed; and in the presence of the lord Pope, if we shall be able to appear before him, we shall do liege homage to him; and we bind our successors and heirs by our wife in perpetuity that they must, without contradiction, perform fealty and recognize liege homage in similar manner to the Supreme Pontiff of that time. In order to make evident this our perpetual obligation and concession we will and establish that from the normal as well as especial revenue of the above-mentioned our kingdoms for all service and custom that we shall be bound to render for them—saving in all respects the penny of St. Peter—the Roman Church shall obtain a thousand mark sterling a year[1], namely on the feast of St. Michael five hundred marks and at Easter five hundred marks; which means seven hundred for the kingdom of England and three hundred for the kingdom of Ireland; saving our jurisdiction, liberties and royal rights ("regalia") for us and our heirs, we wish all the above-said to be valid

---

[1] A mark sterling was worth two-thirds of a pound sterling—very roughly $1,000.00 in modern money. The annual payment to the papacy was thus of the order of one million dollars.

perpetually and we bind ourselves and our successors not to contravene it. And if we or anyone of our successors presumes to attempt this, whoever he may be, if he does not come to his senses after due warning, let him forfeit his rights to the kingdom, whereas this charter of our obligation and concession shall remain always valid.

FORM OF THE OATH OF FEALTY

I, John, by the grace of God king of England and lord of Ireland, from this hour onwards will be faithful to God and St. Peter, and the Roman Church, and my lord Pope Innocent, and to his successors, ascending his See in a Catholic manner; I shall not cause them by any deed, word, consent or counsel to lose their life or limb or to be taken into vile captivity. I will prevent them from suffering damage, if I know, and I will cause the damage to be removed, if I can; or else, I will inform them about it as soon as I can, or tell of it to such person whom I believe for certain will inform them. If they entrust me with any counsel either personally or through their envoys or through their letters, I will keep it secret and will not knowingly reveal it to any one to their harm. I will assist according to my best ability in holding and defending the Patrimony of St. Peter and particularly the kingdom of England and the kingdom of Ireland against all men.

So may God and these holy Gospels help me. . . .

On the 15th day of May, in the 14th year of our reign.

Reading 3

Unam Sanctam, 1302

This emphatic statement of the papal monarchy doctrine is by no means the assertion of papal self-confidence that it might seem. It was issued in November 1302 by Pope Boniface VIII as he was nearing the end of his stormy pontificate. Kings Edward I of England and Philip IV of France had been advancing the doctrine of royal authority against the claims of the international church so tellingly set forth in *Unam Sanctam.* Less than a year after its issue, Boniface was seized by a band of French and Italian troops at his residence at Anagni. Although released shortly thereafter, he died a few weeks later in a state of shock and humiliation.

From *The Crisis of Church and State, 1050–1300*, ed. Brian Tierney; Englewood Cliffs, NJ, 1964, pp. 188-189. Reprinted by permission of Prentice-Hall, Inc.

That there is one holy, Catholic and apostolic church we are bound to believe and to hold, our faith urging us, and this we do firmly believe and simply confess; and that outside this church there is no salvation or remission of sins, as her spouse proclaims in the Canticles, "One is my dove, my perfect one. She is the only one of her mother, the chosen of her that bore her" (Canticles 6:8); which represents one mystical body whose head is Christ, while the head of Christ is God. In this church there is one Lord, one faith, one baptism. At the time of the Flood there was one ark, symbolizing the one church. It was finished in one cubit and had one helmsman and captain, namely Noah, and we read that all things on earth outside of it were destroyed. This church we venerate and this alone, the Lord saying through his prophet, "Deliver, O God, my soul from the sword, my only one from the power of the dog" (Psalm 21:21). He prayed for the soul, that is himself, the head, and at the same time for the body, which he called the one church on account of the promised unity of faith, sacraments and charity of the church. This is that seamless garment of the Lord which was not cut but fell by lot. Therefore there is one body and one head of this one and only church, not two heads as though it were a monster, namely Christ and Christ's vicar, Peter and Peter's successor, for the Lord said to this Peter, "Feed my sheep" (John 21:17). He said "My sheep" in general, not these or those, whence he is understood to have committed them all to Peter. Hence, if the Greeks or any others say that they were not committed to Peter and his successors, they necessarily admit that they are not of Christ's flock, for the Lord says in John that there is one sheepfold and one shepherd.

We are taught by the words of the Gospel that in this church and in her power there are two swords, a spiritual one and a temporal one. For when the apostles said "Here are two swords" (Luke 22:38), meaning in the church since it was the apostles who spoke, the Lord did not reply that it was too many but enough. Certainly anyone who denies that the temporal sword is in the power of Peter has not paid heed to the words of the Lord when he said, "Put up thy sword into its sheath" (Matthew 26:52). Both then are in the power of the church, the material sword and the spiritual. But the one is exercised for the church, the other by the church, the one by the hand of the priest, the other by the hand of kings and soldiers, though at the will and suffrance of the priest. One sword ought to be under the other and the temporal authority subject to the spiritual power. For, while the apostle says, "There is no power but from God and those that are ordained of God" (Romans 13:1), they would not be ordained unless one sword was under the other and, being inferior, was led by the other to the highest things. For, according to the blessed Dionysius, it is the law of divinity for the lowest to be led to the highest through intermediaries. In the order of the universe all things are not kept in order in the same fashion and immediately but the lowest are ordered by the intermediate and inferiors by superiors. But that the spiritual power excels any earthly one in dignity and nobility we ought the more openly to confess in proportion as spiritual things excel temporal ones. Moreover we clearly perceive this from the giving of tithes, from benediction and sanctification, from the acceptance of this power and from the very government of things. For, the truth bearing witness, the spiritual power has to institute the earthly power and to judge it if it has not been good. So is verified the prophecy of Jeremiah [1:10] concerning the church and the power of the church, "Lo, I have set thee this day over the nations and over kingdoms" etc.

Therefore, if the earthly power errs, it shall be judged by the spiritual power, if a lesser spiritual power errs it shall be judged by its superior, but if the supreme spiritual power errs it can be judged only by God not by man, as the apostle witnesses, "The spiritual man judgeth all things and he himself is judged of no man" (1 Corinthians 2:15). Although this authority was given to a man and is exercised by a man it is not human but rather divine, being given to Peter at God's mouth, and confirmed to him and to his successors in him, the rock whom the Lord acknowledged when he said to Peter himself "Whatsoever thou shalt bind" etc. (Matthew 16:19). Whoever therefore resists this power so ordained by God resists the ordinance of God unless, like the Manicheans, he imagines that there are two beginnings, which we judge to be false and heretical, as Moses witnesses, for not "in the beginnings" but "in the beginning" God created heaven and earth (Genesis 1:1). Therefore we declare, state, define and pronounce that it is altogether necessary to salvation for every human creature to be subject to the Roman Pontiff.

Reading 4

William the Conqueror Subdues Northern England

For about five years after his victory at the battle of Hastings in 1066, William the Conqueror and his Normans were kept busy eliminating pockets of English resistance and suppressing native rebellions such as the one described here. Edwin and Morcar, the pre-Conquest earls of Mercia and Northumbria, did not fight at Hastings and were therefore permitted for a time to keep their earldoms.

From Orderic Vitalis, *The Ecclesiastical History*, ed. A. Le Prévost; vol. 2, Paris, 1840, pp. 182–186; tr. David S. Spear.

The passage shows some of the ways in which William consolidated his new regime in England. The author, Orderic Vitalis, was writing a full generation after the event. His sources, oral and written, were generally trustworthy and he used them carefully. But the account of wanton Norman wives which concludes this excerpt is probably exaggerated. Hugh of Grandmesnil did not forfeit his estates, as Orderic suggests, but became a wealthy landholder in central England and bequeathed his lands to one of his sons. Orderic's account of the Norman Conquest is relatively unbiased since he was himself half English and half Norman. He described himself as an "Englishman" but spent his youth and adulthood in the Norman abbey of Saint-Evroul where he died in 1142.

In that same year (1068), the distinguished youths Edwin and Morcar, the sons of Earl Alfgar, rebelled, and as they were joined by many others the entire kingdom of England was in upheaval. King William, however, made peace: in return for count Edwin subduing his brother and nearly a third of England, William promised him his daughter in marriage. But later, owing to the deceitful counsel of the Normans who are a very envious and covetous people, William denied Edwin the hand of the woman for whom he had waited so long. Quite irritated, the two brothers were incited to open rebellion, and a large number of the English and the Welsh soon followed. . . .

[At about this time] Bleddyn king of the Welsh went to the aid of his uncles, bringing a multitude of natives with him. Meeting together, many of the English and Welsh nobles complained about the intolerable injuries and indignities which they had suffered at the hands of the Normans and their companions. Using messengers they succeeded in stirring up the insurgents throughout the island, both in secret and in public. All swore to strive against the Normans and regain their former liberties. Trouble broke out first and most viciously in the furthest regions beyond the Humber, with the rebels garrisoning themselves in the forests, marshes, estuaries, and even in some of the towns. The city of York was the most explosive, and not even the archbishop himself dared to try and quiet it. Many of the natives began to live in tents, scorning houses whose comforts they thought would make them soft. Indeed, it was for this reason that the Normans called them savages.

King William decided to examine carefully even the remote areas of the realm and to garrison the most advantageous locations against the excursions of the enemy. These fortifications, which the Normans called castles, were seldom found in England before this, and because of them the English, even though they were exceptionally warlike and fearless, found their position greatly weakened. The king built a castle at Warwick, and brought Henry the son of Roger of Beaumont to hold it. Edwin and Morcar, considering with their men the dangers of battle, then sought William's forgiveness, which they obtained so far as they were able. The king next erected a castle at Nottingham and commended it to William Peverel.

Hearing of these events the people of York were disinclined to continue their uprising, and promptly gave up the keys of the city to the king, along with some hostages. Since he was a little leary of their loyalty he built a castle right in the town itself, which he handed over to some carefully chosen knights. After this Archill, the most powerful of the Northumbrians, made peace with the king, and gave over his son to William as a hostage. The bishop of Durham also went to the king seeking peace for Malcolm king of the Scots, and brought the conditions back to Scotland. Malcolm, although he was counted on by the English contingent and was prepared to wage a vigorous campaign on their behalf, nonetheless remained quiet when he heard the peace terms which were offered him. He promptly sent his messengers back with the bishop of Durham, and swore through them that he would remain faithful to the king. Thus by preferring peace to war he was able both to further his own interest and to please many of his own people. For the Scots, although certainly hardy in battle, love leisure and quiet as well, not wishing to disturb the affairs of their neighbors, and are more inclined towards the Christian faith than the pursuit of arms. The king then withdrew, careful though to build castles at Lincoln, Huntingdon, and Cambridge, and to entrust them to his strongest men.

At this time certain Norman women, terribly inflamed by the passions of lust, sent messengers to their men demanding that they return home, adding that unless they did so quickly they would take other mates. They did not themselves dare to cross over to their husbands since they were unaccustomed to sailing, nor did they wish to seek after them in England since there the men were constantly armed and making daily expeditions in which no small amount of blood was lost on both sides. The king of course wanted to keep his knights with him under such unstable conditions, and consequently he offered them lands, revenues, and positions of great power, promising them even more when the whole kingdom should be free from the threat of the enemy. The barons and knights were at a loss, for as long as the king and their own brothers and friends remained surrounded and in danger, they realized that they would be labelled cowards or out-and-out deserters. Yet if they remained, their wives would pollute their beds with the stain of infidelity and besmirch the reputations of their offspring. Finally Hugh of Grandmesnil, who oversaw the Gewissae, that is the area around Winchester, and his brother-in-law Humphrey of Tilleul who had commanded Hastings ever since the day it was first built, along with many others, reluctantly departed while their king still labored with the enemy. They returned to their lewd wives in Normandy, but in so doing relinquished their lands, and neither they nor their heirs were able to recover them afterwards.

Reading 5

Henry II's Writ of Novel Disseisin

Feudal societies such as that of post-Conquest England were constantly troubled by disputes over the holding of estates. William the Conqueror and his successors were determined that such disputes be settled peacefully and lawfully, and as time went on the royal judicial system played an increasing role in adjudicating them. King Henry II (1154–1189) took the important step of providing standardized royal writs (brief written commands authenticated by the royal seal) ordering that the local sheriff restore the lands of anyone who had been wrongfully and recently dispossessed. The standardization and expansion of royal justice over local jurisdictions mark the emergence of the English "Common Law," of which Henry II is often called the father.

The king to the sheriff, greeting. N. has complained to me that R. has dispossessed him, unlawfully and without judgment, of his free holding in [such and such a village] since my latest crossing to Normandy. And therefore I command you that, if the aforesaid N. gives you security for prosecuting his claim, you shall have the chattels that were taken from that holding restored to it, and see to it that the aforesaid holding, with its chattels, remains in peace until [such and such a time]. And in the meantime, you shall arrange that twelve free and law-abiding men of the neighborhood inspect that land, and see that their names are recorded in writing. And summon them with proper summoners to appear before me or my justices, prepared to testify concerning the matter. And place under security and safe pledges the aforesaid R., or his bailiff if he himself cannot be found, to be there to hear that testimony. And make certain that the summoners and this writ are also there [at the royal tribunal].

Tr. C. Warren Hollister

Reading 6
Magna Carta, 1215

King John's difficulties (above, p. 158) reached their climax with a major baronial uprising in 1215, as a result of which he was forced to issue a comprehensive charter guaranteeing customary feudal and political rights. Magna Carta is concerned primarily with the rectification of past abuses of feudal privileges, but it also discloses the significant overlap of lord-vassal relationships with the emerging constitutional doctrine of limited monarchy and government under the law. John repudiated Magna Carta shortly after issuing it and died in 1216 in the midst of another baronial rebellion. Magna Carta was reissued repeatedly, with certain variations, during the generations that followed.

John, by the grace of God, king of England, lord of Ireland, duke of Normandy and Aquitaine, and count of Anjou, to the archbishops, bishops, abbots, earls, barons, justiciars, foresters, sheriffs, stewards, servants, and to all his bailiffs and faithful subjects, greeting. Know that we, out of reverence for God and for the salvation of our soul and those of all our ancestors and heirs, for the honour of God and the exaltation of holy church, and for the reform of our realm, on the advice of our venerable fathers, Stephen, archbishop of Canterbury, primate of all England and cardinal of the holy Roman church, [and other bishops and magnates].

[1] In the first place have granted to God, and by this our present charter confirmed for us and our heirs for ever that the English church shall be free, and shall have its rights undiminished and its liberties unimpaired; and it is our will that it be thus observed; which is evident from the fact that, before the quarrel between us and our barons began, we willingly and spontaneously granted and by our charter confirmed the freedom of elections which is reckoned most important and very essential to the English church, and obtained confirmation of it from the lord pope Innocent III; the which we will observe and we wish our heirs to observe it in good faith for ever. We have also granted to all free men of our kingdom, for ourselves and our heirs for ever, all the liberties written below, to be had and held by them and their heirs of us and our heirs.

[2] If any of our earls or barons or others holding of us in chief by knight service dies, and at his death his heir be of full age and owe relief he shall have his inheritance on payment of the old relief, namely the heir or heirs of an earl

From *English Historical Documents, vol. 3, 1189–1327*, ed. and tr. Harry Rothwell; London, Eyre & Spottiswoode, 1975, pp. 316–324. Reprinted by permission.

£100 for a whole earl's barony, the heir or heirs of a baron £100 for a whole barony, the heir or heirs of a knight 100s, at most, for a whole knight's fee; and he who owes less shall give less according to the ancient usage of fiefs.

[3] If, however, the heir of any such be under age and a ward, he shall have his inheritance when he comes of age without paying relief and without making fine.

[4] The guardian of the land of such an heir who is under age shall take from the land of the heir no more than reasonable revenues, reasonable customary dues and reasonable services, and that without destruction and waste of men or goods; and if we commit the wardship of the land of any such to a sheriff, or to any other who is answerable to us for its revenues, and he destroys or wastes what he has wardship of, we will take compensation from him and the land shall be committed to two lawful and discreet men of that fief, who shall be answerable for the revenues to us or to him to whom we have assigned them; and if we give or sell to anyone the wardship of any such land and he causes destruction or waste therein, he shall lose that wardship, and it shall be transferred to two lawful and discreet men of that fief, who shall similarly be answerable to us as is aforesaid.

[5] Moreover, so long as he has the wardship of the land, the guardian shall keep in repair the houses, parks, preserves, ponds, mills and other things pertaining to the land out of the revenues from it; and he shall restore to the heir when he comes of age his land fully stocked with ploughs and the means of husbandry according to what the season of husbandry requires and the revenues of the land can reasonably bear.

[6] Heirs shall be married without disparagement, yet so that before the marriage is contracted those nearest in blood to the heir shall have notice.

[7] A widow shall have her marriage portion and inheritance forthwith and without difficulty after the death of her husband; nor shall she pay anything to have her dower or her marriage portion or the inheritance which she and her husband held on the day of her husband's death; and she may remain in her husband's house for forty days after his death, within which time her dower shall be assigned to her.

[8] No widow shall be forced to marry so long as she wishes to live without a husband, provided that she gives security not to marry without our consent if she holds of us, or without the consent of her lord of whom she holds, if she holds of another.

[9] Neither we nor our bailiffs will seize for any debt any land or rent, so long as the chattels of the debtor are sufficient to repay the debt; nor will those who have gone surety for the debtor be distrained so long as the principal debtor is himself able to pay the debt; and if the principal debtor fails to pay the debt, having nothing wherewith to pay it, then shall the sureties answer for the debt; and they shall, if they wish, have the lands and rents of the debtor un-

til they are reimbursed for the debt which they have paid for him, unless the principal debtor can show that he has discharged his obligation in the matter to the said sureties.

[10] If anyone who has borrowed from the Jews any sum, great or small, dies before it is repaid, the debt shall not bear interest as long as the heir is under age, of whomsoever he holds; and if the debt falls into our hands, we will not take anything except the principal mentioned in the bond.

[11] And if anyone dies indebted to the Jews, his wife shall have her dower and pay nothing of that debt; and if the dead man leaves children who are under age, they shall be provided with necessaries befitting the holding of the deceased; and the debt shall be paid out of the residue, reserving, however, service due to lords of the land; debts owing to others than Jews shall be dealt with in like manner.

[12] No scutage or aid shall be imposed in our kingdom unless by common counsel of our kingdom, except for ransoming our person, for making our eldest son a knight, and for once marrying our eldest daughter; and for these only a reasonable aid shall be levied. Be it done in like manner concerning aids from the city of London.

[13] And the city of London shall have all its ancient liberties and free customs as well by land as by water. Furthermore, we will and grant that all other cities, boroughs, towns, and ports shall have all their liberties and free customs.

[14] And to obtain the common counsel of the kingdom about the assessing of an aid (except in the three cases aforesaid) or of a scutage, we will cause to be summoned the archbishops, bishops, abbots, earls and greater barons, individually by our letters—and, in addition, we will cause to be summoned generally through our sheriffs and bailiffs all those holding of us in chief—for a fixed date, namely, after the expiry of at least forty days, and to a fixed place; and in all letters of such summons we will specify the reason for the summons. And when the summons has thus been made, the business shall proceed on the day appointed, according to the counsel of those present, though not all have come who were summoned. . . .

[20] A free man shall not be amerced for a trivial offence except in accordance with the degree of the offence, and for a grave offence he shall be amerced in accordance with its gravity, yet saving his way of living; and a merchant in the same way, saving his stock-in-trade; and a villein shall be amerced in the same way, saving his means of livelihood—if they have fallen into our mercy: and none of the aforesaid amercements shall be imposed except by the oath of good men of the neighbourhood.

[21] Earls and barons shall not be amerced except by their peers, and only in accordance with the degree of the offence. . . .

[27] If any free man dies without leaving a will, his chattels shall be distributed by his nearest kinsfolk and friends under the supervision of the church, saving to every one the debts which the deceased owed him.

[28] No constable or other bailiff of ours shall take anyone's corn or other chattels unless he pays on the spot in cash for them or can delay payment by arrangement with the seller.

[29] No constable shall compel any knight to give money instead of castle-guard if he is willing to do the guard himself or through another good man, if for some good reason he cannot do it himself; and if we lead or send him on military service, he shall be excused guard in proportion to the time that because of us he has been on service.

[30] No sheriff, or bailiff of ours, or anyone else shall take the horses or carts of any free man for transport work save with the agreement of that freeman.

[31] Neither we nor our bailiffs will take, for castles or other works of ours, timber which is not ours, except with the agreement of him whose timber it is.

[32] We will not hold for more than a year and a day the lands of those convicted of felony, and then the lands shall be handed over to the lords of the fiefs. . . .

[38] No bailiff shall in future put anyone to trial upon his own bare word, without reliable witnesses produced for this purpose.

[39] No free man shall be arrested or imprisoned or disseised or outlawed or exiled or in any way victimised, neither will we attack him or send anyone to attack him, except by the lawful judgment of his peers or by the law of the land.

[40] To no one will we sell, to no one will we refuse or delay right or justice.

[41] All merchants shall be able to go out of and come into England safely and securely and stay and travel throughout England, as well by land as by water, for buying and selling by the ancient and right customs free from all evil tolls, except in time of war and if they are of the land that is at war with us. And if such are found in our land at the beginning of a war, they shall be attached, without injury to their persons or goods, until we, or our chief justiciar, know how merchants of our land are treated who were found in the land at war with us when war broke out; and if ours are safe there, the others shall be safe in our land.

[42] It shall be lawful in future for anyone, without prejudicing the allegiance due to us, to leave our kingdom and return safely and securely by land and water, save, in the public interest, for a short period in time of war— except for those imprisoned or outlawed in accordance with the law of the

kingdom and natives of a land that is at war with us and merchants (who shall be treated as aforesaid). . . .

[45] We will not make justices, constables, sheriffs or bailiffs save of such as know the law of the kingdom and mean to observe it well.

[46] All barons who have founded abbeys for which they have charters of the kings of England or ancient tenure shall have the custody of them during vacancies, as they ought to have.

[47] All forests that have been made forest in our time shall be immediately disafforested; and so be it done with river-banks that have been made preserves by us in our time.

[48] All evil customs connected with forests and warrens, foresters and warreners, sheriffs and their officials, river-banks and their wardens shall immediately be inquired into in each county by twelve sworn knights of the same county who are to be chosen by good men of the same county, and within forty days of the completion of the inquiry shall be utterly abolished by them so as never to be restored, provided that we, or our justiciar if we are not in England, know of it first.

[49] We will immediately return all hostages and charters given to us by Englishmen, as security for peace or faithful service. . . .

[52] If anyone has been disseised of or kept out of his lands, castles, franchises or his right by us without the legal judgment of his peers, we will immediately restore them to him: and if a dispute arises over this, then let it be decided by the judgment of the twenty-five barons who are mentioned below in the clause for securing the peace: for all things, however, which anyone has been disseised or kept out of without the lawful judgment of his peers by King Henry, our father, or by King Richard, our brother, which we have in our hand or are held by others, to whom we are bound to warrant them, we will have the usual period of respite of crusaders, excepting those things about which a plea was started or an inquest made by our command before we took the cross; when however we return from our pilgrimage, or if by any chance we do not go on it, we will at once do full justice therein. . . .

[54] No one shall be arrested or imprisoned upon the appeal of a woman for the death of anyone except her husband.

[55] All fines made with us unjustly and against the law of the land, and all amercements imposed unjustly and against the law of the land, shall be entirely remitted, or else let them be settled by the judgment of the twenty-five barons who are mentioned below in the clause for securing the peace, or by the judgment of the majority of the same, along with the aforesaid Stephen, archbishop of Canterbury, if he can be present, and such others as he may wish to associate with himself for this purpose, and if he cannot be present the business shall nevertheless proceed without him, provided that if any one or more of the aforesaid twenty-five barons are in a like suit, they shall be re-

moved from the judgment of the case in question, and others chosen, sworn and put in their place by the rest of the same twenty-five for this case only. . . .

[60] All these aforesaid customs and liberties which we have granted to be observed in our kingdom as far as it pertains to us towards our men, all of our kingdom, clerks as well as laymen, shall observe as far as it pertains to them towards their men.

[61] Since, moreover, for God and the betterment of our kingdom and for the better allaying of the discord that has arisen between us and our barons we have granted all these things aforesaid, wishing them to enjoy the use of them unimpaired and unshaken for ever, we give and grant them the under-written security, namely, that the barons shall choose any twenty-five barons of the kingdom they wish, who must with all their might observe, hold and cause to be observed, the peace and liberties which we have granted and confirmed to them by this present charter of ours, so that if we, or our justiciar, or our bailiffs or any one of our servants offend in any way against anyone or transgress any of the articles of the peace or the security and the offence be notified to four of the aforesaid twenty-five barons, those four barons shall come to us, or to our justiciar if we are out of the kingdom, and, laying the transgression before us, shall petition us to have that transgression corrected without delay. And if we do not correct the transgression, or if we are out of the kingdom, if our justiciar does not correct it, within forty days, reckoning from the time it was brought to our notice or to that of our justiciar if we were out of the kingdom, the aforesaid four barons shall refer that case to the rest of the twenty-five barons and those twenty-five barons together with the community of the whole land shall distrain and distress us in every way they can, namely, by seizing castles, lands, possessions, and in such other ways as they can, saving our person and the persons of our queen and our children, until, in their opinion, amends have been made; and when amends have been made, they shall obey us as they did before. And let anyone in the land who wishes take an oath to obey the orders of the said twenty-five barons for the execution of all the aforesaid matters, and with them to distress us as much as he can, and we publicly and freely give anyone leave to take the oath who wishes to take it and we will never prohibit anyone from taking it. Indeed, all those in the land who are unwilling of themselves and of their own accord to take an oath to the twenty-five barons to help them to distrain and distress us, we will make them take the oath as aforesaid at our command. And if any of the twenty-five barons dies or leaves the country or is in any other way prevented from carrying out the things aforesaid, the rest of the aforesaid twenty-five barons shall choose as they think fit another one in his place, and he shall take the oath like the rest. In all matters the execution of which is committed to these twenty-five barons, if it should happen that these twenty-five are present yet disagree among themselves about anything, or if some of those summoned will not or

cannot be present, that shall be held as fixed and established which the majority of those present ordained or commanded, exactly as if all the twenty-five had consented to it; and the said twenty-five shall swear that they will faithfully observe all the things aforesaid and will do all they can to get them observed. And we will procure nothing from anyone, either personally or through anyone else, whereby any of these concessions and liberties might be revoked or diminished; and if any such thing is procured, let it be void and null, and we will never use it either personally or through another.

[62] And we have fully remitted and pardoned to everyone all the ill-will, indignation and rancour that have arisen between us and our men, clergy and laity, from the time of the quarrel. Furthermore, we have fully remitted to all, clergy and laity, and as far as pertains to us have completely forgiven, all trespasses occasioned by the same quarrel between Easter in the sixteenth year of our reign and the restoration of peace. And, besides, we have caused to be made for them letters testimonial patent of the lord Stephen archbishop of Canterbury, of the lord Henry archbishop of Dublin and of the aforementioned bishops and of master Pandulf about this security and the aforementioned concessions.

[63] Wherefore we wish and firmly enjoin that the English church shall be free, and that the men in our kingdom shall have and hold all the aforesaid liberties, rights and concessions well and peacefully, freely and quietly, fully and completely, for themselves and their heirs from us and our heirs, in all matters and in all places for ever, as is aforesaid. An oath, moreover, has been taken, as well on our part as on the part of the barons, that all these things aforesaid shall be observed in good faith and without evil disposition. Witness the above-mentioned and many others. Given by our hand in the meadow which is called Runnymede between Windsor and Staines on the fifteenth day of June, in the seventeenth year of our reign.

Reading 7

The Provisions of Oxford, 1258

A long-growing conflict between King Henry III of England (1216–1272) and a powerful group of dissident barons resulted in the Provisions of Oxford, according to which the king was forced to accept a strong element of baronial control in the administration and reform of the realm. The Provisions of Oxford required, for the first time, baronial supervision of the king's council and

Tr. C. Warren Hollister.

of major royal officials. The barons, referring to themselves as the "community" [of the realm], forced the king to summon parliaments regularly and to submit to baronial reforms within the royal household. Although Henry III later repudiated the Provisions, they nevertheless illustrate a significant experiment in joint royal-aristocratic governance and an early effort to create machinery for the limitation of royal authority.

This machinery was complex: the king and the dissident barons were each to choose twelve men to represent their interests. The king's twelve men would then pick two men from among the barons' twelve, and vice-versa. The resulting group of four—two from each side—were then to select fifteen men to constitute the king's council and to supervise the activities of royal officials. This council of fifteen would thus, ideally, represent a balance of royal and baronial interests.

The Provisions of Oxford begin with a section on local governance, followed by lists of the twelve men chosen by the king and the twelve chosen by the barons (referred to collectively in the document as "the twenty-four"), and by a series of oaths by magnates and officials to uphold the Provisions. The document then continues:

The twelve men on the king's side have chosen from the twelve on the community's side Earl Roger Marshal and Hugh Bigot. And the party of the community has chosen from the twelve on the king's side the earl of Warwick and John Mansel. These four men are empowered to elect the king's council. And when they have completed their election, they will designate those whom they have elected to the twenty-four [royal and baronial representatives]. And whatever the majority of them agree upon shall be put into effect. . . .

Concerning the condition of the Holy Church: Let it be noted that the condition of the Holy Church is to be amended by the twenty-four men selected to reform the condition of the English realm, at whatever time and place they think best, in accordance with the authority given them by the sealed writ of the king of England.

Concerning the chief justice: Moreover, let one or two chief justices be appointed, and let him exercise whatever power he has for one year only, so that at the year's end he shall give account of his term before the king and his council, and in his successor's presence.

Concerning the treasurer and the exchequer: The same procedure shall apply to the treasurer, so that he shall give account at the year's end. And, in accordance with the ordinances of the aforesaid twenty-four, other good men shall be appointed to the exchequer, and all revenues from the land shall come there and nowhere else [i.e., not directly into the king's private purse]. And let whatever requires reform be reformed.

Concerning the chancellor: The same procedure shall apply to the chancellor, so that he shall give account of his term at the year's end. And except for routine writs, he shall seal no writs on the king's order alone, but only by the order of the king's council.

Concerning the power of the justices and officials: The chief justice has the power to redress the wrongs done by all other justices, by royal officials, earls, barons, and all others, in accordance with the rightful law of the kingdom. And royal writs are to be pleaded in accordance with the law of the kingdom and at the correct locations. And justices shall accept no gifts except presents of bread, wine, and the like—that is, such food and drink as is customarily brought daily to the tables of important men. And the same regulation shall apply to all the king's counselors and officials. And no official, in connection with a legal hearing or any official responsibility, shall accept any fee, whether by his own hand or through another person in any way at all. And if he is proven guilty, let him be punished along with the person who bribed him. For it is proper that the king should pay his justices and all others who serve him, so that they shall have no need to accept anything from anybody else.

Concerning sheriffs: Sheriffs shall be appointed who are loyal men and trustworthy landholders, so that there shall be a sheriff in every shire who is a feudal tenant in that shire, who will deal well, loyally and justly with the people of the shire. And he shall take no bribes, and shall not serve as sheriff for more than a year at a time. And in the course of the year he shall render his accounts at the exchequer and give account of his term of office. And let the king reimburse him from the royal revenues in proportion to his fiscal responsibilities so that he can govern his shire justly. And neither he nor his officials shall accept bribes. And if they are found guilty of doing so, let them be punished. . . .

Concerning the mint of London: Let it be noted to reform the mint of London, and to reform the condition of the city of London and of all the king's other cities, which have been brought to impoverishment and ruin by arbitrary taxes and other oppressions.

Concerning the household of the king and queen: Let it be noted to reform the household of the king and queen.

Concerning parliaments: how many shall be held each year, and in what manner? Let it be noted that the twenty-four have commanded that there shall be three parliaments every year: the first at the octave of the feast of St. Michael [October 6], the second on the day after Candlemas [February 3], and the third on the first day of June, that is, three weeks before St. John's day. To these three parliaments shall come the [fifteen] elected members of the royal council, even if not summoned, to inspect the condition of the realm and to transact the business of the king and kingdom. And they shall come at other times, at the king's summons, whenever there is need.

Let it further be noted that the community should elect twelve trustworthy men, who shall come to the parliaments, and at other times when there is need and when summoned by the king and council, to transact the business of the king and the kingdom; and the community shall accept as established whatever these twelve men shall do, so as to reduce the cost to the community.

Four men—Earl Marshal, the earl of Warwick, Hugh Bigot and John Mansel—have been chosen by the twenty-four to name the members of the king's council of fifteen. And these fifteen shall be confirmed by the aforesaid twenty-four, or by a majority of them. And the fifteen council members shall have the power to advise the king in good faith on the governance of the realm and on all matters affecting the king and kingdom; and to amend and reform everything that, in their judgment, requires amendment and reform. And they shall have power over the chief justice and all other persons. And if they cannot all be present, whatever the majority decides shall be established. . . .

Reading 8

Philip II of France on the Governance of the Realm, 1190

Philip II "Augustus" (1180–1223) was a contemporary of four successive kings of England: Henry II, Richard I, John, and Henry III. This ordinance, establishing a regency government during Philip's absence on the Third Crusade, contrasts sharply with John's Magna Carta and Henry III's Provisions of Oxford. It projects the image of a king whose duties to his subjects are governed by conscience rather than by baronial pressures.

In the name of the holy and indivisible Trinity. Amen. Philip, by the grace of God King of the French.

It is the duty of a King to look after the interests of his subjects by all possible means and to place the public welfare before his own private advantage. Since we are most eagerly and with all our strength fulfilling our vow to make a journey to aid the Holy Land, on the advice of the Most High we have determined to ordain how to deal with the business of the kingdom that must be transacted and how to dispose of our last mortal possessions if we should die upon the journey.

First, therefore, we ordain that our bailiffs shall in each provostship on our estates appoint four wise and law-abiding men who will bear honest witness, and the business of the village shall be transacted only with their advice or with that of at least two of them. At Paris, however, we appoint six

From *Sources for the History of Medieval Europe*, ed. and tr. Brian Pullan; Oxford, Basil Blackwell, 1966, pp. 254–257. Reprinted by permission.

honest and law-abiding men whose names are T[hibaud le Riche], A[thon de la Grève], E[brouin le Changeur], R[obert of Chartres], B[audouin Bruneau?] and N[icolas Boisseau?].

In lands of ours which have been specified by name, we have appointed our bailiffs, who shall each month fix one day called the assize, on which all who make a complaint shall receive justice and their rights without delay through the bailiffs, and we shall likewise receive justice and our rights; and a record shall be kept there of all fines which are due to us.

Further, it is our will and command that our dearest mother Queen Adèle, with our dearest uncle and vassal William, Archbishop of Reims, shall every four months fix one day on which they shall hear at Paris the complaints of the men of our Kingdom, and there deal with them to the honour of God and the profit of the realm.

We further ordain that on that day representatives of each of our villages and also our bailiffs who hold assizes shall appear before them to describe in their presence the affairs of our land.

If any of our bailiffs has committed a crime, other than murder, robbery, homicide or treason, and if the Archbishop, the Queen and others who attend to hear of the offences committed by our bailiffs are agreed upon this, we order them to inform us, three times in every year, by letters written on the aforesaid days, which bailiff has offended, and what he has done, and from whom he has received money, gifts or services for causing us or our vassals to lose their rights.

Our bailiffs shall in a similar fashion send us information about our provosts.

The Queen and Archbishop shall not be empowered to remove our bailiffs from their bailiwicks save for murder, robbery, homicide or treason; nor shall bailiffs have the power to remove provosts, save for one of these crimes. We, on God's advice, once these persons have informed us of the facts of the case, will inflict a punishment which will serve as a fitting deterrent to others.

Likewise, the Queen and Archbishop shall report to us three times a year concerning the state of our realm and its affairs.

If it happens that an episcopal see[1] or the headship of a royal abbey falls vacant, we wish the canons of the church or the monks of the monastery which is vacant to come before the Queen and Archbishop, as they would come before us, and ask them for freedom to elect; and we wish the Queen and Archbishop to grant this to them without opposition. We advise the canons and monks to elect a pastor who will be pleasing to God and useful to the realm. The Queen and Archbishop shall keep the *regalia* in their hands until

---

[1] An episcopal see is a bishopric.

the chosen candidate has been consecrated and blessed, and then the *regalia* shall be handed to him without opposition.

We further ordain that if a prebend or ecclesiastical benefice falls vacant, when the *regalia* come into our hands, the Queen and Archbishop shall confer them in the best and most honourable fashion possible upon honourable and learned men, taking the advice of Brother Bernard. Our donations, which we have made by letters patent, shall be excepted from this.

We forbid all prelates of churches and vassals of ours to pay *taille*[2] or other taxes whilst we are on God's service. If the Lord God's will be done and death befalls us, we strictly forbid all men of our land, both clergy and laity, to pay *taille* until our son—may God keep him safe and sound for his service—reaches the age at which, by the grace of the Holy Spirit, he can rule the Kingdom.

Should anyone wish to make war upon our son, and the revenues that he has be not sufficient, then all our vassals must assist him with their persons and their property, and the churches shall extend to him the aid which they are accustomed to render to us.

We forbid our provosts and bailiffs to arrest any man or seize his property, whilst he is willing to give good guarantors that he will appear for trial in our court, except in cases of homicide, murder, robbery or treason.

We further ordain that all our revenues, dues and emoluments shall be brought to Paris at three dates: firstly on the Feast of St. Remigius, secondly at the Purification of the Blessed Virgin and thirdly on Ascension Day; and they shall be handed over to our aforesaid burghers, and to Pierre le Maréchal. Should any of these happen to die, Guy de Garlande shall appoint another in his place.

When our revenues are received, Adam, our clerk, shall be present and record the receipts; and each of the burghers shall have a key to each of the coffers in the Temple in which our treasure is stored, and the Temple itself shall have one. We will give instructions in our letters as to how much of this treasure shall be sent to us.

We ordain that, should we happen to die on the journey we are making, the Queen and Archbishop and the Bishop of Paris, and the Abbots of St. Victor and St. Denis, and Brother Bernard shall divide our treasure into two parts. They shall distribute one-half as they choose in order to repair churches which have been destroyed as a result of our wars, so that the worship of God can take place within them. They shall give some of the same half to those who have been ruined by our taxes; and the rest of the same half to those whom they choose and whom they believe to be most in need, for the salvation of our

[2]A specific type of direct tax.

soul and that of our father King Louis and those of our ancestors. We order the guardians of our treasure and all the men of Paris to keep the other half of the treasure for the needs of our son until he reaches an age at which he can rule the Kingdom with the advice of God and by his own intellect.

If death should befall both us and our son, we order the aforesaid seven men to distribute our treasure as they choose for the sake of our soul and his. As soon as the news of our death arrives, we wish our treasure, wherever it is, to be taken to the house of the Bishop of Paris, and there kept under guard, and afterwards it shall be disposed of as we have ordained.

We instruct the Queen and Archbishop to keep in their own hands as many as they decently can of the honours, such as abbeys, deaneries and certain other offices, which are in our gift when they fall vacant until we return from serving God; and those that they cannot retain, they shall give and assign in a godly fashion on the advice of Brother Bernard and they shall do this to the honour of God and the profit of the realm. But should we die on the journey, we wish them to give the honours and offices in the churches to those whom they perceive to be most worthy of them.

That this may be firmly established, we order this charter to be authenticated by our seal and by the addition of the royal signature below.

Done at Paris, in the year of the Incarnate Word 1190, in the eleventh year of our reign, with those whose names and signatures are appended below present in our palace. The signature of Count Thibaut, our Seneschal. The signature of Guy the Butler. The signature of Matthew the Chamberlain. The signature of Ralph the Constable. Given at a time when the Chancery was vacant.

Reading 9

The Mise of Amiens, 1264

The Mise ("settlement") of Amiens discloses the growing differences between French and English conceptions of royal governance. In reading it, one should recall some of the earlier documents in this chapter: John's oath to Innocent III (the popes remained nominal overlords of England throughout the thirteenth century); Henry III's Provisions of Oxford of 1258 (a central issue in the Mise of Amiens); and the immediately preceding ordinance of Philip II.

From *Documents of the Baronial Movement of Reform and Rebellion, 1258–1267*, selected by R.E. Treharne and edited by I.J. Sanders; Oxford, 1973, pp. 287–291. Reprinted by permission of Oxford University Press.

St. Louis IX of France (1226–1270) was so deeply and widely respected for his sense of justice and Christian obligation that he was called upon to arbitrate the dispute between Henry III of England and his dissident barons. Louis and Henry were brothers-in-law, married to two noble sisters from Provence (southern France). The "aliens" referred to in this document were countrymen of Henry's queen who had followed her to England and sifted into positions of power and influence. St. Louis' settlement was motivated less by his in-law relationship than by his concept of the traditional prerogatives of the French monarchy and his resulting insensitivity to English notions of joint royal-baronial governance. Henry's baronial opponents rejected the Mise of Amiens and led the kingdom into civil war.

[Clauses 1–7 deal largely with protocol.]

8. Moreover the king of England on the one side, and the barons on the other side have agreed to accept our [Louis IX] arbitration in all disputes which have arisen by occasion of these issues between them since the feast of All Saints' [1 November], down to the day of St. Lucy [13 December] recently past, and have promised on oaths, sworn touching the holy gospels, that they will observe in good faith whatever we ordain or decree upon the above matter or on any of them, provided we shall declare before Whitsuntide [8 June] next our award on these matters and upon all others which may happen meanwhile to have been attempted, arising out of the matters submitted to our award or in connection with them.

9. Accordingly we, for this purpose, summoned the parties to Amiens, and the king appeared before us in person, and certain of the barons appeared personally and others by proctors; and we heard the proposals of both sides and fully understood the replies and counter-arguments of the parties. We concluded that through the provisions, ordinances, statutes, and obligations of Oxford and through those issues which had arisen from them or had followed in consequence of them, the rights and honour of the king had been greatly harmed, the realm disturbed, churches oppressed and plundered, and that very heavy losses had befallen other persons of the realm, both ecclesiastical and secular, native and alien, and that there was good reason to fear that still worse would follow in the future; and we received the counsel of good and great men.

10. In the name of the Father, and of the Son, and of the Holy Spirit, by our award or ordinance we quash and invalidate all these provisions, ordinances, and obligations, or whatever else they may be called, and whatever has arisen from them or has been occasioned by them; especially since it is apparent that the pope, by his letters, has already declared them quashed and invalid; and we decree that both the king and the barons, with all others who agreed to the present compromise, and who in any way had bound

themselves to oberve them, shall now entirely acquit and absolve themselves from them.

11. And we also add that no one shall make new statutes in virtue of these provisions, obligations, or ordinances, or in virtue of any power hitherto granted by the king in consequence of them; nor shall anyone hold or observe any enactments hitherto made by virtue of them, nor by reason of the non-observance of them ought anyone to be held the mortal enemy, or any other kind of enemy, of anyone, nor suffer any penalty therefore.

12. We also decree that all documents made concerning or by occasion of the provisions are invalid and of no effect, and we command that they shall be restored by the barons to the king of England, and handed back to him.

13. In particular, we declare and ordain that whatever castles were handed over to be kept as security, or by reason of the provisions and are still held back, shall be freely restored by the barons to the king, to be held by the king as he held them before the time of the provisions.

14. Next, we declare and ordain that the king shall freely be allowed to appoint, institute, dismiss, and remove at his own free will the chief justiciar, the chancellor, the treasurer, the councillors, the lesser justices, sheriffs, and all other officials and servants of his realm and of his household, as he did and had the power to do before the time of the provisions.

15. Further, we reject and quash the statute made declaring that the realm of England should in future be governed by native-born men, and that aliens must depart, never to return, save those whose stay the faithful men of the realm might in common accept.

16. And we decree by our award that aliens shall be allowed to stay in the realm securely, and that the king can safely call to his counsel both aliens and natives whom he may think useful and faithful to him, as he had power to do before this time.

17. Further, we decree and ordain that the said king shall have full power and free authority in his kingdom and in all that pertains to it, and shall be in that same state and fullness of power, in and for all things, that he enjoyed before this time.

18. But we do not wish or intend, by the present ordinance, to derogate in any way from the royal privileges, charters, liberties, statutes and laudable customs of the realm of England which were in force before the time of the provisions.

19. We decree that the lord king shall fully pardon the barons, and shall renounce all rancour which he may have against them by reason of these disputes, and that the barons shall do likewise to him, and that in future neither shall harm nor offend the other, either by himself or through another, in any matter which was submitted to our arbitration.

20. We have declared this our ordinance or award at Amiens on the morrow of St. Vincent the Martyr [23 January], in the month of January in the year 1263.[1] In testimony of this we have had our seal affixed to these present letters. Done in the year, month, day and place aforesaid.

Reading 10

Louis IX Receives Certain Relics

Matthew Paris, a monk of St. Albans Abbey, was born around 1200 and died in or shortly after 1259. He was an Englishman who, despite his name, was probably neither born nor educated in Paris. He was thus a contemporary but not a countryman of St. Louis. Nevertheless, he was in a position to be well informed about the affairs of Western Christendom: St. Albans was a much visited abbey, a day's journey from London on the main road to the north. Matthew was personally acquainted with Henry III, his queen Eleanor of Provence, and important barons, bishops, and royal officials.

The passage below illustrates the importance of relics and religious ceremonial in intensifying the sense of holiness associated with the French monarchy. The relics described here were among the most significant in Christendom. Whether the cross in question was actually the "True Cross" remains a matter of debate, but it did have a verifiable pedigree running back to the fourth century. St. Louis took relics very seriously and was not easily fooled. His "beautiful chapel at Paris" described toward the end of the passage is known as La Sainte-Chapelle and remains to this day one of the architectural marvels of Europe.

In this year, [1241] the holy cross of our Lord, which, after the time of Saladin, had remained at Damietta until the unfortunate battle, in which that city had been first gained and afterwards lost, when it fell into the hands of the Saracens, was brought into the kingdom of France, by the agency of the French king and his mother, Blanche, and by the grace of Christ seconding their pious wishes: they gave a large sum of money in order to obtain posses-

From Matthew Paris, *History of the English*, tr. J.A. Giles; vol. 1, London, Henry G. Bohn, 1852.

[1]It was common practice in the Middle Ages to date the beginning of the year to Easter. Historians therefore adjust events occurring between January 1 and Easter to the following year; hence, January 23, 1264.

sion of the same. When this cross was first sold, it was bought by the Venetians for twenty thousand pounds, and they obtained it from the two sons of J., king of Jerusalem, who wanted money to make war on the Greeks; and afterwards Baldwin pawned it for a still larger sum of money, and lastly sold it to Louis, the French king.

On the Friday next preceding Easter-day, on which day our Lord Jesus Christ was nailed to the life-giving-cross for the redemption of the world, this said cross was carried to Paris from the church of St. Antoine, where it had been placed on a vehicle of some kind, on which the king mounted with the two queens, namely, Blanche of Castile, his mother, and Margaret of Provence, his wife, and his brothers, and in the presence of the archbishops, bishops, abbots, and other religious men, as well as the French nobles, and surrounded by a countless host of people, who were awaiting this glorious sight with great joy of heart, raised the cross above his head with tears, whilst the prelates who were present cried with a loud voice, "Behold the cross of our Lord." After all had worshipped it with due reverence and devotion, the king himself, barefooted, ungirt, and with his head bare, and after a fast of three days, following the example of the noble triumpher, the august Heraclius, carried it in wool to the cathedral church of Notre Dame at Paris; the brothers of the king, too, after having purified themselves by similar acts of devotion, by confessions, fasting, and prayers, followed him on foot with the two queens.

They also carried the crown of thorns (which divine mercy had, as has been before stated, given to the kingdom of France the year before), and raising it on high on a similar vehicle to the other, presented it to the gaze of the people. Some of the nobles supported the arms of the king and his brothers, whilst carrying this pious burden, lest they should become fatigued by holding their hands constantly raised, and give way beneath this priceless treasure. This was done circumspectly at the wish of the prelates, that so holy a thing might be handled reverently by those whose prudent conduct had gained so much glory, after the example of Heraclius, whom we have before mentioned. When they arrived at the cathedral church, all the bells in the city were set ringing, and after special prayers had been solemnly read, the king returned to his great palace, which is in the middle of the city, carrying his cross, his brothers carrying the crown, and the priests following in a regular procession (a sight more solemn or more joyful than which the kingdom of France had never seen), and each and all then, with clasped hands, glorified God, who thus showed his especial love for the French kingdom above all others, and for affording to it his consolation and protection.

Thus, therefore, our Lord Jesus Christ, the King of kings, the Lord of lords, who judgments are a great deep, in whose hands are the hearts of kings, giving health to whomsoever he wills, in a short space of time endowed and enriched the kingdom of France with these three precious gifts, namely, the aforesaid crown and cross of our Lord, of which we have now made mention, and the body of the blessed Edmund of Canterbury, the archbishop and confessor, which was now manifestly shining forth with unusual miracles. The French king therefore ordered a chapel of handsome structure, suitable for the reception of his said treasure, to be built near his palace, and in it he afterwards placed the said relics with due honour. Besides these the French king had, in his beautiful chapel at Paris, the garment belonging to Christ, the lance, that is to say, the iron head of the lance, and the sponge, and other relics besides; on which account the pope granted an indulgence of forty days to all who went to them in the chapel at Paris for the sake of paying their devotions.

Reading 11

Philip IV's Destruction of the Knights Templars

Giovanni Villani was born in Florence around 1275 and died in 1348, a victim of the Black Death. Unlike most of the chroniclers in our sourcebook, Villani was a layman and a townsman, and his accounts of the political events of his time are shrewdly realistic. But the distinction between monk-historians and burgher-historians should not be overstressed: monks such as Matthew Paris were intimately acquainted with affairs of the world, and townsmen like Villani could comfortably ascribe historical events to divine providence. Villani had traveled widely—through Italy, France, and The Netherlands— before settling down as a Florentine civic official. He knew France well and was a younger contemporary of Philip IV, "the Fair."

Some modern specialists have argued that Philip IV actually did believe the false charges against the Knights Templars and that his motives were at once financial and religious. Whatever the case, the Templars were a tempting prey to a financially strapped monarchy. Having originated in the twelfth century as an austere crusading order, the Templars had gradually grown wealthy through their involvement in international banking. Both Philip IV and his English contemporary Edward I were in desperate need of money to conduct their wars. They enriched their treasuries by persecuting and expelling both the Templars and the Jews from their respective realms.

In the year 1307, before the king of France (Philip IV) departed from the court at Poitiers, he accused and denounced the master and the Order of the

From *Villani's Chronicle*, tr. Rose E. Selfe, ed. Philip H. Wicksteed; London, Archibald Constable & Co., Ltd., 1906, pp. 377–381. Revised by David S. Spear.

Temple to the Pope. Incited thereto by his officers and by desire of gain, he charged them with certain crimes and errors of which he had been informed the Templars were guilty. The first accusation came from a prior of the said Order, of Monfaucon in the region of Toulouse, a man of evil life and a heretic who, for all his faults was condemned to perpetual imprisonment in Paris by the grand master. Finding himself in prison with one Noffo Dei, of our city of Florence, a man full of all vices, these two men wickedly and maliciously invented the said false charge in hope of gain and of being set free from prison by aid from the king. But not long afterwards each of them came to a bad end, since Noffo was hanged and the prior stabbed. Hoping thus to move the king to seek his gain, they brought the accusation before his officers. The officers in turn brought it before the king who, moved by avarice, made secret arrangements with the Pope, causing him to promise to destroy the Order of the Templars by charging them with many articles of heresy. But it is said that it was more in hope of extracting great sums of money from them, and by reason of offence taken against the master of the Temple and the Order, that the king acted as he did. And the Pope, in order to rid himself of the king of France (already acting in this way when he agreed to condemn Pope Boniface) promised that he would do this.

Therefore, when the king had departed, on the day named in his letters, he caused all the Templars to be seized throughout the whole world, and all their churches and mansions and possessions, which were almost innumerable in power and riches, to be sequestered. All those in the realm of France the king caused to be occupied by his court, and at Paris Jacques de Molay the master of the Temple was taken, along with sixty knights, friars, and gentlemen. They were charged with certain articles of heresy, and certain vile sins against nature which they were said to practice among themselves, and that at their profession they swore to support the Order right or wrong, and that their worship was idolatrous, and that they spat upon the cross, and that when their master was consecrated it was secretly and in private, and that their predecessors had caused the Holy Land to be lost by treachery, and King Louis [IX: St. Louis] and his followers to be taken at Monsura.

When sundry proofs had been given by the king of the truth of these charges, he had them punished by diverse tortures that they might confess, but it was found that they would not confess nor acknowledge anything. After keeping them a long time in prison in great misery, and not knowing how to put an end to their trial, fifty-six of the said Templars were at last brought to a great wooded part at Saint Antoine outside Paris (and also at Senlis). There each one was bound to a stake and fires set little by little to their feet and legs, all the while admonished that if any of them would acknowledge their errors and sins they would be set free. During the martyrdom, in spite of exhortations by their kinsfolk and friends to confess and not to allow themselves to be thus vilely slain, not a single one of them confessed. Instead, with weeping and cries they defended themselves as being innocent and faithful Christians, calling upon Christ and Saint Mary and the other saints. But by the said martyrdom— all of them burning to ashes—they ended their lives.

The master along with the brother of the dauphin of Auvergne, Brother Hugh of Peraud, and another of the leaders of the Order, who had been officers and treasurers of the king of France, were all brought to Poitiers before the Pope (with the king of France also present), where they were promised forgiveness if they would acknowledge their error and sin. It is said that they confessed something to that effect. When, however, they returned to Paris, two cardinal legates arrived to give sentence and condemn the Order upon said confession, and to impose some discipline upon the said master and his companions. After the legates had mounted the great scaffold, opposite the church of Notre Dame, and had read the indictment, the said master of the Temple rose to his feet demanding to be heard. When silence was proclaimed, he denied that such heresies and sins as they had been charged with were ever true, and maintained that the rule of their Order had been holy and just and catholic, but that he was certainly worthy of death and would endure it in peace, for it was through fear of torture and by the persuasions of the Pope and the king that he had deceitfully been persuaded to confess. With the discourse thus broken off, and the sentence not fully delivered, the cardinals and the other prelates departed from that place. And having held counsel with the king, the said master and his companions were made martyrs in the Isle de Paris before the hall of the king in the same manner as the rest of their brethren. The master, even while slowly burning to death, continually repeated that the Order and their religion were catholic and righteous, and commended himself to God and Saint Mary; and likewise did the brother of the dauphin. Brother Hugh of Peraud and the other, through fear of martyrdom, confessed and confirmed that which they had said before the Pope and the king. Thus they escaped, although afterwards they died miserably.

Athough it was said by many that they were slain and destroyed wrongly and wickedly, their property was nevertheless seized. It was later granted in privilege by the Pope to the Order of the Hospitallers, but they were required to recover and redeem it from the king of France and the other princes and lords for so great a sum (to say nothing of the interest to be paid), that the Order of the Hospitallers was, and is now, poorer in its property than it was before. Perhaps, then, God brought this miraculously about in order to show how things were. Afterwards the king of France and his sons had much shame and adversity, both because of this sin and of the capture of Pope Boniface, as hereafter shall be related. And note that the night after the said master and his companion were martyred, their ashes and bones were collected as sacred relics by friars and other religious persons, and carried away to holy places. In this manner was destroyed and brought to nought the rich and powerful Order of the Temple at Jerusalem, in the year of Christ 1310.

CHAPTER 7

The Culture of Christendom

High-medieval Western Europe produced an immense variety of poetry, prose fiction, and treatises on the liberal arts, technology, law, medicine, political thought, and philosphy. We have chosen to focus this chapter on the major philosophers of the period rather than to serve up a smorgasbord of literary forms. You will find examples of high-medieval poetry and fiction in Chapter 14 of Hollister's *Medieval Europe: A Short History*.

St. Anselm (d. 1109), the first important speculative philosopher of the period, was a monk of deep piety, penetrating intellect, and political acumen whose "ontological proof" of God (document 1), although rejected by some high-medieval theologians, is debated in the pages of philosophy journals to this day. Our excerpts from the writings of Peter Abelard (d. 1142) exemplify the twelfth-century intellectual shift from monasteries to urban schools. Abelard's autobiography (document 2) bears witness to the increased self-awareness that marked twelfth-century culture, and his *Ethics* (document 3) carries this new self-awareness to the point of distinguishing sharply between an act and the intention behind it. Abelard's psychologically sophisticated emphasis on intent, or motive, was reflected in the codes and customs of high-medieval law.

The work of the Franciscan Roger Bacon (d. 1292) shows the growing interest among some medieval thinkers in mathematical and experimental science (document 4). Conversely, the two passages from the great Dominican philosopher St. Thomas Aquinas (d. 1274) illustrate his characteristic confidence in the power of the human intellect, the intelligibility of the cosmos, and the compatibility of faith and reason (documents 5 and 6).

Reading 1

St. Anselm's Proslogion

A native of northwestern Italy, St. Anselm (d. 1109) migrated to Normandy to become a monk, and later abbot, of the monastery of Bec. In 1093 he became archbishop of Canterbury and was twice exiled as a result of conflicts with the Anglo-Norman monarchy over ecclesiastical liberties.

Anselm was a devotee of St. Augustine (d. 430), who was himself influenced by Plato's doctrine of the superiority of meditation to observation. Notice that Anselm's ontological argument is more nearly a meditation than a formal proof, and that it depends on pure reason rather than on the workings of the physical world. One must bear in mind that Anselm is addressing monks rather than students or skeptics. He is writing to believers, with the aim of helping them to understand more fully the faith to which they have already committed their lives.

After I had published, at the solicitous entreaties of certain brethren, a brief work (the *Monologium*) as an example of meditation on the grounds of faith, in the person of one who investigates, in a course of silent reasoning with himself, matters of which he is ignorant; considering that this book was knit together by the linking of many arguments, I began to ask myself whether there might be found a single argument which would require no other for its proof than itself alone; and alone would suffice to demonstrate that God truly exists, and that there is a supreme good requiring nothing else, which all other things require for their existence and well-being; and whatever we believe regarding the divine Being.

Although I often and earnestly directed my thought to this end, and at some times that which I sought seemed to be just within my reach, while again it wholly evaded my mental vision, at last in despair I was about to cease, as if from the search for a thing which could not be found. But when I wished to exclude this thought altogether, lest, by busying my mind to no purpose, it should keep me from other thoughts, in which I might be successful; then more and more, though I was unwilling and shunned it, it began to force itself upon me, with a kind of importunity. So, one day, when I was exceedingly wearied with resisting its importunity, in the very conflict of my thoughts, the proof of which I had despaired offered itself, so that I eagerly embraced the thoughts which I was strenuously repelling.

Thinking, therefore, that what I rejoiced to have found, would, if put in writing, be welcome to some readers, of this very matter, and of some others, I

From *The Basic Writings of St. Anselm*, tr. S.N. Deane; La Salle, Ill., The Open Court Publishing Co., 1903, pp. 1–11.

have written the following treatise, in the person of one who strives to lift his mind to the contemplation of God, and seeks to understand what he believes. In my judgment, neither this work nor the other, which I mentioned above, deserved to be called a book, or to bear the name of an author; and yet I thought they ought not to be sent forth without some title by which they might, in some sort, invite one into whose hands they fell to their perusal. I accordingly gave each a title, that the first might be known as, An Example of Meditation on the Grounds of Faith, and its sequel as, Faith Seeking Understanding.

Be it mine to look up to thy light, even from afar, even from the depths. Teach me to seek thee, and reveal thyself to me when I seek thee, for I cannot seek thee, except thou teach me, nor find thee, except thou reveal thyself. Let me seek thee in longing, let me long for thee in seeking; let me find thee in love, and love thee in finding. Lord, I acknowledge and I thank thee that thou hast created me in this thine image, in order that I may be mindful of thee, may conceive of thee, and love thee; but that image has been so consumed and wasted away by vices, and obscured by the smoke of wrong-doing, that it cannot achieve that for which it was made, except thou renew it, and create it anew. I do not endeavor, O Lord, to penetrate thy sublimity, for in no wise do I compare my understanding with that; but I long to understand in some degree thy truth, which my heart believes and loves. For I do not seek to understand that I may believe, but I believe in order to understand. For this also I believe,—that unless I believed, I should not understand.

And so, Lord, do thou, who dost give understanding to faith, give me, so far as thou knowest it to be profitable, to understand that thou art as we believe; and that thou art that which we believe. And, indeed, we believe that thou art a being than which nothing greater can be conceived. Or is there no such nature, since the fool hath said in his heart, there is no God? (Psalms xiv. I). But, at any rate, this very fool, when he hears of this being of which I speak—a being than which nothing greater can be conceived—understands what he hears, and what he understands is in his understanding; although he does not understand it to exist.

For, it is one thing for an object to be in the understanding, and another to understand that the object exists. When a painter first conceives of what he will afterwards perform, he has it in his understanding, but he does not yet understand it to be, because he has not yet performed it. But after he has made the painting, he both has it in his understanding, and he understands that it exists, because he has made it.

Hence, even the fool is convinced that something exists in the understanding, at least, than which nothing greater can be conceived. For, when he hears of this, he understands it. And whatever is understood, exists in the understanding. And assuredly that, than which nothing greater can be conceived, cannot exist in the understanding alone. For, suppose it exists in the understanding alone: then it can be conceived to exist in reality; which is greater.

Therefore, if that, than which nothing greater can be conceived, exists in the understanding alone, the very being, than which nothing greater can be conceived, is one, than which a greater can be conceived. But obviously this is impossible. Hence, there is no doubt that there exists a being, than which nothing greater can be conceived, and it exists both in the understanding and in reality.

And it assuredly exists so truly, that it cannot be conceived not to exist. For, it is possible to conceive of a being which cannot be conceived not to exist; and this is greater than one which can be conceived not to exist. Hence, if that, than which nothing greater can be conceived, can be conceived not to exist, it is not that, than which nothing greater can be conceived. But this is an irreconcilable contradiction. There is, then, so truly a being than which nothing greater can be conceived to exist, that it cannot even be conceived not to exist; and this being thou art, O Lord, our God.

So truly, therefore, dost thou exist, O Lord, my God, that thou canst not be conceived not to exist; and rightly. For, if a mind could conceive of a being better than thee, the creature would rise above the Creator; and this is most absurd. And, indeed, whatever else there is, except thee alone, can be conceived not to exist. To thee alone, therefore, it belongs to exist more truly than all other beings, and hence in a higher degree than all others. For, whatever else exists does not exist so truly, and hence in a less degree it belongs to it to exist. Why, then, has the fool said in his heart, there is no God (Psalms xiv. I), since it is so evident, to a rational mind, that thou dost exist in the highest degree of all? Why, except that he is dull and a fool?

But how has the fool said in his heart what he could not conceive; or how is it that he could not conceive what he said in his heart—since it is the same to say in the heart, and to conceive?

But, if really, nay, since really, he both conceived, because he said in his heart; and did not say in his heart, because he could not conceive; there is more than one way in which a thing is said in the heart or conceived. For, in one sense, an object is conceived, when the word signifying it is conceived; and in another when the very entity, which the object is, is understood.

In the former sense, then, God can be conceived not to exist; but in the latter, not at all. For no one who understands what fire and water are can conceive fire to be water, in accordance with the nature of the facts themselves, although this is possible according to the words. So, then, no one who understands what God is can conceive that God does not exist; although he says these words in his heart, either without any or with some foreign, signification. For, God is that than which a greater cannot be conceived. And he who thoroughly understands this, assuredly understands that this being so truly exists, that not even in concept can it be non-existent. Therefore, he who understands that God so exists, cannot conceive that he does not exist.

I thank thee, gracious Lord, I thank thee; because what I formerly believed by thy bounty, I now so understand by thine illumination, that if I were unwilling to believe that thou dost exist, I should not be able not to understand this to be true.

What art thou, then, Lord God, than whom nothing greater can be conceived? But what art thou, except that which, as the highest of all beings, alone exists through itself, and creates all other things from nothing? For, whatever is not this is less than a thing which can be conceived of. But this cannot be conceived of thee. What good, therefore, does the supreme Good lack, through which every good is? Therefore, thou art just, truthful, blessed, and whatever it is better to be than not to be. For it is better to be just than not just; better to be blessed than not blessed.

Reading 2
Peter Abelard, The History of My Misfortunes

The excerpts below deal with Abelard's celebrated love affair with Heloise. They also disclose, in rich detail, his life at the Paris schools and the rough-and-tumble world of shotgun weddings in the twelfth century.

And so, after a few days, I returned to Paris, and there for several years I peacefully directed the school which formerly had been destined for me, nay, even offered to me, but from which I had been driven out. At the very outset of my work there, I set about completing the glosses on Ezekiel which I had begun at Laon. These proved so satisfactory to all who read them that they came to believe me no less adept in lecturing on theology than I had proved

From *Historia Calamitatum, The Story of My Misfortunes. An Autobiography of Peter Abelard*, tr. Henry A. Bellows; St. Paul, Minn., Thomas A. Boyd, 1922, pp. 14–22, 29–30. Reprinted by permission of Macmillan Publishing Co., Inc.

myself to be in the field of philosophy. Thus my school was notably increased in size by reason of my lectures on subjects of both these kinds, and the amount of financial profit as well as glory which it brought me cannot be concealed from you, for the matter was widely talked of. But prosperity always puffs up the foolish, and worldly comfort enervates the soul, rendering it an easy prey to carnal temptations. Thus I, who by this time had come to regard myself as the only philosopher remaining in the whole world, and had ceased to fear any further disturbance of my peace, began to loosen the rein on my desires, although hitherto I had always lived in the utmost continence. And the greater progress I made in my lecturing on philosophy or theology, the more I departed alike from the practice of the philosophers and the spirit of the divines in the uncleanness of my life. For it is well known, I think, that philosophers, and still more those who have devoted their lives to arousing the love of sacred study, have been strong above all else in the beauty of chastity.

Thus did it come to pass that while I was utterly absorbed in pride and sensuality, divine grace, the cure for both diseases, was forced upon me, even though I would have preferred to shun it. First was I punished for my sensuality, and then for my pride. For my sensuality I lost those things whereby I practiced it; for my pride, engendered in me by my knowledge of letters—and it is even as the Apostle said: "Knowledge puffeth itself up" (1 Cor. viii, 1)—I knew the humiliation of seeing burned the very book in which I most gloried.

Now there dwelt in that same city of Paris a certain young girl named Heloise, the niece of a canon who was called Fulbert. Her uncle's love for her was equalled only by his desire that she should have the best education which he could possibly procure for her. Of no mean beauty, she stood out above all by reason of her abundant knowledge of letters. Now this virtue is rare among women, and for that very reason it doubly graced the maiden, and made her the most worthy of renown in the entire kingdom. It was this young girl whom I, after carefully considering all those qualities which are apt to attract lovers, determined to unite with myself in the bonds of love, and indeed the thing seemed to me very easily done. So distinguished was my name, and I possessed such advantages of youth and comeliness, that no matter what woman I might favour with my love, I dreaded rejection of none. Then, too, I believed that I could win the maiden's consent all the more easily by reason of her knowledge of letters and her zeal therefor; so, even if we were parted, we might yet be together in thought with the aid of written messages. Perhaps, too, we might be able to write more boldy than we could speak, and thus at all times could we live in joyous intimacy.

Thus, utterly aflame with my passion for this maiden, I sought to discover means whereby I might have daily and familiar speech with her, thereby the more easily to win her consent. For this purpose I persuaded the girl's uncle, with the aid of some of his friends, to take me into his household—for he dwelt near my school—in return for the payment of a small sum. In all this the man's simplicity was nothing short of astounding to me; I should not have been more struck with wonder if he had entrusted a tender lamb to the care of a ravenous wolf. When he had thus given her into my charge, not only to be taught but even to be disciplined, what had he done but to give free scope to my desires, and to offer me every opportunity, even if I had not sought it, to bend her to my will with threats and blows if I failed to do so with caresses? There were, however, two things which particularly served to allay any foul suspicion: his own love for his niece, and my former reputation for continence.

Why should I say more? We were united first in the dwelling that sheltered our love, and then in the hearts that burned with it. Under the pretext of study we spent our hours in the happiness of love, and learning held out to us the secret opportunities that our passion craved. Our speech was more of love than of the books which lay open before us; our kisses far outnumbered our reasoned words. Our hands sought less the book than each other's bosoms; love drew our eyes together far more than the lesson drew them to the pages of our text. In order that there might be no suspicion, there were, indeed, sometimes blows, but love gave them, not anger; they were the marks, not of wrath, but of a tenderness surpassing the most fragrant balm in sweetness. What followed? No degree in love's progress was left untried by our passion, and if love itself could imagine any wonder as yet unknown, we discovered it. And our inexperience of such delights made us all the more ardent in our pursuit of them, so that our thirst for one another was still unquenched.

In measure as this passionate rapture absorbed me more and more, I devoted ever less time to philosophy and to the work of the school. Indeed it became loathsome to me to go to the school or to linger there; the labour, moreover, was very burdensome, since my nights were vigils of love and my days of study. My lecturing became utterly careless and lukewarm; I did nothing because of inspiration, but everything merely as a matter of habit. I had become nothing more than a reciter of my former discoveries, and though I still wrote poems, they dealt with love, not with the secrets of philosphy. Of these songs you yourself well know how some have become widely known and have been sung in many lands, chiefly, I think, by those who delighted in the things of this world. As for the sorrow, the groans, the lamentations of my students when they perceived the preoccupation, nay, rather the chaos, of my mind, it is hard even to imagine them.

It was not long after this that Heloise found that she was pregnant, and of this she wrote to me in the utmost exultation, at the same time asking me to consider what had best be done. Accordingly, on a night when her uncle was absent, we carried out the plan we had determined on, and I stole her secretly away from her uncle's house, sending her without delay to my own country.[1] She remained there with my sister until she gave birth to a son, whom she named Astrolabe. Meanwhile her uncle, after his return, was almost mad with grief; only one who had then seen him could rightly guess the burning agony of his sorrow and the bitterness of his shame. And in order to make amends even beyond his extremest hope, I offered to marry her whom I had seduced, provided only the thing could be kept secret, so that I might suffer no loss of reputation thereby. To this he gladly assented, pledging his own faith and that of his kindred, and sealing with kisses the pact which I had sought of him— and all this that he might the more easily betray me. . . .

After our little son was born, we left him in my sister's care, and secretly returned to Paris. A few days later, in the early morning, having kept our nocturnal vigil of prayer unknown to all in a certain church, we were united there in the benediction of wedlock, her uncle and a few friends of his and mine being present. We departed forthwith stealthily and by separate ways, nor thereafter did we see each other except rarely and in private, thus striving our utmost to conceal what we had done. But her uncle and those of his household, seeking solace for their disgrace, began to divulge the story of our marriage, and thereby to violate the pledge they had given me on this point. Heloise, on the contrary, denounced her own kin and swore that they were speaking the most absolute lies. Her uncle, aroused to fury by this, punished her repeatedly. No sooner had I learned this than I sent her to a convent of nuns at Argenteuil, not far from Paris, where she herself had been brought up and educated as a young girl. I had them make ready for her all the garments of a nun, suitable for the life of a convent, excepting only the veil, and these I bade her put on.

When her uncle and his kinsmen heard of this, they were convinced that now I had completely played them false and had rid myself forever of Heloise by forcing her to become a nun. Violently incensed, they laid a plot against me, and one night, while I, unsuspecting, was asleep in a secret room in my lodgings, they broke in with the help of one of my servants, whom they had bribed. There they had vengeance on me with a most cruel and most shameful punishment, such as astounded the whole world, for they cut off those parts of my body with which I had done that which was the cause of their sorrow. This done, straightway they fled, but two of them were captured, and suffered the loss of their eyes and their genital organs. One of these two was the aforesaid servant, who, even while he was still in my service, had been led by his avarice to betray me.

---

[1] Abelard came from Brittany in western France.

Reading 3
Peter Abelard, Ethics

The actual title of this work is *Know Thyself*. It is a discourse on the nature of vice and, for its time, a highly original inquiry into the relationship of act and intent in human behavior. Abelard's emphasis on intent was so extreme as to render his ethical criteria impractical to those who could not read minds. His successors, drawing back from his radical subjectivity, achieved a more even balance between deed and motive.

There are four things which we have put forward in order carefully to distinguish them from each other, namely the vice of the mind which makes us prone to sinning and then the sin itself which we fixed in consent to evil or contempt of God, next the will for evil and the doing of evil. Just as, indeed, to will and to fulfil the will are not the same, so to sin and to perform the sin are not the same. We should understand the former to relate to the consent of the mind by which we sin, the latter to the performance of the action when we fulfil in a deed what we have previously consented to. When we say that sin or temptation occurs in three ways, namely in suggestion, pleasure, and consent, it should be understood in this sense, that we are often led through these three to the doing of sin. This was the case with our first parents. Persuasion by the devil came first, when he promised immortality for tasting the forbidden tree. Pleasure followed, when the woman, seeing the beautiful fruit and understanding it to be sweet to eat, was seized with what she believed would be the pleasure of the food and kindled a longing for it. Since she ought to have checked her longing in order to keep the command, in consenting she was drawn into sin. And although she ought to have corrected the sin through repentance in order to deserve pardon, she finally completed it in deed. And so she proceeded to carry through the sin in three stages. Likewise we also frequently arrive by these same steps not at sinning but at the carrying through of sin, namely by suggestion, that is, by the encouragement of someone who incites us externally to do something which is not fitting. And if we know that doing this is pleasurable, even before the deed our mind is seized with the pleasure of the deed itself and in the very thought we are tempted through pleasure. When in fact we assent to this pleasure through consent, we sin. By these three we come at last to the execution of the sin.

There are those who would like carnal suggestion to be included in the term suggestion, even if there is no person making a suggestion—for instance, if someone on seeing a woman falls into lust for her. But this suggestion, it seems, should really be called nothing other than pleasure. Indeed this pleasure, which has become almost necessary, and others of its kind which, we observed above, are not sin, are called by the Apostle human temptation when he says: "Let no temptation take hold on you, but such as is human. And God is faithful, who will not suffer you to be tempted above that which you are able; but will also make issue with temptation, that you may be able to bear it." Now, temptation is generally said to be any inclination of the mind, whether a will or consent, to do something which is not fitting. But human temptation, such as carnal concupiscence or the desire for delicious food, is said to be that without which human infirmity can now scarcely or can never survive. He asked to be set free from these who said: "Deliver me from my necesssities, O Lord," that is, from these lustful temptations which have now become almost natural and necessary, lest they lead to consent; alternatively, let me really be free of them at the end of this life full of temptations. So, what the Apostle says, "Let no temptation take hold on you, but such as is human," is as an opinion very like saying: "If the mind is inclined by pleasure which is, as we have said, human temptation, let it not lead as far as consent, in which sin consists." He says, as if someone were asking by what virtue of ours we can resist those lusts: "God is faithful who will not suffer you to be tempted," that is as if to say: "Rather than rely on ourselves we should trust in him who, promising help for us, is true in all his promises," that is, he is faithful, so in everything faith should clearly be put in him. Then indeed he does not allow us to be tempted above that which we are able, since he moderates his human temptation with his mercy, so that it does not press us into sin by more than we are able to bear in resisting it. However, he then in addition turns this very temptation to our advantage when he trains us by it, so that eventually when it occurs it can bother us less and so that we should now have less fear of the attack of an enemy over whom we have already triumphed and whom we know how to manage. Every struggle which we have not hither-to experienced is borne more severely and is dreaded more. But when it comes regularly to the victorious, its power and its dread alike vanish.

Of the Suggestions of Demons

Suggestions are made not only by men but also by demons, because they too sometimes incite us to sin, less by words than by deeds. By their subtle talent as much as by their long experience they are certainly experts in the nature of things and for this are called demons, that is, knowledgeable; they know the natural powers of things by which human weakness may easily be stirred to lust or to other impulses. Sometimes by God's leave they send some into languor and then provide the remedies for those who beseech them, and when they cease to afflict they are often thought to cure. In Egypt they were in the end allowed through the magicians to do many things marvellously against Moses, in reality by the natural power of things which they knew. They should not be called creators of what they have made so much as compositors; for instance, if anyone, following the example in Virgil, having pounded the flesh of a bull should by his labour bring about from this the making of bees, he should be called not so much a creator of bees as a preparer of nature. And so, by this expertise which they have with the natures of things, demons provoke us to lust or to other passions of the mind, bringing them by every possible stratagem while we are unawares, whether setting them in taste or in bed or placing them by no matter what means inside or outside us. There are certainly many forces in herbs or seeds or in the natures of trees as much as of stones which are suitable for provoking or soothing our minds; those who carefully learn to know them can easily do this.

That a Work is Good by Reason of a Good Intention

We say that an intention is good, that is, right in itself, but that an action does not bear anything good in itself but proceeds from a good intention. Whence when the same thing is done by the same man at different times, by the diversity of his intention, however, his action is now said to be good, now bad, and so it seems to fluctuate around the good and the bad, just as this proposition "Socrates is seated" or the idea of it fluctuates around the true and the false, Socrates being at one time seated, at another standing. Aristotle says that the way in which this change in fluctuating around the true and the false happens here is not that what changes between being true and being false undergoes anything by this change, but that the subject, that is Socrates, himself moves from sitting to standing or vice versa.

Whence an Intention Should be Said to be Good

There are those who think that an intention is good or right whenever someone believes he is acting well and that what he does is pleasing to God, like the persecutors of the martyrs mentioned by Truth in the Gospel: "The hour cometh that whosoever killeth you will think that he doth a service to God." The Apostle had compassion for the ignorance of such as these when he said: "I bear them witness that they have a zeal for God, but not according to knowledge," that is, they have great fervour and desire in doing what they believe to be pleasing to God. But because they are led astray in this by the zeal or the eagerness of their minds, their intention is in error and the eye of their heart is not simple, so it cannot see clearly, that is, guard itself against error. And so the Lord, in distinguishing works according to right or wrong intention, carefully called the mind's eye, that is, the intention, sound and, as it were, free of dirt so that it can see clearly; or, conversely, dark when he said: "If thy eye be sound thy whole body shall be full of light," that is, if the intention was right, the whole mass of works coming from it, which like physical things can be seen, will be worthy of the light, that is, good; conversely also. And so an intention should not be called good because it seems to be good but because in addition it is just as it is thought to be, that is, when, believing that one's objective is pleasing to God, one is in no way deceived in one's own estimation. Otherwise even the unbelievers themselves would have good works just like ourselves, since they too, no less than we, believe they will be saved or will please God through their works.

That There is no Sin Unless it is Against Conscience

However, if one asks whether those persecutors of the martyrs or of Christ sinned in what they believed to be pleasing to God, or whether they could without sin have forsaken what they thought should definitely not be forsaken, assuredly, according to our earlier description of sin as contempt of God or consenting to what one believes should not be consented to, we cannot say that they have sinned in this, nor is anyone's ignorance a sin or even the unbelief with which no one can be saved. For those who do not know Christ and therefore reject the Christian faith because they believe it to be contrary to God, what contempt of God have they in what they do for God's sake and therefore think they do well— especially since the Apostle says: "If our heart do not reprehend us, we have confidence towards God"? As if to say: where we do not presume against our conscience our fear of being judged guilty of fault before God is groundless; alternatively, if the ignorance of such men is not to be imputed to sin at all, how does the Lord pray for his crucifiers, saying: "Father, forgive them, for they know not what they do," or Stephen, taught by this example, say in prayer for those stoning him: "Lord, lay not this sin to their charge"? For there seems no need to pardon where there was no prior fault; nor is pardon usually said to be anything other than the remission of a punishment earned by a fault. Moreover, Stephen manifestly calls sin that which came from ignorance.

Reading 4

Roger Bacon on Experimental Science

The Oxford Franciscan Roger Bacon (d. 1292) explored such subjects as optics, alchemy and languages. The excerpt below is a brief and rather clouded summary, from the last part of Bacon's *Opus Majus*, of the necessity for experimentation. Bacon's work, like that of many of his contemporaries, deals with the themes of reason and faith, tradition and innovation. It shows that the "experimental sciences" were still infused with theology and tinged with alchemy and magic. It also discloses the degree to which Bacon, and other scholars of his time, had absorbed the philosophical and scientific legacy of Classical Antiquity.

Having laid down fundamental principles of the wisdom of the Latins so far as they are found in language, mathematics, and optics, I now wish to unfold the principles of experimental science, since without experience nothing can be sufficiently known. For there are two modes of acquiring knowledge, namely, by reasoning and experience. Reasoning draws a conclusion and makes us grant the conclusion, but does not make the conclusion certain, nor does it remove doubt so that the mind may rest on the intuition of truth, unless the mind discovers it by the path of experience; since many have the arguments relating to what can be known, but because they lack experience they neglect the arguments, and neither avoid what is harmful nor follow what is good. For if a man who has never seen fire should prove by adequate reasoning that fire burns and injures things and destroys them, his mind would not be satisfied thereby, nor would he avoid fire, until he placed his hand or some combustible substance in the fire, so that he might prove by experience that which reasoning taught. But when he has had actual experience of combustion his mind is made certain and rests in the full light of truth. Therefore reasoning does not suffice, but experience does.

This is also evident in mathematics, where proof is most convincing. But the mind of one who has the most convincing proof in regard to the equilateral triangle will never cleave to the conclusion without experience, nor will he heed it, but will disregard it until experience is offered him by the intersection of two circles, from either intersection of which two lines may be drawn to the extremities of the given line; but then the man accepts the conclusion without any question. Aristotle's statement, then, that proof is reasoning that causes us to know is to be understood with the proviso that the proof is accompanied by its

From *The Opus Majus of Roger Bacon*, tr. Robert Belle Burke; Philadelphia, University of Pennsylvania Press, 1928, pp. 583–585, 587. Reprinted by permission.

appropriate experience, and is not to be understood of the bare proof. His statement also in the first book of the Metaphysics that those who understand the reason and the cause are wiser than those who have empiric knowledge of a fact, is spoken of such as know only the bare truth without the cause. But I am here speaking of the man who knows the reason and the cause through experience. These men are perfect in their wisdom, as Aristotle maintains in the sixth book of the *Ethics*, whose simple statements must be accepted as if they offered proof, as he states in the same place.

He therefore who wishes to rejoice without doubt in regard to the truths underlying phenomena must know how to devote himself to experiment. For authors write many statements, and people believe them through reasoning which they formulate without experience. Their reasoning is wholly false. For it is generally believed that the diamond cannot be broken except by goat's blood, and philosophers and theologians misuse this idea. But fracture by means of blood of this kind has never been verified, although the effort has been made; and without that blood it can be broken easily. For I have seen this with my own eyes, and this is necessary, because gems cannot be carved except by fragments of this stone.

But experience is of two kinds; one is gained through our external senses, and in this way we gain our experience of those things that are in the heavens by instruments made for this purpose, and of those things here below by means attested by our vision. Things that do not belong in our part of the world we know through other scientists who have had experience of them. As, for example, Aristotle on the authority of Alexander sent two thousand men through different parts of the world to gain experimental knowledge of all things that are on the surface of the earth, as Pliny bears witness in his Natural History. This experience is both human and philosophical, as far as man can act in accordance with the grace given him; but this experience does not suffice him, because it does not give full attestation in regard to things corporeal owing to its difficulty, and does not touch at all on things spiritual. It is necessary, therefore, that the intellect of man should be otherwise aided, and for this reason the holy patriarchs and prophets, who first gave sciences to the world, received illumination within and were not dependent on sense alone. The same is true of many believers since the time of Christ. For the grace of faith illuminates greatly, as also do divine inspirations, not only in things spiritual, but in things corporeal and in the sciences of philosophy; as Ptolemy states in the *Centilogium*, namely, that there are two roads by which we arrive at the knowledge of facts, one through the experience of philosophy, the other through divine inspiration, which is far the better way, as he says.

Since this Experimental Science is wholly unknown to the rank and file of students, I am therefore unable to convince people of its utility unless at the same time I disclose its excellence and its proper signification. This science alone, therefore, knows how to test perfectly what can be done by nature, what by the effort of art, what by trickery, what the incantations, conjurations, invocations, deprecations, sacrifices, that belong to magic, mean and dream of, and what is in them, so that all falsity may be removed and the truth alone of art and nature may be retained. This science alone teaches us how to view the mad acts of magicians, that they may be not ratified but shunned, just as logic considers sophistical reasoning.

Reading 5
St. Thomas Aquinas on Faith and Reason

St. Thomas Aquinas, the most renowned philosopher of the Middle Ages, was born in southern Italy in 1225—the seventh son of an aristocratic family part German, part Italian, part Norman. After six years of study at the University of Naples, he joined the recently founded Dominican Order and traveled northward to study and teach at such intellectual centers as Cologne and Paris. After a distinguished career of teaching and voluminous writing, he died in 1274 at the age of 49.

As a believer in human reason, Aquinas absorbed himself in Greek philosophy, particularly the writings of Aristotle—the greatest logician who had ever lived and, in Aquinas's judgment, "the Philosopher." In his *Summa Contra Gentiles* ("Summa against the unbelievers"), Aquinas deliberately avoids appeals to Biblical authority and limits himself to arguments from reason alone. Here, as in his other works, he explores the relationship of faith and reason, finding them distinct but compatible. Notice how Aquinas, following Aristotle, differs from St. Anselm on the importance of sense perceptions as sources of human knowledge.

Not every truth is to be made known in the same way, *and it is the part of an educated man to seek for conviction in each subject, only so far as the nature of the subject allows,* as the Philosopher most rightly observes as quoted by Boethius. It is therefore necessary to show first of all in what way it is possible to make known the aforesaid truth.

Now in those things which we hold about God there is truth in two ways. For certain things that are true about God wholly surpass the capability of

From *The Summa Contra Gentiles of Saint Thomas Aquinas*, tr. The English Dominican Fathers; London, Burns, Oates & Washbourne, Ltd., 1924, pp. 4–5, 9–10, 14–17. Reprinted by permission.

human reason, for instance that God is three and one: while there are certain things to which even natural reason can attain, for instance that God exists, that God is one, and others like these, which even the philosophers proved demonstratively of God, being guided by the light of natural reason.

That certain divine truths wholly surpass the capability of human reason, is most clearly evident. For since the principle of all the knowledge which the reason acquires about a thing, is the understanding of that thing's essence, because according to the Philosopher's teaching the principle of a demonstration is *what a thing is*, it follows that our knowledge about a thing will be in proportion to our understanding of its essence. Wherefore, if the human intellect comprehends the essence of a particular thing, for instance a stone or a triangle, no truth about that thing will surpass the capability of human reason. But this does not happen to us in relation to God, because the human intellect is incapable by its natural power of attaining to the comprehension of His essence: since our intellect's knowledge, according to the mode of the present life, originates from the senses: so that things which are not objects of sense cannot be comprehended by the human intellect, except in so far as knowledge of them is gathered from sensibles. Now sensibles cannot lead our intellect to see in them what God is, because they are effects unequal to the power of their cause. And yet our intellect is led by sensibles to the divine knowledge so as to know about God that He is, and other such truths, which need to be ascribed to the first principle. Accordingly some divine truths are attainable by human reason, while others altogether surpass the power of human reason.

It may appear to some that those things which cannot be investigated by reason ought not to be proposed to man as an object of faith: because divine wisdom provides for each thing according to the mode of its nature. We must therefore prove that it is necessary also for those things which surpass reason to be proposed by God to man as an object of faith.

For no man tends to do a thing by his desire and endeavour unless it be previously known to him. Wherefore since man is directed by divine providence to a higher good than human frailty can attain in the present life, as we shall show in the sequel, it was necessary for his mind to be bidden to something higher than those things to which our reason can reach in the present life, so that he might learn to aspire, and by his endeavours to tend to something surpassing the whole state of the present life. And this is especially competent to the Christian religion, which alone promises goods spiritual and eternal: for which reason it proposes many things surpassing the thought of man: whereas the old law which contained promises of temporal things, proposed few things that are above human inquiry. It was with this motive that the philosophers, in order to wean men from sensible pleasures to virtue, took care to show that there are other goods of greater account than those which appeal to the senses, the taste of which things affords much greater delight to those who devote themselves to active or contemplative virtues.

Again it is necessary for this truth to be proposed to man as an object of faith in order that he may have truer knowledge of God. For then alone do we know God truly, when we believe that He is far above all that man can possibly think of God, because the divine essence surpasses man's natural knowledge, as stated above. Hence by the fact that certain things about God are proposed to man, which surpass his reason, he is strengthened in his opinion that God is far above what he is able to think.

There results also another advantage from this, namely, the checking of presumption which is the mother of error. For some there are who presume so far on their wits that they think themselves capable of measuring the whole nature of things by their intellect, in that they esteem all things true which they see, and false which they see not. Accordingly, in order that man's mind might be freed from this presumption, and seek the truth humbly, it was necessary that certain things far surpassing his intellect should be proposed to man by God.

Now though the aforesaid truth of the Christian faith surpasses the ability of human reason, nevertheless those things which are naturally instilled in human reason cannot be opposed to this truth. For it is clear that those things which are implanted in reason by nature, are true, so much so that it is impossible to think them to be false. Nor is it lawful to deem false that which is held by faith, since it is so evidently confirmed by God. Seeing then that the false alone is opposed to the true, as evidently appears if we examine their definitions, it is impossible for the aforesaid truth of faith to be contrary to those principles which reason knows naturally.

Again. The same thing which the disciple's mind receives from its teacher is contained in the knowledge of the teacher, unless he teach insincerely, which it were wicked to say of God. Now the knowledge of naturally known principles is instilled into us by God, since God Himself is the author of our nature. Therefore the divine Wisdom also contains these principles. Consequently whatever is contrary to these principles, is contrary to the divine Wisdom; wherefore it cannot be from God. Therefore those things which are received by faith from divine revelation cannot be contrary to our natural knowledge.

Moreover. Our intellect is stayed by contrary arguments, so that it cannot advance to the knowledge of truth. Wherefore if conflicting knowledges were instilled into us by God, our intellect would thereby be hindered from knowing the truth. And this cannot be ascribed to God.

Furthermore. Things that are natural are unchangeable so long as nature remains. Now contrary opinions cannot be together in the same subject.

Therefore God does not instil into man any opinion or belief contrary to natural knowledge.

From this we may evidently conclude that whatever arguments are alleged against the teachings of faith, they do not rightly proceed from the first self-evident principles instilled by nature. Wherefore they lack the force of demonstration, and are either probable or sophistical arguments, and consequently it is possible to solve them.

It is evident that the intention of the wise man must be directed to the twofold truth of divine things and to the refutation of contrary errors: and that the research of reason is able to reach to one of these, while the other surpasses every effort of reason. And I speak a twofold truth of divine things, not on the part of God Himself Who is Truth one and simple, but on the part of our knowledge, the relation of which to the knowledge of divine things varies.

Wherefore in order to deduce the first kind of truth we must proceed by demonstrative arguments whereby we can convince our adversaries. But since such arguments are not available in support of the second kind of truth, our intention must be not to convince our opponent by our arguments, but to solve the arguments which he brings against the truth, because, as shown above, natural reason cannot be opposed to the truth of faith. In a special way may the opponent of this kind of truth be convinced by the authority of Scripture confirmed by God with miracles: since we believe not what is above human reason save because God has revealed it. In support, however, of this kind of truth, certain probable arguments must be adduced for the practice and help of the faithful, but not for the conviction of our opponents, because the very insufficiency of these arguments would rather confirm them in their error, if they thought that we assented to the truth of faith on account of such weak reasonings.

Reading 6

St. Thomas Aquinas on Faith, Hope, and Love

These excerpts from Aquinas's *Summa Theologica* draw together several of the themes dealt with by the writers in this chapter. The word "charity," as Aquinas uses it, might better be translated as "love," except that in Aquinas's mind "charity" is a particular form of love. The "theological vir-

From *An Aquinas Reader*, ed. Mary T. Clark; New York, Image Books, 1972, pp. 404–408. Copyright 1972 by Mary T. Clark. Reprinted by permission of Doubleday & Company, Inc.

tues" that he discusses here were introduced by St. Paul in his First Epistle
to the Corinthians (13:13): "Meanwhile these three remain: faith, hope and
love [or charity]; and the greatest of these is love."

None of the philosophers before the coming of Christ could by bending
all effort to the task know as much about God and things necessary for eternal
life as, after the coming of Christ, a little old woman knows through her faith.

The object of every science includes two things: first, what is materially
known and is, one might say, the material object, and second, that by which it
is known, or the formal aspect of an object. Hence in the science of geometry
the conclusions are what is materially known, whereas the medium of
demonstration, whereby the conclusions are deduced, is the formal aspect of
the science.

So if in faith we are referring to the object's formal aspect, this is nothing
other than the first truth. For the faith we mean only assents to what is revealed by God. Thus the medium through which faith comes is the divine
truth. But if we are referring to what faith assents to, materially, not only God
but many other things are included, and yet they only fall within the assent of
faith as related to God, since through some effects of the divine action, man is
assisted on his way toward the enjoyment of God. So even from this viewpoint
the object of faith is the first truth, since what falls within faith does so insofar
as it is related to God, just as the medical art's object is health, since it considers things only in relation to health.

Action from a power or a durable dispostion depends upon how the
power or disposition is related to its object. But there are three aspects to the
object of faith. Because *to believe* is the intellect's act insofar as the will moves
it to assent. . . the object of faith can be referred to intellect or to the will,
which moves the intellect.

In reference to intellect, two things are notable with regard to faith's object: One of these is the material object of faith, and in this sense an act of
faith is *to believe in a God* (since, as explained, only what refers to God is proposed to our faith); the other is the formal aspect of the object—this is the
medium whereby we assent to this or that point of faith, and in this way an act
of faith is *to believe God* because, as explained, the formal object of faith is
the first truth, to which man adheres so that for its sake he assents to whatever
he believes.

Third, if we look at the object of faith in respect to the intellect as moved
by the will, an act of faith is *to believe in God*; for the first truth is related to
the will under its aspect of end.

. . . The act of faith is directed to the object of the will, i.e., the good, as to its end; and this good that is the end of faith, the divine good, is the proper object of charity, so that insofar as the act of faith is perfected and formed through charity, charity is called the form of faith.

A theological virtue is one having God as that to which it adheres. This adherence occurs in two ways: first, for its own sake; second, because through it something else is had. Thus charity makes us cling to God for his own sake, uniting our minds to God by the emotion of love.

Hope and faith, on the other hand, make man cling to God as to a principle whereby other things come to us. Now, from God we get both knowledge of truth and perfect goodness, so that faith makes us cling to God as our source in knowing the truth since we believe that what God declares is true, whereas hope makes us cling to God as our source of perfect goodness, i.e., inasmuch as through hope we trust the divine assistance to become happy.

According to the philosopher (Aristotle: Ethics VIII, 2, 3) not all love can be characterized as friendship, only love expressing benevolence, i.e., loving someone by wanting his good. But if we do not want good for the one we love, but for ourselves (as we are said to love wine, or a horse, etc.), it is a sort of concupiscence rather than love of friendship. For to speak of having friendship for wine or for a horse is absurd.

Yet friendship does not amount to well-wishing but requires mutual love, inasmuch as friendship is between friend and friend, and well-wishing itself is based upon a kind of communication.

Thus, since God communicates his happiness to us, there must be between man and God a communication upon which some kind of friendship is based, of which it is written (1 Cor. 1: 9): "God is faithful: by whom you are called unto the fellowship of his Son."

The love that is based upon this communication is charity, and so it is clear that charity is the friendship of man for God.

. . . There is no perfect action coming from an active power unless through some form, as the principle of that action, it is connatural to that power. So God, who moves all things to their appropriate ends, gave to each thing its form whereby it tends to the end he appointed; and thus he "ordereth all things sweetly" (Wis. 8: 1). But it is clear that the act of charity is beyond the will's nature, so that without a form being superadded to the natural power inclining it toward the act of love, this very act would be less perfect than the natural acts and the acts of the other powers, nor would it be easy and pleasurable to do. But clearly such is not the case, because no virtue has such a strong tendency toward its act as charity does, nor does any virtue operate with as great pleasure. So for us to act with charity there is required some habitual form superadded to the natural power, inclining that power to the act of charity and making it act with ease and pleasure.

Every accident is inferior in being to substance, because substance has existence through itself, whereas an accident has its existence in another. But under its species aspect, an accident resulting from its subject's principles is inferior to its subject as any effect is inferior to its cause; but an accident resulting from a participation in some higher nature is superior to its subject inasmuch as it is a likeness of that higher nature, just as light is superior to the diaphanous body.

In this sense charity is superior to the soul because it is a participation in the Holy Spirit.

God is the object of faith, which assents to propositions concerning God under the formal aspect of their being revealed by God:

. . . The object of any knowing habit [in this case, that of faith] has two aspects, namely, that which is materially known, which is, as it were, the material object, and that through which it is known, which is the formal notion of the object. Thus, in the science of geometry, what are materially known are the conclusions, while the formal notion under which they are known constitutes the middles of demonstration, through which the conclusions are known. Hence, in the faith, if we consider the formal notion of its object, it is nothing other than the first truth [i.e., God as the guarantor of all truth]. For the faith of which we are speaking does not assent to anything except insofar as it is revealed by God. Hence it is founded upon the divine truth as a middle [of demonstration, whence derives the certitude of the conclusions]. But if we consider materially the things to which faith assents, not only is it God, but also many other things, which, however, do not fall under the assent of faith except insofar as they have some order to God, namely, as through certain effects of the divinity, man is aided in his tending toward divine fruition [e.g., by faith in the sacraments, in the divine foundation of the Church, etc.].

This revelation is contained in Scripture (and tradition), and appropriately summarized under certain articles of faith.

. . . The truth of the faith is contained diffusedly in sacred Scripture, and in various manners, and obscurely in some. Hence, in order to bring forth the truth of faith from sacred Scripture there is required long study and training. But all those for whom it is necessary to know the truth of faith cannot arrive at this—a great number, being occupied with other concerns, cannot devote themselves to study. Therefore it was necessary that, from what was set forward in sacred Scripture, a certain clear summary be gathered together, to be proposed for belief by all. This summary is not *added to* sacred Scripture, but is, rather, *drawn from* sacred Scripture.

Part Three

THE LATE MIDDLE AGES

The late Middle Ages (*c.* 1300–1500) are difficult to characterize. The era was one of plague, depression, and strife, but it also witnessed the Italian Renaissance, the invention of printing, and the early voyages of discovery.

The Hundred Years' War (1337–1453) brought death, starvation, and intermittent anarchy to the French countryside while driving the English monarchy to the brink of bankruptcy and forcing it to make significant concessions to Parliament. England suffered widespread disorder, a bloodcurdling peasants' revolt, the deposition and murder of two kings, and a drawn-out civil war between rival aristocratic factions—the so-called "Wars of the Roses" (1455–1485). Spain, too, was afflicted by civil strife, as were Italy and central Europe. Yet by the close of the period strong monarchies had reemerged in France, England, and Spain, and the Italian Renaissance had reached its height.

The late-medieval Church was similarly troubled. The popes moved from faction-ridden Rome to Avignon in 1309 and remained there for more than a century. Between 1378 and 1415 the Church was torn by schism as two popes, and later three, contended for the spiritual supremacy of Christendom. The period ended with the papacy reunited and planted firmly back in Rome, but drained of much of its former prestige and international authority. The Protestant Reformation was just beyond the horizon.

The civil and economic unrest of the late Middle Ages was aggravated enormously by the onset of bubonic plague. Descending on Europe in 1348, the Black Death carried off a third of its population in the ensuing two years and returned periodically during the next three centuries. As a consequence of plague, warfare, and famine, Europe's population was lower in 1500 than in 1300, and most of its major cities had diminished accordingly. But in the last half of the fifteenth century the population reversed its long downward trend and commerce began to revive. By 1500 there were clear signs that Europe had surmounted its late-medieval crisis. Western Civilization was moving into an era of renewed prosperity and global expansion.

CHAPTER 8

Constitutional Europe

The Hundred Years' War widened the gulf between the French and English systems of royal governance, propelling France toward the absolutism of early-modern times while advancing the authority of Parliament in England. Sir John Fortescue, writing in the fifteenth century, distinguishes sharply between the two regimes (document 1). The documents that follow illustrate important stages in the growth of parliamentary power in England (document 2) and the thoughts of two perceptive Frenchmen, one writing at the beginning of the period and one toward the end, on monarchical authority in France (documents 3 and 4).

The German monarchy (or Holy Roman Empire), battered by generations of struggle with the papacy and German princes, emerged from the Middle Ages in a crippled condition (document 5). The Roman papacy was similarly weakened by its long exile in Avignon, its lapse into schism, its conflicts with church councils, and its declining moral reputation (documents 6–8).

Reading 1

Sir John Fortescue on the English and French Monarchies

Sir John Fortescue (*c.* 1394–*c.* 1476) was a distinguished English jurist who served as chief justice of the King's Bench. Shifting political configurations resulting from the Wars of the Roses drove him for a time into exile in France but did not diminish his admiration for the English system of government. In the following passage from *The Governance of England* (*c.* 1470), Fortescue contrasts French "royal lordship" with English "political and royal lordship." His bias toward the English system will be evident.

There are two types of kingdoms, one of which is called a royal lordship, and the other is called a political and royal lordship.[1] They differ in that the first king may rule his people by such laws as he makes himself, and therefore he may set taxes and other impositions on them as he himself wishes, without their assent. The second king may not rule his people by laws other than those they assent to, and therefore he may set no impositions upon them without their own assent.

It may perhaps be marvelled at by some men why one realm is a royal lordship alone and the prince rules it by his law, called the royal law, and why another kingdom is a royal and political lordship and the prince rules it by a law called the royal and political law, since these two princes are of equal stature. This doubt may be answered in this manner: that the first constitution of these two realms upon the incorporation of them is the cause of this diversity. Now it seems to me it is shown openly enough why one king rules royally alone and the other politically and royally: for one kingdom began of and by the might of the prince, and the other began by the desire and institution of the people of the prince.

Now the French king reigns upon his people royally; yet neither St. Louis, once king there, nor any of his progenitors ever set taxes or other impositions upon the people of that land without the assent of the Three Estates, which, when they are assembled, are like the parliament in England.[2] And many of his successors kept this order until recently, when Englishmen made such war in

From Sir John Fortescue, *The Governance of England*, ed. and tr. Charles Plummer; Oxford, The Clarendon Press, 1885, pp. 109–115. Revised by Joe W. Leedom.

[1] The Latin for these two types of government, a *dominium regale* and a *dominium politicum et regale*, was widely used in later discussions of the English government.

[2] The first Estates General, as the French parliament came to be known, did not actually meet until 1303.

France that the Three Estates dared not come together. And so because of that, and because of the great necessity which the French king had of good for the defence of that land, he took it upon himself to set taxes and other impositions upon the commons without the assent of the Three Estates; yet he would not and has not set such charges upon the nobles for fear of rebellion. And because the commons there, though they have grouched, have not rebelled and are not ready to rebel, the French kings have every year since set such charges upon them, and augmented such charges, so that the commons are so impoverished and destroyed that they may hardly live. Truly they live in the most extreme poverty and misery, though they dwell in the most fertile land in the world. And because of this the French king does not have men of his own realm able to defend it, except for the nobles who bear no such impositions; rather, the king is forced to make his armies and retinues for the defence of his land up of foreigners, Scots, Spaniards, men of Germany, and of other nations, or else all his enemies might overrun him, for he has no defences of his own, except his castles and fortresses. Lo, this is the fruit of his royal law.

If the realm of England, which is an island, were ruled under such a law and such a prince, it would then be a prey to all other nations, and they would conquer, rob, or devour it, as was proved in the time of the Britons. But this land is ruled under a better law, and therefore the people of it are not in such penury, but rather they are wealthy and have all things necessary to the sustenance of nature. And so they are mighty, and able to resist the adversaries of this realm, and to beat other realms that do, or would do them wrong. Lo, this is the fruit of the royal and political law under which we live.

Reading 2

Documents Relating to Crown and Parliament in England

These documents illustrate the changing relationship between crown and parliament during the period of the Hundred Years' War, and the split within parliament between lords and commons. It was the commons (smallholding shire knights and representatives from towns) who wrung the most important privileges from the financially strapped monarchy. Step by step, the crown was surrendering its initiative as parliament established control over

From *Sources of English Constitutional History*, ed. and tr. Carl Stephenson and Frederick George Marcham; vol. I, rev. ed., New York, Harper & Row, 1972, pp. 217–218, 223–224, 258–259, 265. Copyright 1937 by Harper & Row, Publishers, Inc. Reprinted by permission of the publishers.

direct taxation and used that power to compel the king to grant its petitions. On the principle of "redress before supply," parliament was insisting that the king enact its petitions into law without alteration. Behind the mask of courtly and respectful language, one can discern some sharp-eyed negotiating over difficult constitutional issues.

A. PARLIAMENT OF 1348

. . . Whereupon the knights of the shires and the others of the commons were told that they should withdraw together and take good counsel as to how, for withstanding the malice of the said enemy and for the salvation of our said lord the king and his kingdom of England, our lord the king could be aided to his greatest advantage and to the least burdening of his people; and that, as soon as they had come to a decision, they should notify our lord the king and the lords of his council. The which knights and others of the commons took counsel on the matter day after day and at last gave their response to the following effect:

. . . Thus the said poor commons, to their own excessive hurt, grant to our lord the king three fifteenths,[1] to be levied during three years, beginning at Michaelmas next;[2] on condition that in each of these years one fifteenth, and nothing in addition, shall be levied in equal portions at two terms of the year, Michaelmas and Easter, and that this aid shall be assigned and kept solely for the war of our lord the king and shall in no way be assigned to [pay] old debts. . . .

And afterwards the said commons were told that all individual persons who wished to present petitions in this parliament should present them to the chancellor; and that the petitions touching the commons [in general] should be presented to the clerk of the parliament. The which commons presented their petitions to the said clerk in the manner following:

. . . Item, the commons pray that the petitions presented in the last parliament by the said commons and fully answered and granted by our said lord the king and the prelates and lords of the land, shall be observed; and that, by no bill presented in this parliament in the name of the commons or of any one else, shall the responses already granted be changed: for the commons acknowledge no such bill as may be presented by any one to effect the contrary. Response: At an earlier time the king, by the advice of the prelates and lords of the land, made answer to the petitions of the commons regarding the law of

---

[1]A "fifteenth" was a tax of one-fifteenth of the value of all movable goods. Unlike modern taxes, which are levied on real estate or income, these assessments applied to the worth of an individual's holdings.

[2]Michaelmas, or the Mass of St. Michael the Archangel, is celebrated on September 29.

the land, [to the effect] that neither the laws held and accustomed in times past nor the process of the same [law of the land] so accustomed in the past could be changed without making a new statute—to do which the king could not then and cannot now see his way. But as soon as he can see his way [to do so], he will bring the lords and the skilled men of his council before him and by their advice and counsel will ordain concerning such articles and others that involve amendment of the law; so that right and equity shall be enforced for all and each of his lieges and subjects. . . .

B. SECOND STATUTE OF 14 EDWARD III: PARLIAMENTARY CONTROL OF DIRECT TAXES (1340)

. . . Whereas the prelates, earls, barons, and commons of our realm, in our present parliament summoned at Westminster . . . , of their free will and grace have granted us, in aid of advancing the great enterprises that we have before us both on this side of the sea and beyond it, the ninth sheaf, the ninth fleece, and the ninth lamb[3] . . . ; and [whereas] the citizens of cities and the burgesses of boroughs [have granted] the true ninth of all their goods; and [whereas] foreign merchants and other men who live neither from trade nor from flocks of sheep, [have granted] the fifteenth of their goods, rightly [assessed] according to value: we, desirous of providing indemnity for the said prelates, earls, barons, and others of the said commonalty, and also for the citizens, burgesses, and merchants aforesaid, will and grant for us and our heirs to the same prelates, earls, barons, and commons, [and to the same] citizens, burgesses, and merchants, that this grant now chargeable shall not at another time be treated as a precedent or work to their prejudice in the future; and that henceforth they shall be neither charged nor burdened to make common aid or to sustain charge except by the common assent of the prelates, earls, and barons, and of the other lords and commons of our said realm of England, and this in parliament; and that all profits arising from the said aid, and from wardships, marriages, customs, and escheats, together with other profits arising from the kingdom of England, shall be devoted and spent to maintain the safeguarding of our said kingdom of England and [to advance] our wars in Scotland, France, and Gascony, and nowhere else during the [continuance of] the said wars. . . .

And whereas the said prelates, earls, barons, and commons, for the sake of the great enterprises which we have undertaken, have granted at our request that we may levy 40s. on each sack of wool passing beyond sea from now until the feast of Pentecost next; and 40s. on every three hundred wool-fells; and 40s. on a last of leather: we . . . have granted that, after the said feast of

[3]That is, a tax of one-ninth of the value of goods.

Pentecost to come in one year, neither we nor our heirs shall demand, assess, levy, or cause to be levied more than half a mark of custom on a sack of wool throughout all England, half a mark on three hundred wool-fells, and one mark on a last of leather. . . .

C. THE PARLIAMENT OF 1401

On Saturday, January 22, the commons of the realm . . . set forth to our lord the king that in several parliaments during times past their common petitions had not been answered before they had made their grant to our lord the king of some aid or subsidy. And therefore they prayed our same lord the king that, for the great ease and comfort of the said commons, our lord the king might be pleased to grant to the same commons that they could have knowledge of the responses to their said petitions before any such grant had thus been made. To which it was replied that the king wished to confer on this matter with the lords of the parliament and thereupon do what seemed best to him by the advice of the said lords. And afterwards, that is to say, on the last day of the parliament, the response was given that such procedure had been unknown and unaccustomed in the time of any of his progenitors or predecessors—[namely] that they should have any answer to their petitions, or knowledge of it, before they had set forth and completed all their other business in parliament, whether it was the making of any grant or something else. And, in conclusion, the king wished in no way to change the good customs and usages of ancient times. . . .

D. THE PARLIAMENT OF 1414

Item, it is to be remembered that in this parliament the commons presented to our most sovereign lord the king a petition of which the tenor is word for word as follows:

Our sovereign lord, your humble and true lieges who have come on behalf of the commons of your land pray your righteousness that—whereas it has ever been their liberty and freedom that no statute or law should be made unless they have thereto given their assent, and in consideration of the fact that the commons of your land, who now are and ever have been a member of your parliament, have the power of assenting as well as of petitioning—from this time forward, on complaint by the commons asking remedy for any mischief either by the mouth of the speaker of the commons or else by written petition, no law shall thereupon be made and engrossed as a statute and a law with either additions or subtractions which in any particular or particulars change the meaning and intent as requested by the mouth of the speaker or the aforesaid petitions drawn up in writing after the manner aforesaid, without the assent of the aforesaid commons. It is to be understood, our sovereign lord, that if the commons either orally or in writing make two or three requests of you, or as many as please them, they have no intention whatsoever but that it shall always be in the freedom of your high regality to grant whichever of them you please and to refuse the rest.

Response: The king grants of his especial grace that, in connection with the petitions of his commons, nothing contrary to their request shall henceforth be enacted, whereby they shall be bound without their assent; saving always to our liege lord his real prerogative to grant and deny what may please him of their petitions and requests aforesaid. . . .

Reading 3

John of Paris on the French Monarchy

John of Paris (d. 1306), one of medieval Europe's most skillful political thinkers, was a firm supporter of the regime of King Philip the Fair. John's treatise *On Royal and Papal Power* thus reflects the self-image of the French monarchy at the opening of the late Middle Ages. Notice the contrast between John of Paris's views and those of Sir John Fortescue.

When considering the nature of royal government the following definition of the correct sense of the word kingdom should be known: it is the government of a perfect or self-sufficient community by one man for the sake of the common good. In this definition "government" is the genus: "community" is added to differentiate it from government where each governs himself either by natural instinct, as is the case with animals, or by reason, as is the case with those who live a solitary life. "Perfect" serves to distinguish the community from the family which is not self-sufficient for anything more than a short period of time and not for all the needs of life as is the community, as the Philosopher teaches in the first book of his *Politics*. "For the sake of the common good" is included in the definition to distinguish it from oligarchy, tyranny and democracy, in which the ruler seeks nothing but his own good, especially in a tyranny. "By one man" is included to distinguish it from an aristocracy, that is the rule of the best men, where government in accordance with virtue is in the hands of a few.

From John of Paris, *On Royal and Papal Power*, tr. J.A. Watt; Toronto, 1971, pp. 76–79. Copyright 1971 by The Pontifical Institute of Mediaeval Studies, Toronto. Reprinted by permission.

Government as defined above has its roots in natural law and the law of nations. For since man is by nature created a political and civil animal, as is said in Book 1 of the *Politics*—the Philosopher deduces this from man's need for food, clothing and protection which man in isolation cannot supply for himself and from man's speech, the purpose of which is communication with others; these considerations apply to man only—he must of necessity live in a community and in such a community as is self-sufficient in all life's necessaries. The community of the family or of the village is not self-sufficient but the city-state or kingdom is, for in a single household or village are not to be found all those necessities of food, clothing and protection for a man's whole life as can be found in a city-state or kingdom. A society in which everyone seeks only his own advantage will collapse and disintegrate unless it is ordered to the good of all by some one ruler who has charge of the common good, just as a man's body would collapse if there were not in it some general force directing the common good of the members as a whole.

Government of a community is more effective when conducted by one man according to virtue, than when exercised by many or few virtuous men. This is clear from the weighing-up of a number of points: firstly, considering power: virtue is more united and therefore the stronger in one ruler than when divided among many. Secondly, considering the unity and peace which rulers seek to provide for their communities: there can be no community where unity and concord is missing. But the single ruler better upholds that unity of a community which gives it its being than the rule of many; so therefore the rule of one man according to virtue will the better keep peace, and concord among citizens will not easily be broken. Thirdly, a single ruler has a sharper eye for the common good than many rulers can have even if they are ruling according to virtue. For the more who, as rulers, stand apart from the mass of the community, so the less do the remainder, the ruled, represent what is common, and vice versa. Hence the Philosopher says that among all the different types of constitution directed to the interest of those who rule, the tyrant is the worst because his object is his own advantage and not the advantage of those he governs. Fourthly, in the law of nature all government is reduced to overall unity just as in any body composed of a mixture of parts there is one element which is master over the others. For example, in the heterogeneous human body, there is a principal member in the whole man and the soul contains all the elements. Animals which herd together and for whom it is natural to live in society are subject to one ruler.

From these arguments it is clear that it is both necessary and advantageous for man to live in society and especially in such a society as a city or kingdom which is self-sufficient in everything that pertains to the whole of life, and especially, too, under the government of one who rules the common good, who is called king. It is clear also that this sort of government derives from natural law in that man is a civil or political and social animal.

Reading 4

Philippe de Commynes on the French Monarchy

One of the most gifted French historians of the late Middle Ages, Philippe de Commynes (d. 1509) dealt astutely with the reigns of Louis XI (1461–1483) and Charles VIII (1483–1498). Compare the opinions of Commynes and Fortescue on the taxation power of the French crown.

Of all the kings in this world ours has least reason to say: "I have the privilege of levying on my subjects what I please." And those who ascribe these words to him to make him appear greater do him no honor; on the contrary, they cause him to be hated and feared by his neighbors, who would not want to live under his domination for anything in the world. But if our king, or those who want to exalt him or promote his reputation, were to say: "I have subjects who are so good and loyal that they never refuse me anything I request of them, and I am more feared and better obeyed by my subjects than any other prince in the world; my subjects endure all misfortunes and afflictions with more patience than any others, and bear less resentment for past sufferings," it seems to me that this would be very much to his credit, and I am sure that this is so. He should not say: "I take whatever I want and it is my prerogative, which I intend to keep." King Charles V [of France] never used such terms. As a matter of fact I have never heard any king say this, but I have heard it from their servants, who thought that they were doing their master a good turn. But, in my opinion, they misunderstood the interests of their lord, and they spoke this way in order to show humility before him and because they did not know what they were saying.

As an example of the goodness of the French, the first instance which comes to mind from our time is the convocation of the three estates in Tours [in 1484], after the decease of our good master, King Louis, may he rest in peace, which took place in 1483. It might have been thought at the time that

From *The Memoirs of Philippe de Commynes,* ed. Samuel Kinser, tr. Isabelle Cazeaux; Columbia, S.C., 1969, pp. 359–361. Copyright University of South Carolina Press, 1969. Reprinted by permission.

such an assembly would be dangerous, and some persons of low estate and little virtue said then, and many times since, that it was a crime of lese majesty to consider having a meeting of the estates, and that it would only serve to diminish the authority of the king. But these are the very persons who commit a crime against God, the king, and the people. These words serve only those who are in positions of authority and esteem without having deserved it in any way, who are not qualified for their office, and who have never done anything except whisper in ears and talk about things of little value; these people are opposed to these great assemblies for fear that they may be recognized for what they are and that their practices may be condemned.

At the time everyone, whether of high, middle, or low rank, considered the kingdom to be very costly to maintain, for the people had endured and suffered for twenty years and more great and horrible taxes, and which amounted to some three million francs a year more than ever before. For Charles VII never levied more than 1,800,000 francs a year, and King Louis, his son, in the year of his death, raised 4,700,000 francs, not including funds for artillery and other supplies. And it was indeed pitiful to see and hear of the poverty of the people. But one good thing about our good master was that he did not hoard anything in the treasury; he collected everything and spent everything. He built large edifices to fortify and defend the towns and other places of the kingdom, and he did this to a much larger extent than all the kings who preceded him. He was very generous to the churches. In certain respects it would have been better if he had been less liberal, because he robbed the poor to give to those who had no need of it. In short, no one is perfect in this world.

And in this kingdom, which was so oppressed in many ways after the death of our king, was there any division against the king who now reigns? Did princes and their subjects rise up in arms against their young king? Did they wish to replace him with another? Did they wish to deprive him of his authority? Did they want to restrain him so that he would be unable to perform his role as a king and issue commands? Certainly not. Still, there were some people vainglorious enough to say that such things would have happened, had they not prevented it. People did the opposite of everything I said in my questions: for all of them came to him, whether they were princes, lords, or ordinary townsmen; all of them acknowledged him as their king and swore allegiance to him. The princes and the lords made their requests humbly, on their knees, handing in their demands in the form of petitions, and they established a council to which twelve of them were named. And then the king, who was only thirteen years old, gave orders, according to the advice of this council.

At the above-mentioned assembly of the three estates, certain requests and remonstrances were made with great humility for the good of the kingdom, always remitting everything to the king's good pleasure and that of his council, and granting him whatever was asked of them, and whatever was shown by written documents to be necessary for the king's expenses, without saying anything. And the sum requested was 2,500,000 francs, which was enough, and all that heart could desire, and, if anything, it was too much rather than too little, unless something else should come up. And the estates begged that at the end of two years they should meet again, and in case the king did not have enough money, they would grant him as much as he pleased; and if he were engaged in war or if anyone were to offend him, they would put at his disposal their persons and their possessions without refusing him anything that he might need.

Is it with such subjects, who give so liberally to him, that the king should allege a privilege of being able to take at his pleasure? Would it not be fairer to God and to the world to raise money in this manner than with unordered will? For no prince can levy taxes otherwise than by authorization, as I said, unless he does it by tyranny and is excommunicated. But many are so stupid that they do not know what they can do or not in this respect.

Reading 5

The Golden Bull of Emperor Charles IV, 1356

The Golden Bull of 1356 is important less as an agent of constitutional change than as a recognition and regularization of political arrangements that had long been developing. The document must be read very carefully. Some of its phrases are empty verbiage, whereas its utter silence on the traditional papal role in disputed elections is most eloquent. The pope's exclusion from German politics should be understood in the light of Charles IV's prior concession to the papacy that he would exercise no authority in Italy without papal permission. In short, Germany and Italy were becoming disentangled at last.

Charles IV pretends that the Golden Bull is a product of imperial initiative, but its provisions were actually hammered out in an imperial assembly of German princes. The Bull describes the emperor in grandiose terms as "ruler of the world," yet it is designed, point by point, to enhance

From *Select Historical Documents of the Middle Ages*, ed. and tr. Ernest F. Henderson; London, G. Bell and Sons, Ltd., 1892, pp. 220–221; and *A Source Book for Mediaeval History*, ed. and tr. O.J. Thatcher and E.N. McNeal; New York, Charles Scribner's Sons, 1905, pp. 284–285, 287–290, 292, 294–295, 300.

the authority of the seven electorial princes and to assure the autonomy and indivisibility of their dominions at imperial expense. Charles was himself both emperor and, as hereditary king of Bohemia, an electoral prince. A careful reading will disclose the identities of the other six electors.

In the name of the holy and indivisible Trinity, amen. Charles the Fourth, by the favor of divine mercy emperor of the Romans, always august, and king of Bohemia, as a perpetual memorial does this. Every kingdom divided against itself shall be desolated, for its princes have become the companions of thieves. Tell us, pride, how would you have reigned over Lucifer had you not had discord to aid you? Tell us, hateful Satan, how would you have cast Adam out of paradise if you had not divided him from his obedience? You have often spread discord among the seven electors of the holy empire, through whom the holy empire ought to be illuminated.

We, through the office by which we possess the imperial dignity, are doubly bound—both as emperor and by the electoral right that we enjoy—to put an end to future danger of discord among the electors themselves, to whose number we, as king of Bohemia, are known to belong. And so we have promulgated, decreed, and recommended for ratification these laws for the purpose of cherishing unity among the electors, and of bringing about a unanimous election, and of closing all avenues to that detestable discord and to the dangers that arise from it. This we have done in our solemn court at Nuremburg, in session with all the electoral princes, after mature deliberation, from the fullness of our imperial power, in the year of our Lord 1356, on the 10th day of January, in the 10th year of our reign as king of Bohemia, the 1st as emperor.

We decree and determine by this imperial edict that, whenever the electoral princes are summoned according to the ancient and praiseworthy custom to meet and elect a king of the Romans and future emperor, each one of them shall be bound to furnish on demand an escort and safe-conduct to his fellow electors or their representatives, within his own lands and as much farther as he can, for the journey to and from the city where the election is to be held. Any electoral prince who refuses to furnish escort and safe-conduct shall be liable to the penalties for perjury and to the loss of his electoral vote for that occasion.

If there should arise any enmity or hostility between two electoral princes, it shall not be allowed to interfere with the safe-conduct which each is bound to furnish to the other on the occasion of the election, under penalty of being declared guilty of perjury, and being deprived of his vote for that occasion, as described above.

The above decrees concerning safe-conduct are to be understood to mean that any person, whether expressly named or not, from whom safe-conduct is demanded on the occasion of the election, must furnish it in good faith within his own lands, and as much farther as he can, under the penalties described above.

It shall be the duty of the archbishop of Mainz to send notice of the approaching election to each of the electoral princes by his messenger bearing letters patent, containing the following: first, the date on which the letter should reach the prince to whom it is directed; then the command to the electoral prince to come or send his representatives to Frankfort on the Main, three months from that date, such representatives being duly accredited by letters bearing the great seal of the prince, and giving them full power to vote for the king of the Romans and future emperor. The form of the letter of notification and of the credentials of the representatives are appended to this document, and we hereby command that these forms be used without change.

When the news of the death of the king of the Romans has been received at Mainz, within one month from the date of receiving it the archbishop of Mainz shall send notices of the death and of the approaching election to all the electoral princes. But if the archbishop neglects or refuses to send such notices, the electoral princes are commanded on their fidelity to assemble on their own motion and without summons at the city of Frankfort within three months from the death of the emperor, for the purpose of electing a king of the Romans and future emperor.

(Mass shall be celebrated on the day after the arrival of the electors. The archbishop of Mainz administers this oath, which the other electors repeat:)

"I, archbishop of Mainz, archchancellor of the empire for Germany, electoral prince, swear on the holy gospels here before me, and by the faith which I owe to God and to the holy Roman empire, that with the aid of God, and according to my best judgment and knowledge, I will cast my vote, in this election of the king of the Romans and future emperor, for a person fitted to rule the Christian people. I will give my voice and vote freely, uninfluenced by any agreement, price, bribe, promise, or anything of the sort, by whatever name it may be called. So help me God and all the saints."

After the electors have taken this oath, they shall proceed to the election, and shall not depart from Frankfort until the majority have elected a king of the Romans and future emperor, to be ruler of the world and of the Christian people. If they have not come to a decision within thirty days from the day on which they took the above oath, after that they shall live upon bread and water and shall not leave the city until the election has been decided.

Such an election shall be as valid as if all the princes had agreed unanimously and without difference upon a candidate. If any one of the princes or his representatives has been hindered or delayed for a time, but arrives before the election is over, he shall be admitted and shall take part in the election at the stage which had been reached at the time of his arrival. According to the ancient and approved custom, the king of the Romans elect, immediately after his election and before he takes up any other business of the empire, shall confirm and approve by sealed letters for each and all of the electoral princes, ecclesiastical and secular, the privileges, charters, rights, liberties, concessions, ancient customs, and dignities, and whatever else the princes held and possessed from the empire at the time of the election; and he shall renew the confirmation and approval when he becomes emperor. The original confirmation shall be made by him as king, and the renewal as emperor. It is his duty to do this graciously and in good faith, and not to hinder the princes in the exercise of their rights.

In the case where three of the electors vote for a fourth electoral prince, his vote shall have the same value as that of the others to make a majority and decide the election. . . .

To prevent any dispute arising between the archbishops of Trier, Mainz, and Cologne, electoral princes of the empire, as to their priority and rank in the diet, it has been decided and is hereby decreed with the advice and consent of all the electoral princes, ecclesiastical and secular, that the archbishop of Trier shall have the seat directly opposite and facing the emperor; that the archbishop of Mainz shall have the seat at the right of the emperor when the diet is held in the diocese or province of Mainz, or anywhere in Germany except in the diocese of Cologne; that the archbishop of Cologne shall have the seat at the right of the emperor when the diet is held in the diocese or province of Cologne, or anywhere in Gaul or Italy.

. . . It is known and recognized throughout the world, that the king of Bohemia, the count palatine of the Rhine, the duke of Saxony, and the margrave of Brandenburg, by virtue of the principalities which they possess, have the right to vote in the election of the king of the Romans along with their coelectors, the ecclesiastical princes, and that they with the ecclesiastical princes are the true and legal electoral princes of the holy empire. In order to prevent disputes arising among the sons of these secular electoral princes in regard to the electoral authority and vote, which would be productive of delays dangerous to the state and other evils, we have fixed the succession by the present law which shall be valid forever. On the death of one of the secular electoral princes his right, voice, and vote in the election shall descend to his first-born son who is a laymen; if the son has died before this, to the son's first-born son who is a layman. If the first-born lay son of the elector has died without legitimate lay sons, by virtue of the present law the succession shall go to the elector's next oldest lay son and then to his heirs, and so on according to the law of primogeniture. In case the heir is under age the paternal uncle of the heir shall act as guardian and administrator until the heir comes of age, which shall be, in the case of electoral princes, at eighteen years. Then the guardian shall immediately surrender to him the electoral vote and authority and all the possessions of the electorate.

When any electorate falls vacant for lack of heirs, the emperor or king of the Romans shall have the power to dispose of it, as if it reverted to the empire, saving the rights, privileges, and customs of the kingdom of Bohemia, according to which the inhabitants of that kingdom have the right to elect their king in case of a vacancy.

We decree also that no count, baron, noble, vassal, burggrave, knight, client, citizen, burgher, or other subject of the churches of Cologne, Mainz, or Trier, of whatever status, condition or rank, shall be cited, hailed, or summoned to any authority before any tribunal outside of the territories, boundaries, and limits of these churches and their dependencies, or before any judge, except the archbishops and their judges. . . . We refuse to hear appeals based upon the authority of others over the subjects of these princes; if these princes are accused by their subjects of injustice, appeal shall lie to the imperial diet, and shall be heard there and nowhere else. . . .

We extend this right by the present law to the secular electoral princes, the count palatine of the Rhine, the duke of Saxony, and the margrave of Brandenburg, and to their heirs, successors, and subjects forever.

It is known that the right of voting for the king of the Romans and future emperor inheres in certain principalities, the possessors of which have also the other offices, rights, and dignities belonging to these principalities. We decree, therefore, by the present law that the electoral vote and other offices, dignities, and appurtenances shall always be so united and conjoined that the possessor of one of these principalities shall possess and enjoy the electoral vote and all the offices, dignities, and appurtenances belonging to it, that he shall be regarded as electoral prince, that he and no other shall be accepted by the other electoral princes and admitted to participation in the election and all other acts which regard the honor and advantage of the holy empire, and that no one of these rights, which are and ought to be inseparable, shall ever be taken from him. And if through error or by any other means any decision or sentence is issued by any judge against the present law, it shall be void.

Reading 6

Petrarch's Description of the Papal
Court at Avignon, *c*. 1340–1353

This somber portrait of the Avignon papacy, by the Italian humanist Petrarch (1304–1374), illustrates at once the papacy's diminishing reputation and Petrarch's addiction to rhetorical exaggeration. He was by no means the first critic to contrast papal wealth with apostolic poverty, nor were the Roman popes of the High Middle Ages immune from such criticism. But Petrarch's blade is particularly sharp and well-polished, and his identification of fourteenth-century Avignon with ancient, hedonistic Babylon gained wide circulation.

. . . Now I am living in France, in the Babylon of the West. The sun in its travels sees nothing more hideous than this place on the shores of the wild Rhone, which suggests the hellish streams of Cocytus and Acheron. Here reign the successors of the poor fishermen of Galilee; they have strangely forgotten their origin. I am astounded, as I recall their predecessors, to see these men loaded with gold and clad in purple, boasting of the spoils of princes and nations; to see luxurious palaces and heights crowned with fortifications, instead of a boat turned downwards for shelter.

Instead of holy solitude we find a criminal host and crowds of the most infamous satellites; instead of soberness, licentious banquets; instead of pious pilgrimages, unnatural and foul sloth; instead of the bare feet of the apostles, the snowy coursers of brigands fly past us, the horses decked in gold and fed on gold, soon to be shod with gold, if the Lord does not check this slavish luxury. In short, we seem to be among the kings of the Persians or Parthians, before whom we must fall down and worship, and who cannot be approached except presents be offered. O ye unkempt and emaciated old men, is it for this you labored? Is it for this that you have sown the field of the Lord and watered it with your holy blood? But let us leave the subject.

From *Readings in European History*, vol. I, ed. James H. Robinson; Boston, Ginn & Company, 1904, pp. 502–503.

Reading 7

The Declaration of the Cardinals, 1378

Under strong international pressure, the Avignon pope Gregory XI moved the papal court back to Rome. Like many of his predecessors, he found the city difficult to govern, and he decided to return to Avignon. But Gregory died in 1378 before he could carry out his plan, and the resulting events, related here by the cardinals, gave rise to the great schism. Having declared their election of the Italian Urban VI null and void, they elected another pope and returned with him to Avignon. Urban VI stayed on in Rome and appointed new cardinals.

The Declaration of the Cardinals thus pinpoints the origin of the schism, but it is not so much an objective account of events as a self-serving interpretation of them. Other sources make it clear that the cardinals elected Urban VI willingly, *before* being pressured by a mob of Romans who were unaware of the election. As archbishop of Bari, Urban had been an efficient but colorless ecclesiastical administrator. As pope he surprised everyone by launching a campaign against clerical wealth and taking steps to reduce the cardinals' revenues. It was at that point that they repudiated Urban, fled Rome, and manufactured their cover story.

. . . After the apostolic seat was made vacant by the death of our lord, pope Gregory XI, who died in March, we assembled in conclave for the election of a pope, as is the law and custom, in the papal palace, in which Gregory had died. . . . Officials of the city with a great multitude of the people, for the most part armed and called together for this purpose by the ringing of bells, surrounded the palace in a threatening manner and even entered it and almost filled it. To the terror caused by their presence they added threats that unless we should at once elect a Roman or an Italian they would kill us. They gave us no time to deliberate but compelled us unwillingly, through violence and fear, to elect an Italian without delay. In order to escape the danger which threatened us from such a mob, we elected Bartholomew, archbishop of Bari, thinking that he would have enough conscience not to accept the election, since everyone knew that it was made under such wicked threats. But he was unmindful of his own salvation and burning with ambition, and so, to the great scandal of the clergy and of the Christian people, and contrary to the laws of the church, he accepted this election which was offered him, although not all the cardinals were present at the election, and it was extorted from us by the threats and demands of the officials and people of the city. And although such

From *A Source Book for Mediaeval History*, ed. and tr. O.J. Thatcher and E.N. McNeal; New York, Charles Scribner's Sons, 1905, pp. 325–326.

an election is null and void, and the danger from the people still threatened us, he was enthroned and crowned, and called himself pope and apostolic. But according to the holy fathers and to the law of the church, he should be called apostate, anathema, Antichrist, and the mocker and destroyer of Christianity.

Reading 8

Decrees of the Conciliar Movement

The great schism stimulated a movement by reform-minded churchmen to reorganize ecclesiastical governance on more or less the parliamentary model, with the papacy sharing its authority with Church councils. The following documents illustrate the rise and fall of the conciliar movement.

The Council of Pisa (documents A and B) elected a "conciliar" pope but failed in its attempt to dethrone the popes of Rome and Avignon, both of whom asserted the traditional claim that the pope could be judged by no one. Against this claim, the churchmen at Pisa, and later at Constance (documents C, D, and E), affirmed the power of councils over popes and demanded that councils be convened on a regular basis. But the Council of Constance's success in healing the schism diminished the need of conciliar governance. Councils continued to meet regularly until the mid-fifteenth century, when the conciliar movement disintegrated under the pressure of papal opposition (document F).

A. THE COUNCIL OF PISA CLAIMS JURISDICTION, 1409

This holy and general council, representing the universal church, decrees and declares that the united college of cardinals was empowered to call the council, and that the power to call such a council belongs of right to the aforesaid holy college of cardinals, especially now when there is a detestable schism. The council further declared that this holy council, representing the universal church, caused both claimants of the papal throne to be cited in the gates and doors of the churches of Pisa to come and hear the final decision [in the matter of the schism] pronounced, or to give a good and sufficient reason why such sentence should not be rendered.

B. THE OATH OF REFORM FROM THE COUNCIL OF PISA, 1409

We, each and all, bishops, priests, and deacons of the holy Roman church, congregated in the city of Pisa for the purpose of ending the schism and of

From *A Source Book for Mediaeval History*, ed. and tr. O.J. Thatcher and E.N. McNeal; New York, Charles Scribner's Sons, 1905, pp. 327–332.

restoring the unity of the church, on our word of honor promise God, the holy Roman church, and this holy council now collected here for the aforesaid purpose, that, if any one of us is elected pope, he shall continue the present council and not dissolve it, nor, so far as is in his power, permit it to be dissolved until, through it and with its advice, a proper, reasonable, and sufficient reformation of the universal church in its head and in its members shall have been accomplished.

C. "HAEC SANCTA" FROM THE COUNCIL OF CONSTANCE, 1415

This holy synod of Constance, being a general council, and legally assembled in the Holy Spirit for the praise of God and for ending the present schism, and for the union and reformation of the church of God in its head and in its members, in order more easily, more securely, more completely, and more fully to bring about the union and reformation of the church of God, ordains, declares, and decrees as follows: And first it declares that this synod, legally assembled, is a general council, and represents the catholic church militant and has its authority directly from Christ; and everybody, of whatever rank or dignity, including also the pope, is bound to obey this council in those things which pertain to the faith, to the ending of this schism, and to a general reformation of the church in its head and members. Likewise it declares that if anyone, of whatever rank, condition, or dignity, including also the pope, shall refuse to obey the commands, statutes, ordinances, or orders of this holy council, or of any other holy council properly assembled, in regard to the ending of the schism and to the reformation of the church, he shall be subject to the proper punishment; and unless he repents, he shall be duly punished; and if necessary, recourse shall be had to other aids of justice.

D. THE REFORM PROGRAM OF THE COUNCIL OF CONSTANCE, 1417

The holy council at Constance determined and decreed that before this holy council shall be dissolved, the future pope, by the grace of God soon to be elected, with the aid of this holy council, or of men appointed by each nation, shall reform the church in its head and in the Roman curia, in conformity to the right standard and good government of the church. And reforms shall be made in the following matters: 1. In the number, character, and nationality of the cardinals. 2. In papal reservations. 3. In annates, and in common services and little services. 4. In the granting of benefices and expectancies. 5. In determining what cases may be tried in the papal court. 6. In appeals to the papal court. 7. In the offices of the *cancellaria*, and of the penitentiary. 8. In the exemptions and incorporations made during the schism. 9. In the matter of commends. 10. In the confirmation of elections. 11. In the disposition of the income of churches, monasteries, and benefices during the time when they are vacant.[1] 12. That no ecclesiastical property be alienated. 13. It shall be determined for what causes and how a pope may be disciplined and deposed. 14. A plan shall be devised for putting an end to simony. 15. In the matter of dispensations. 16. In the provision for the pope and cardinals. 17. In indulgences. 18. In assessing tithes.

E. "FREQUENS" FROM THE COUNCIL OF CONSTANCE, 1417

A good way to till the field of the Lord is to hold general councils frequently, because by them the briers, thorns, and thistles of heresies, errors, and schisms are rooted out, abuses reformed, and the way of the Lord made more fruitful. But if general councils are not held, all these evils spread and flourish. We therefore decree by this perpetual edict that general councils shall be held as follows: The first one shall be held five years after the close of this council, the second one seven years after the close of the first, and forever thereafter one shall be held every ten years. One month before the close of each council the pope, with the approval and consent of the council, shall fix the place for holding the next council. If the pope fails to name the place the council must do so.

F. "EXECRABILIS": PIUS II DENOUNCES CONCILIARISM, 1460

The execrable and hitherto unknown abuse has grown up in our day, that certain persons, imbued with the spirit of rebellion, and not from a desire to secure a better judgment, but to escape the punishment of some offence which they have committed, presume to appeal from the pope to a future council, in spite of the fact that the pope is the vicar of Jesus Christ and to him, in the person of St. Peter, the following was said: "Feed my sheep" [John 21:16] and "Whatsoever thou shalt bind on earth shall be bound in heaven" [Matt. 16:18]. Wishing therefore to expel this pestiferous poison from the church of Christ and to care for the salvation of the flock entrusted to us, and to remove every cause of offence from the fold of our Saviour, with the advice and consent of our brothers, the cardinals of the holy Roman church, and of all the prelates, and of those who have been trained in the canon and civil law, who are at our court, and with our own sure knowledge, we condemn all such appeals and prohibit them as erroneous and detestable.

---

[1]Annates, expectancies, and similar financial measures were payments made to the papacy by appointees to ecclestical offices.

9

Echoes of the Future

The documents that follow provide an appropriately confused picture of the fourteenth and fifteenth centuries as an era of death, disorder, and renaissance. The Black Death (document 1) produced enormous suffering, grief, and economic upheaval. The elimination of one-third of the population resulted in a violent shift from land shortage to labor shortage, prompting property holders great and small to seek legislation to freeze wages (document 2). These laws, along with other grievances, drove the peasantry into revolt, first in France and then in England (document 3). But amid the horrors of plague and civil strife, European commerce remained lively (document 4) and European culture continued to flourish.

The fifteenth century marks the apex of the Italian Renaissance. A glance at Renaissance writings, no less than at Renaissance art, discloses a characteristic blend of classicism, secularism, and Christianity. Renaissance humanists such as Coluccio Salutati could write about Christian virtue and salvation (document 5) while popes such as Nicholas V were collecting classical books and showering patronage on classical scholars (document 6). A similar mixture of Christian and worldly motives underlay the early voyages of exploration (document 7). They were seen at the time both as ventures into the unknown and as continuations of the crusading movement.

Reading 1

Boccaccio's Decameron on the Black Death in Florence, 1348

This eyewitness account is provided by the Florentine humanist, Giovanni Boccaccio (1313–1375), one of the best minds and keenest observers of his time. Except for a touch of civic pride, Boccaccio writes with remarkable objectivity.

In the year of our Lord 1348, there happened at Florence, the finest city in all Italy, a most terrible plague; which, whether owing to the influence of the planets, or that it was sent from God as a just punishment for our sins, had broken out some years before in the Levant, and after passing from place to place and making incredible havoc all the way, had now reached the west. There, spite of all the means that art and human foresight could suggest, such as keeping the city clear from filth, the exclusion of all suspected persons, and the publication of copious instructions for the preservation of health, and notwithstanding manifold humble supplications offered to God in processions and otherwise, it began to show itself in the spring of the aforesaid year, in a sad and wonderful manner. Unlike what had been seen in the east, where bleeding from the nose is the fatal prognostic, here there appeared certain tumors in the groin or under the arm-pits, some as big as a small apple, others as an egg; and afterwards purple spots in most parts of the body; in some cases large and but few in number, in others smaller and more numerous—both sorts the usual messengers of death. To the cure of this malady neither medical knowledge nor the power of drugs was of any effect; whether because the disease was in its own nature mortal, or that the physicians (the number of whom, taking quacks and women pretenders into the account, was grown very great) could form no just idea of the cause, nor consequently devise a true method of cure; whichever was the reason, few escaped; but nearly all died the third day from the first appearance of the symptoms, some sooner, some later, without any fever or other accessory symptoms. What gave the more virulence to this plague, was that, by being communicated from the sick to the hale, it spread daily, like fire when it comes in contact with large masses of combustibles. Nor was it caught only by conversing with or coming near the sick, but even by touching their clothes, or anything that they had before touched. It is wonderful, what I am going to mention; and had I not seen it with my own eyes, and were there not many witnesses to attest it besides myself, I should

From *The First Century of Italian Humanism*, ed. Ferdinand Schevill; New York, F.S. Crofts & Co., 1928, pp. 32–34.

never venture to relate it, however worthy it were of belief. Such, I say, was the quality of the pestilential matter, as to pass not only from man to man, but, what is more strange, it has been often known, that anything belonging to the infected, if touched by any other creature, would certainly infect and even kill that creature in a short space of time. One instance of this kind I took particular notice of: the rags of a poor man just dead had been thrown into the street. Two hogs came up, and after rooting amongst the rags and shaking them about in their mouths, in less than an hour they both turned round and died on the spot.

These facts, and others of the like sort, occasioned various fears and devices amongst those who survived, all tending to the same uncharitable and cruel end; which was, to avoid the sick and every thing that had been near them, expecting by that means to save themselves. And some, holding it best to live temperately and to avoid excesses of all kinds, made parties and shut themselves up from the rest of the world; eating and drinking moderately of the best, and diverting themselves with music and such other entertainments as they might have within doors; never listening to anything from without to make them uneasy. Others maintained free living to be a better preservative, and would balk no passion or appetite they wished to gratify, drinking and revelling incessantly from tavern to tavern, or in private houses (which were frequently found deserted by the owners and therefore common to every one), yet strenuously avoiding, with all this brutal indulgence, to come near the infected.

And such, at that time, was the public distress that the laws, human and divine, were no more regarded; for the officers, to put them in force, being either dead, sick, or in want of persons to assist them, every one did just as he pleased. A third sort of people chose a method between these two: not confining themselves to rules of diet like the former, and yet avoiding the intemperance of the latter; but eating and drinking what their appetites required, they walked everywhere with perfumes and nosegays to smell to, as holding it best to corroborate the brain: for the whole atmosphere seemed to them tainted with the stench of dead bodies, arising partly from the distemper itself, and partly from the fermenting of the medicines within them. Others with less humanity, but perchance, as they supposed, with more security from danger, decided that the only remedy for the pestilence was to avoid it. Persuaded, therefore, of this and taking care for themselves only, men and women in great numbers left the city, their houses, relations, and effects, and fled into the country, as if the wrath of God had been constrained to visit those only within the walls of the city, or else concluding that none ought to stay in a place thus doomed to destruction.

Reading 2

The Ordinance of Laborers, 1349

Edward III of England (1327–1377) sent copies of this ordinance to all his sheriffs. Its purpose is self-explanatory.

The king to the sheriff of Kent, greeting. Because a great part of the people, and especially of workmen and servants, have lately died in the pestilence, many seeing the necessities of masters and great scarcity of servants, will not serve unless they may receive excessive wages, and others preferring to beg in idleness rather than by labor to get their living; we, considering the grievous incommodities which of the lack especially of plowmen and such laborers may hereafter come, have upon deliberation and treaty with the prelates and the nobles and learned men assisting us, with their unanimous counsel ordained:

That every man and woman of our realm of England, of what condition he be, free or bond, able in body, and within the age of sixty years, not living in merchandize, nor exercising any craft, nor having of his own whereof he may live, nor land of his own about whose tillage he may occupy himself, and not serving any other; if he be required to serve in suitable service, his estate considered, he shall be bound to serve him which shall so require him; and take only the wages, livery, meed, or salary which were accustomed to be given in the places where he oweth to serve, the twentieth year of our reign of England, or five or six other common years next before.[1] Provided always, that the lords be preferred before others in their bondmen or their land tenants, so in their service to be retained; so that, nevertheless, the said lords shall retain no more than be necessary for them. And if any such man or woman being so required to serve will not do the same, and that be proved by two true men before the sheriff, bailiff, lord, or constable of the town where the same shall happen to be done, he shall immediately be taken by them or any of them, and committed to the next gaol, there to remain under strait keeping, till he find surety to serve in the form aforesaid.

From *Translations and Reprints from the Original Sources of European History*, vol. 2; Philadelphia, University of Pennsylvania Press, 1902, pp. 3–5.

[1]That is, wages were to be fixed at pre-plague levels paid in 1347 or before.

If any reaper, mower, other workman or servant, of what estate or condition he be, retained in any man's service, do depart from the said service without reasonable cause or license, before the term agreed, he shall have pain of imprisonment; and no one, under the same penalty, shall presume to receive or retain such a one in his service.

No one, moreover, shall pay or promise to pay to anyone more wages, liveries, meed, or salary than was accustomed, as is before said; nor shall anyone in any other manner demand or receive them, upon pain of doubling of that which shall have been so paid, promised, required or received, to him who thereof shall feel himself aggrieved; and if none such will sue, then the same shall be applied to any of the people that will sue; and such suit shall be in the court of the lord of the place where such case shall happen.

And if lords of towns or manors presume in any point to come against this present ordinance, either by them or by their servants, then suit shall be made against them in the form aforesaid, in the counties, wapentakes, and trithings, or such other courts of ours, for the penalty of treble that so paid or promised by them or their servants. And if any before this present ordinance hath covenanted with any so to serve for more wages, he shall not be bound, by reason of the said covenant, to pay more than at another time was wont to be paid to such a person; nor, under the same penalty, shall presume to pay more.

And because many strong beggars, as long as they may live by begging, do refuse to labor, giving themselves to idleness and vice, and sometimes to theft and other abominations; no one upon the said pain of imprisonment, shall, under the color of pity or alms, give anything to such, who are able to labor, or presume to favor them in their idleness, so that thereby they may be compelled to labor for their necessary living.

Reading 3

An Account of the English Peasants' Revolt of 1381

This detailed description is drawn from the "Anonimalle Chronicle," written in French by an unknown monk of St. Mary's, York. It is the most authoritative surviving history of the Revolt and may well have drawn some of its information from a lost London chronicle. The writer was a contemporary, and, notwithstanding his obvious hostility toward the rebels, his ac-

From *The Great Revolt of 1381*, ed. C.W.C. Oman; Oxford, The Clarendon Press, 1906, pp. 186–205.

count is generally trustworthy. A careful examination of the rebels' goals will suggest the reasons for his hostility.

The author uses the term "commons" (lower case) to mean "common folk," not members of parliament.

Because in the year 1380 the subsidies were over lightly granted at the Parliament of Northampton and because it seemed to divers Lords and to the Commons that the said subsidies were not honestly levied, but commonly exacted from the poor and not from the rich, to the great profit and advantage of the tax-collectors, and to the deception of the King and the Commons, the Council of the King ordained certain commissions to make inquiry in every township how the tax had been levied. Among these townships was Fobbing, whose people made answer that they would not pay a penny more, because they already had a receipt for the said subsidy. On which the said Thomas[1] threatened them angrily, and he had with him two sergeants-at-arms of our Lord the King. And for fear of his malice the folks of Fobbing took counsel with the folks of Corringham, and the folks of these two places made levies and assemblies, and sent messages to the men of Stanford to bid them rise with them, for their common profit.

And because of these occurrences Sir Robert Belknap, Chief Justice of the King's Bench, was sent into the county, with a commission, and indictments against divers persons were laid before him, and the folks of the countryside were in such fear that they were proposing to abandon their homes. Wherefore the commons rose against him, and came before him, and told him that he was a traitor to the King, and that it was of pure malice that he would put them in default, by means of false inquests made before him. And they took him, and made him swear on the Bible that never again would he hold such a session, nor act as a justice in such inquests. And they made him give them a list of the names of all the jurors, and they took all the jurors they could catch, and cut off their heads, and cast their houses to the ground. So the said Sir Robert took his way home without delay. And afterwards the said commons assembled together, before Whitsunday, to the number of some 50,000, and they went to the manors and townships of those who would not rise with them, and cast their houses to the ground or set fire to them.

And after this the commons of Kent gathered together in great numbers day after day, without a head or a chieftain, and the Friday after Whitsunday[2] came to Dartford. And there they took counsel, and made proclamation that none who dwelt near the sea in any place for the space of twelve leagues,

[1]A royal tax collector, Thomas Bampton.
[2]7 June 1381.

should come out with them, but should remain to defend the coasts of the sea from public enemies, saying among themselves that they were more kings than one, and they would not suffer or endure any other king but King Richard.

Those who came from Maidstone took their way with the rest of the commons through the countryside. And there they made chief over them Wat Tyler of Maidstone, to maintain them and be their councillor. And on the Monday next after Trinity Sunday[3] they came to Canterbury, before the hour of noon; and 4,000 of them entering into the Minster at the time of High Mass, there made a reverence and cried with one voice to the monks to prepare to choose a monk for Archbishop of Canterbury, "for he who is Archbishop now is a traitor, and shall be decapitated for his iniquity." And so he was within five days after! And when they had done this, they went into the town to their fellows, and with one assent they summoned the Mayor, the bailiffs, and the commons of the said town, and examined them whether they would with good will swear to be faithful and loyal to King Richard and to the true commons of England or no. Then the mayor answered that they would do so willingly, and they made their oath to that effect. Then they (the rebels) asked them if they had any traitors among them, and the townsfolk said that there were three, and named their names. These three the commons dragged out of their houses and cut off their heads. And afterwards they took 500 men of the town with them to London, but left the rest to guard the town.

At this time the commons had as their councillor a chaplain of evil disposition named Sir John Ball, which Sir John advised them to get rid of all the lords, and of the archbishop and bishops, and abbots, and priors, and most of the monks and canons, saying that there should be no bishop in England save one archbishop only, and that he himself would be that prelate, and they would have no monks or canons in religious houses save two, and that their possessions should be distributed among the laity. For which sayings he was esteemed among the commons as a prophet, and laboured with them day by day to strengthen them in their malice—and a fit reward he got, when he was hung, drawn, and quartered, and beheaded as a traitor.

And the said commons had among themselves a watchword in English, "With whome haldes you?"; and the answer was, "With kinge Richarde and the true commons"; and those who could not or would not so answer were beheaded and put to death.

At this time the King was in a turret of the great Tower of London, and could see the manor of the Savoy and the Hospital of Clerkenwell, and the house of Simon Hosteler near Newgate, and John Butterwick's place, all on fire at once.

[3]10 June.

And next day, Friday, the commons of the countryside and the commons of London assembled in fearful strength, to the number of 100,000 or more, besides some four score who remained on Tower Hill to watch those who were in the Tower. And some went to Mile End, on the Brentwood Road, to wait for the coming of the King, because of the proclamation that he had made. But some came to Tower Hill, and when the King knew that they were there, he sent them orders by messenger to join their friends at Mile End, saying that he would come to them very soon.

And at this time the King made the commons draw themselves out in two lines, and proclaimed to them that he would confirm and grant it that they should be free, and generally should have their will, and that they might go through all the realm of England and catch all traitors and bring them to him in safety, and then he would deal with them as the law demanded.

Under colour of this grant Wat Tyler and [some of] the commons took their way to the Tower, to seize the Archbishop, while the rest remained at Mile End. There they cut off the heads of Master Simon Sudbury, Archbishop of Canterbury, and of Sir Robert Hales, Prior of the Hospital of St. John's, Treasurer of England, and of Sir William Appleton, a great lawyer and surgeon, and one who had much power with the king and the Duke of Lancaster.

At this moment the Mayor of London, William Walworth, came up, and the King bade him go to the commons, and make their chieftain come to him. And when he was summoned by the Mayor, by the name of Wat Tyler of Maidstone, he came to the King with great confidence, mounted on a little horse, that the commons might see him. And he dismounted, holding in his hand a dagger which he had taken from another man, and when he had dismounted he half bent his knee, and then took the King by the hand, and shook his arm forcibly and roughly, saying to him, "Brother, be of good comfort and joyful, for you shall have, in the fortnight that is to come, praise from the commons even more than you have yet had, and we shall be good companions." And the King said to Walter [= Wat], "Why will you not go back to your own country?": But the other answered, with a great oath, that neither he nor his fellows would depart until they had got their charter such as they wished to have it, and had certain points rehearsed, and added to their charter which they wished to demand. And he said in a threatening fashion that the lords of the realm would rue it bitterly if these points were not settled to their pleasure. Then the King asked him what were the points which he wished to have revised, and he should have them freely, without contradiction, written out and sealed. Thereupon the said Walter rehearsed the points which were to be demanded; and he asked that there should be no law within the realm save the law of Winchester, and that from henceforth there should be no outlawry in any process of law, and that no lord should have lordship save civilly, and that there should be equality among all people save only the King, and that the goods of Holy Church should not remain in the hands of the religious, nor of parsons and vicars, and other churchmen; but that clergy already in possession should have a sufficient sustenance from the endowments, and the rest of the goods should be divided among the people of the parish. And he demanded that there should be only one bishop in England and only one prelate, and all the lands and tenements now held by them should be confiscated, and divided among the commons, only reserving for them a reasonable sustenance. And he demanded that there should be no more villeins in England, and no serfdom or villeinage, but that all men should be free and of one condition. To this the King gave an easy answer, and said that he should have all that he could fairly grant, reserving only for himself the regality of his crown. And then he bade him go back to his home, without making further delay.

At this time a certain valet from Kent, who was among the King's retinue, asked that the said Walter, the chief of the commons, might be pointed out to him. And when he saw him, he said aloud that he knew him for the greatest thief and robber in all Kent.

And for these words Wat tried to strike him with his dagger, and would have slain him in the King's presence; but because he strove so to do, the Mayor of London, William Walworth, reasoned with the said Wat for his violent behaviour and spite, done in the King's presence, and arrested him. And because he arrested him, the said Wat stabbed the Mayor with his dagger in the stomach in great wrath. But, as it pleased God, the Mayor was wearing armour and took no harm, but like a hardy and vigorous man drew his cutlass, and struck back at the said Wat and gave him a deep cut on the neck, and then a great cut on the head. And during this scuffle one of the King's household drew his sword, and ran Wat two or three times through the body, mortally wounding him.

And when the commons saw that their chieftain, Wat Tyler, was dead in such a manner, they fell to the ground there among the wheat, like beaten men, imploring the King for mercy for their misdeeds. And the King benevolently granted them mercy, and most of them took to flight.

Afterwards the King sent out his messengers into divers parts, to capture the malefactors and put them to death. And many were taken and hanged at London, and they set up many gallows around the City of London, and in other cities and boroughs of the south country. At last, as it pleased God, the King seeing that too many of his liege subjects would be undone, and too much blood spilt, took pity in his heart, and granted them all pardon, on condition that they should never rise again, under pain of losing life or members, and that each of them should get his charter of pardon, and pay the King as fee for his seal twenty shillings, to make him rich. And so finished this wicked war.

Reading 4

The Legal Status of the German Hansa, 1469

This document was written in response to an inquiry from the court of King Edward IV of England asking what provisions of the law applied to the Hanseatic League of German Cities (the *Hansa Theutonica*). It clarifies the nature, operation, and presuppositions of this commercial confederation by explaining what it was not.

It is incorrect to assert that there has existed in Germany from time immemorial a *societas*, a *collegium* and a *universitas* generally called *Hansa Theutonica* etc. For, most honourable fathers, with all due respect to the royal majesty, the *Hansa Theutonica* is not a *societas*: for it knows no community of property either in whole or in part, since no common property exists within the *Hansa Theutonica*; neither is it a *societas* for specific commercial enterprises, as within the *Hansa Theutonica* each trades on his own account, and profit and loss from trade falls to each individually. Now as the law knows no other form of society than the said three forms, it has been established that the *Hansa Theutonica* is not a *societas*.

Neither is it a *collegium*, because in law the joining together of several into a single entity is called a *collegium*: the *Hansa Theutonica* is, however, made up of widely separated towns, as the royal letters acknowledge. It is therefore clear that the *Hansa Theutonica* is not a *collegium*. Nor is it a *universitas*, for in both civil and canon law it is required that a community, to merit the name of *universitas*, should hold its property in common, have a common treasury, a common seal, a common syndic and a common business manager; but nothing of this kind is to be found within the *Hansa Theutonica*. It is therefore not a *universitas*.

And furthermore . . . the *Hansa Theutonica* came into being through agreement and alliance of different towns; but it is clear beyond all doubt that a mere grouping of towns can produce in law neither a *societas* nor a *collegium* nor a *universitas*, for which many other qualities are essential.

But the *Hansa Theutonica* is . . . a firm *confederatio* of many cities, towns and communities for the purpose of ensuring that business enterprises by land and sea should have a desired and favourable outcome and that there should

From Philippe Dollinger, *The German Hansa*, tr. D.S. Ault and S.H. Steinberg; London, Macmillan & Co., Ltd., 1970, pp. 411–413. Reprinted by permission of St. Martin's Press, Inc., and Macmillan & Co., Ltd.

be effective protection against pirates and highwaymen, so that their ambushes should not rob merchants of their goods and valuables.

The *Hansa Theutonica* is not controlled by the merchants; on the contrary each city and each town has its own lords and its own magistracy by whom its affairs are directed. For the *Hansa Theutonica*, as has been shown, is nothing other than a kind of alliance between towns, which does not release the towns from the jurisdiction of those lords who ruled over them previously: on the contrary they remain subject in all things to these lords as they were before, and continue to be governed by them.

Moreover the *Hansa Theutonica* has neither seal nor council in common. Indeed the situation does not allow the existence of a common seal. But when for essential purposes letters are written in the name of the whole *Hansa Theutonica*, they are sealed with the seal of the town in which they were written, as can easily be seen from the documents and warrants sent to you recently, most honourable fathers, in the name of the whole *Hansa Theutonica*: they were not sealed with some seal common to the whole *Hansa Theutonica*, but with the seal of the town of Lübeck, where they were written.

The *Hansa Theutonica* has no common council; but each town sends delegates, with instructions, who are not called councillors but delegates, whenever it is necessary to deliberate on matters pending. . . .

Neither the *Hansa Theutonica* nor any one of the towns has the power to summon assemblies and fix meetings; instead the towns of the Hansa assemble whenever there are questions to be discussed by common agreement in a certain place and decide among themselves what they consider necessary for the good of their merchants. Also up to the present no Hansa town has taken precedence over the others. Rather do the towns decide among themselves which ones are particularly concerned in the matters at issue and these, according to the importance of the matter, notify the other towns that they are to send delegates.

Reading 5

Coluccio Salutati, Letter to Pellegrino on the Active Life

Coluccio Salutati (1331–1406) was a major Florentine humanist and civic official who in 1375 became chancellor of Florence. His writings stress the connection between humanistic scholarship and service to the city-state. In his letter to Pellegrino, Salutati praises the active life over the contemplative life in the context of Christian piety and salvation. In another of his letters, however, he praises the monastic life, thus reflecting the medieval rhetorical tradition of celebrating the virtues of both action and contemplation.

In some respects Salutati is simply echoing St. Francis (see p. 139) while in others he is expressing the new civic humanism of the Renaissance. Can you separate the old ideas from the new?

Do not believe, my Pellegrino, that to flee from turmoil, to avoid the view of pleasant things, to enclose oneself in a cloister, or to isolate oneself in a hermitage, constitute the way of perfection. Within yourself is that which imprints upon your work the title of perfection, which receives those things which do not touch you, rather cannot touch you, if your mind and your spirit withdraws within itself, if it does not search outside of itself. If the spirit will not receive within itself these exterior objects—the square, the forum, the court, the most crowded place of the city, they will be for you a very remote retreat and a perfect solitude. If instead, either in the recollection of distant things or in the fascination of present ones, our spirit turns outwardly, I do not know what it profits to live a solitary life. For it is a characteristic of the spirit to think always of something, whether this be a thing comprehended by the senses, represented by the memory, constructed by the power of the intellect, or created by the feeling of desire. And tell me, Pellegrino, who do you believe was more beloved by God: Paul,[1] the inactive hermit, or the busy Abraham? Among the superior ones, there are more who dedicate themselves to the active life than occupy themselves solely with spiritual things, just as there are many more who save themselves in the active life than are chosen from the contemplative life.

You should not be pleased with your prayers; you should not believe that you have approached more closely to heaven; you should not condemn me for remaining in the secular world. Without doubt you, fleeing from the world,

From *Renaissance Italy: Was It the Birthplace of Modern Europe?* ed. Gene A. Brucker; New York, Holt, Rinehart, and Winston, Inc., 1958, pp. 35–36. Reprinted by permission of Gene A. Brucker and the publisher.

[1]St. Paul the Hermit (d. *c.* 347), not Paul the Apostle.

can fall from heaven to earth, while I, remaining in the world, can raise my heart to heaven. And if you provide for, serve, and think of your family, children, relatives, friends, you cannot fail to raise your heart to the heavens and please God. Perhaps, occupied in mundane things, you will please Him more, since you will not aspire for yourself alone to be in communion with God, but in conjunction with Him, who holds dear the things necessary for the family, pleasing to friends, salutary for the state, you will labor, to the extent that He gives you the opportunity.

And thus to conclude, while contemplation is better, more divine, and more sublime, still it must be united with action. Nor is it always necessary to remain fixed in that summit of speculation. And tell me, I pray you, what is examined in the Last Judgment, if not the works of mercy, even though neglected or incomplete? Whoever will have clothed the nude, fed the hungry, given drink to the thirsty, buried the dead, released the imprisoned, he will hear that most sweet appeal: "Come, blessed by My Father, enjoy the Kingdom prepared for you from the beginning of the world."

Reading 6

Vespasiano on the Founding of the Papal Library by Nicholas V

Vespasiano (1421–1498) was a writer and bookseller who, it is said, was put out of business by the influx of inexpensive printed books. In this selection from his *Lives of the Artists*, Vespasiano praises Pope Nicholas V (1447–1455) for founding the Vatican Library and supporting humanist scholars. In both these activities, Nicholas was playing the role of an enlightened Renaissance despot.

Owing to the jubilee of 1450 a great quantity of money came in by this means to the apostolic see, and with this the pope commenced building in many places, and sent for Greek and Latin books, wherever he was able to find them, without regard to price. He gathered together a large band of writers, the best that he could find, and kept them in constant employment. He also summoned a number of learned men, both for the purpose of composing new works and of translating such existing works as were not already translated, giving them most abundant provision for their needs meanwhile; and when the

From *Readings in European History*, vol. 1, ed. James Harvey Robinson; Boston, Ginn & Company, 1904, pp. 529–530.

works were translated and brought to him, he gave them large sums of money, in order that they should do more willingly that which they undertook to do.

He made great provision for the needs of learned men. He gathered together great numbers of books upon every subject, both Greek and Latin, to the number of five thousand volumes. So at his death it was found by inventory that never since the time of Ptolemy had half that number of books of every kind been brought together. All books he caused to be copied, without regard to what it cost him, and there were few places where his Holiness had not copiers at work. When he could not procure a book for himself in any way, he had it copied.

After he had assembled at Rome, as I said above, many learned men at large salaries, he wrote to Florence to Messer Giannozzo Manetti, that he should come to Rome to translate and compose for him. And when Manetti left Florence and came to Rome, the pope, as was his custom, received him with honor, and assigned to him, in addition to his income as secretary, six hundred ducats, urging him to attempt the translation of the books of the Bible and of Aristotle, and to complete the book already commenced by him, *Contra Judaeos et gentes;* a wonderful work, if it had been completed, but he carried it only to the tenth book. Moreover he translated the New Testament, and the Psalter, . . . with five apologetical books in defense of this Psalter, showing that in the Holy Scriptures there is not one syllable that does not contain the greatest of mysteries.

It was Pope Nicholas' intention to found a library in St. Peter's, for the general use of the whole Roman curia, which would have been an admirable thing indeed, if he had been able to carry it out, but death prevented his bringing it to completion. He illumined the Holy Scriptures through innumerable books, which he caused to be translated; and in the same way with the works of the pagans, including certain works upon grammar, of use in learning Latin—the *Orthography* of Messer Giovanni Tortelle, who was of his Holiness' household and worked upon the library, a worthy book and useful to grammarians; the *Iliad* of Homer; Strabo's *De situ orbis* he caused to be translated by Guerrino, and gave him five hundred florins for each part—that is to say, Asia, Africa, and Europe; that was in all fifteen hundred florins. Herodotus and Thucydides he had translated by Lorenzo Valla, and rewarded him liberally for his trouble; Xenophon and Diodorus, by Messer Poggio; Polybius, by Nicolo Perotto, whom, when he handed it to him, he gave five hundred brand-new papal ducats in a purse, and said to him that it was not what he deserved, but that in time he would take care to satisfy him.

Reading 7

Azurara on the Motives of Prince Henry the Navigator

Gomes Eannes de Azurara (d. 1474) was advanced to the offices of chief archivist and royal chronicler of the kingdom of Portugal a year after he wrote this account. He is our best authority for the early Portugese voyages down the west coast of Africa sponsored by Prince Henry the Navigator (1394–1460)—whom Azurara calls "the Lord Infant" or "the Prince." Prince Henry played a part in the Portugese capture of the North African port of Ceuta in 1415. Afterward, from his court at Sagres in Portugal, he collected geographical and navigational data from the expeditions that he sent westward to the Atlantic islands and southward down the African coast. Azurara, writing as a court historian, is obviously providing an unflawed portrait.

We imagine that we know a matter when we are acquainted with the doer of it and the end for which he did it. And since in former chapters we have set forth the Lord Infant as the chief actor in these things, giving as clear an understanding of him as we could, it is meet that in this present chapter we should know his purpose in doing them. And you should note well that the noble spirit of this Prince, by a sort of natural constraint, was ever urging him both to begin and to carry out very great deeds. For which reason, after the taking of Ceuta he always kept ships well armed against the Infidel, both for war, and because he had also a wish to know the land that lay beyond the isles of Canary and Cape Bojador [Morocco], since before his own time, neither by writings, nor by the memory of man, was known with any certainty the nature of the land beyond that Cape. Some said indeed that Saint Brandan had passed that way; and there was another tale of two galleys rounding the Cape, which never returned. But this doth not appear at all likely to be true, for it is not to be presumed that if the said galleys went there, some other ships would not have endeavoured to learn what voyage they had made. And because the said Lord Infant wished to know the truth of this—since it seemed to him that if he or some other lord did not endeavour to gain that knowledge, no mariners or merchants would ever dare to attempt it—(for it is clear that none of them ever trouble themselves to sail to a place where there is not a sure and certain hope of profit)—and seeing also that no other prince took any pains in this matter, he sent out his own ships against those parts, to have manifest certainty of

From *The Chronicle of the Discovery and Conquest of Guinea*, vol. 1, tr. C.R. Beazley and E. Prestage; London, Hakluyt Society Publications, Inc., 1899, pp. 27–30.

them all. And to this he was stirred up by his zeal for the service of God and of the King Edward his Lord and brother, who then reigned. And this was the first reason of his action.

The second reason was that if there chanced to be in those lands some population of Christians, or some havens, into which it would be possible to sail without peril, many kinds of merchandise might be brought to this realm, which would find a ready market, and reasonably so, because no other people of these parts traded with them, nor yet people of any other that were known; and also the products of this realm might be taken there, which traffic would bring great profit to our countrymen.

The third reason was that, as it was said that the power of the Moors in that land of Africa was very much greater than was commonly supposed, and that there were no Christians among them, nor any other race of men; and because every wise man is obliged by natural prudence to wish for a knowledge of the power of his enemy; therefore the said Lord Infant exerted himself to cause this to be fully discovered, and to make it known determinately how far the power of those infidels extended.

The fourth reason was because during the one and thirty years that he had warred against the Moors, he had never found a Christian king, nor a lord outside this land, who for the love of our Lord Jesus Christ would aid him in the said war. Therefore he sought to know if there were in those parts any Christian princes, in whom the charity and the love of Christ was so ingrained that they would aid him against those enemies of the faith.

The fifth reason was his great desire to make increase in the faith of our Lord Jesus Christ and to bring to Him all the souls that should be saved—understanding that all the mystery of the Incarnation, Death, and Passion of our Lord Jesus Christ was for this sole end—namely the salvation of lost souls—whom the said Lord Infant by his travail and spending would fain bring into the true path. For he perceived that no better offering could be made unto the Lord than this; for if God promised to return one hundred goods for one, we may justly believe that for such great benefits, that is to say for so many souls as were saved by the efforts of this Lord, he will have so many hundreds of guerdons in the kingdom of God, by which his spirit may be glorified after this life in the celestial realm. For I that wrote this history saw so many men and women of those parts turned to the holy faith, that even if the Infant had been a heathen, their prayers would have been enough to have obtained his salvation. And not only did I see the first captives, but their children and grandchildren as true Christians as if the Divine grace breathed in them and imparted to them a clear knowledge of itself.

But over and above these five reasons I have a sixth that would seem to be the root from which all the others proceeded: and this is the inclination of the heavenly wheels. For, as I wrote not many days ago in a letter I sent to the

Lord King, that although it be written that the wise man shall be Lord of the stars, and that the courses of the planets (according to the true estimate of the holy doctors) cannot cause the good man to stumble; yet it is manifest that they are bodies ordained in the secret counsels of our Lord God and run by a fixed measure, appointed to different ends, which are revealed to men by his grace, through whose influence bodies of the lower order are inclined to certain passions. And if it be a fact, speaking as a Catholic, that the contrary predestinations of the wheels of heaven can be avoided by natural judgment with the aid of a certain divine grace, much more does it stand to reason that those who are predestined to good fortune, by the help of this same grace, will not only follow their course but even add a greater increase to themselves.